PRACTICAL AI FOR THE REST OF US

PRACTICAL AI FOR THE REST OF US

WHAT AI CAN DO FOR YOU, STARTING TODAY

JEFF KUEHN

Published by WOCxO, LLC
Maryland, United States
www.wocxo.com

ISBN 978-1-972970-00-3 (Paperback)
ISBN 978-1-972970-01-0 (Hardcover)
ISBN 978-1-972970-02-7 (eBook)

First Edition, 2026

This book is for informational and educational purposes only and does not constitute professional, legal, financial, or medical advice. Consult qualified professionals for guidance specific to your situation.
AI tools, features, and pricing described here reflect information available as of early 2026. The AI landscape changes rapidly — verify current details at practicalaibook.ai before making decisions.

For Alex, whose stories inspired me to finally write mine. And for our kids, who remind me every day that the future is worth getting ready for.

"I am not afraid of computers. I am afraid of the lack of them."
— Isaac Asimov

COMPANION WEBSITE & QR CODES

YOUR BRIDGE BETWEEN THIS BOOK AND THE EVER-CHANGING WORLD OF AI

Why a Companion Website?

AI tools change their interfaces and features constantly. Screenshots from a printed book can become outdated within months. The companion website at practicalaibook.ai keeps every chapter's walk-throughs, screenshots, and exercises current. When something changes, a menu moves, a feature gets renamed, pricing updates, we update the website so you're never stuck following outdated instructions.

The site is free to access. No account required.

✦✦✦

What You'll Find Online

Chapter Walkthroughs: Updated screenshots and step-by-step instructions for every exercise in the book

Video Demonstrations: Short video tutorials showing key tasks in real time

Prompt Library: All 50+ prompts from Appendix B in a searchable, copy-paste format

Tool Comparison Chart: The latest version of Appendix A with current pricing and features

Community Forum: Connect with other readers, share tips, and ask questions

Monthly Updates: A change log showing what's been updated and why

Bonus Content: Extra exercises, deep dives, and reader-submitted use cases

Accessibility Resources: Screen-reader friendly versions, large-print guides, and multilingual content

✦✦✦

Chapter-by-Chapter Quick Reference

Throughout this book, you'll see references to the companion website. Here's a quick reference for every chapter's online page. In the printed edition, QR codes appear at the start of each chapter for quick access.

Chapter Resources

Intro. Why You Need This Book — practicalaibook.ai/introduction

1. What Is AI, Really? — practicalaibook.ai/chapter/1
2. Your AI Starter Kit — practicalaibook.ai/chapter/2
3. Talking to AI: The Art of the Prompt — practicalaibook.ai/chapter/3
4. AI at Home — practicalaibook.ai/chapter/4
5. AI at Work — practicalaibook.ai/chapter/5
6. AI for Parents & Educators — practicalaibook.ai/chapter/6
7. AI for Small Business Owners — practicalaibook.ai/chapter/7

8. AI for Creative Projects — practicalaibook.ai/chapter/8
9. Staying Safe and Smart — practicalaibook.ai/chapter/9
10. Building Your AI Workflow — practicalaibook.ai/chapter/10
11. What's Coming Next — practicalaibook.ai/chapter/11
12. Appendix A. AI Tool Comparison Chart — practicalaibook.ai/appendix/a
13. Appendix B. Prompt Library — practicalaibook.ai/prompts
14. Appendix C. Glossary
15. Appendix D. Resources & Further Reading — practicalaibook.ai/resources

✦✦✦

Using QR Codes

In the printed edition, each chapter opens with a QR code that takes you directly to that chapter's companion page. To scan: Open your phone's camera app (iPhone or Android), point it at the QR code, and tap the link that appears. No special app needed.

If scanning doesn't work, just type the URL from the table above into any web browser. In the digital edition of this book, all companion site links are clickable directly—no scanning required.

✦✦✦

Staying Connected

Sign up for our monthly email at practicalaibook.ai/updates to get notified when we add new content or when major tool changes affect the book's exercises.

Found something outdated or have a suggestion? Email us at hello@practicalaibook.ai or use the feedback form on any chapter page. This book stays current because readers like you help us catch what's changed.

This book was designed to be a starting point, not a final destination. The companion website ensures your journey continues long after you turn the last page. We'll see you online at practicalaibook.ai.

WHY YOU NEED THIS BOOK

EVEN IF YOU THINK YOU DON'T

My wife Alexandra writes children's books. Beautiful ones, actually, the kind with soft illustrations and sentences that land just right. She is thoughtful, creative, and deeply patient with people who have questions. She is considerably less patient with technology.

A few years ago, she came to me with that look on her face, the one that means "explain this to me like I'm five, and don't you dare use an acronym." She'd heard about AI. It was everywhere: the news, her author community, the dinner table at every social event we'd attended in the past six months. People were using it to write things. To make pictures. To "do stuff." What stuff? What things? And was she supposed to be worried? Excited? Both?

"Just tell me what it actually is," she said. "In plain English."

I opened my mouth, and immediately realized I was about to make the classic tech-person mistake. I was about to explain it correctly instead of usefully. I was about to say "large language model" and "neural network" and "natural language processing," and she was going to look at me the way I look at our HVAC unit when it starts making a new sound: acknowledgment that something is clearly happening in there, but no idea what to do about it.

So I stopped. And I started over.

"Imagine," I said, "the world's most well-read intern. They've read basically every book, article, manual, recipe, legal brief, and Reddit thread ever published in human history. They can't go get you coffee, they can't remember your conversation from yesterday unless you remind them, and they will sometimes confidently make things up, so you have to double-check important stuff. But if you ask them a question or give them a task, they'll take a real swing at it in about three seconds."

She thought about that for a moment.

"Okay," she said. "So how do I use it?"

That's the question this book answers.

✦✦✦

I've spent my career in technology. I'm the Chief Technology Officer at Colossal LLC, where we build AI solutions for government agencies and enterprise clients. I've been talking about artificial intelligence professionally for years. I understand the technical side.

And because of that, I've watched something that bothers me quite a bit: the people who most need to understand AI are the people least likely to get a straight answer about it.

If you're a developer or a researcher or a startup founder, there is no shortage of resources. There are entire universities and conference circuits and venture capital firms dedicated to helping you navigate this space.

But if you're a retired teacher trying to figure out whether this technology could help you, or a small business owner wondering if you're falling behind your competitors, or a parent trying to understand what your kid is doing with it and whether you should be concerned, the options are pretty bleak. Most AI books are either too technical (written by engineers for engineers), too abstract (big ideas, no practical steps), or too hyped up (THIS CHANGES EVERYTHING, starting next Tuesday).

Nobody had written the book for the rest of us.

So I did.

✦✦✦

Who This Book Is For

This book is for you if any of the following describes you:

• You've heard about AI tools like ChatGPT, Claude, or Gemini and you're curious but haven't tried them, or you've tried them once and weren't sure what to do.

• You're worried you're falling behind and you'd like to catch up without having to take a class or read a textbook.

• You run a small business and you've heard competitors are using AI, and you want to know what that means.

• You're a parent or teacher trying to understand what kids are using this for and how to think about it.

• You're in the workforce and you want to work smarter, not just harder.

• You're retired, or close to it, and you'd like technology to be a useful tool rather than a source of frustration.

• You're creative (a writer, a photographer, a musician, a hobbyist) and you want to know whether AI can be a collaborator rather than a threat.

• You're just someone who wants to make sense of the world you're living in.

This book is not for people who want to build AI systems, write code, or start a tech company. That's a different book. This is the one for people who want to use AI, intelligently, practically, and without losing their minds.

✦✦✦

What You'll Find Inside

We start where everyone should start: understanding what AI is. Not the science fiction version, not the Silicon Valley hype version, but the honest, practical version you can actually use. (Chapter 1. It's good. Pour yourself a coffee.)

From there, Chapter 2 helps you get set up, which tools are available, how much they cost, and how to get started today without needing any special equipment or expertise.

Chapter 3 is the heart of the book. It's where you'll learn the PRIME framework, a simple, five-step approach to working with AI that my team at Colossal LLC developed from teaching hundreds of people how to get dramatically better results. I'll explain it fully when we get there, but the short version is this: most people get mediocre results from AI because they're using it like a search engine. PRIME teaches you to work with it like a collaborator. The difference is remarkable.

The rest of the book is about putting all of this to work in your real life. We cover AI at home (Chapter 4), AI at work (Chapter 5), AI for parents and educators (Chapter 6), AI for small businesses (Chapter 7), and AI for creative projects (Chapter 8). Chapter 9 covers something that doesn't get nearly enough attention: how to stay safe and smart, understanding AI's limitations, recognizing misinformation, and protecting yourself from the ways this technology can be used against you, not just for you.

Chapter 10 pulls everything together by helping you build an AI workflow that fits your life. And Chapter 11 takes a grounded, honest look at what's coming next. Not with dramatic predictions or robot apocalypse warnings, but with the practical question Dave the plumber asks at the end of the book: "What do I need to pay attention to?"

✦✦✦

The People You'll Meet

One of the things I believe most deeply about learning is that we don't remember principles, we remember people. So instead of walking you through abstract examples, this book follows a cast of real-feeling characters who are learning to use AI in ways that are directly relevant to their lives.

You'll meet Dave, a plumber from Pennsylvania who's pretty handy with a pipe wrench and considerably less confident with a smartphone. His college-age daughter has been trying to get him to pay attention to AI for months, and he's got the polite skepticism of someone who's seen a lot of tech trends come and go. Dave opens the book and closes it, and his journey across those eleven chapters is, I think, the best argument I can make for why this matters.

You'll meet Rosa, a retired schoolteacher in her late sixties who is more capable than most people give her credit for, and who discovers in these pages that AI is the first technology that has ever worked the way her brain works. Her story is one of the most affecting things I've written.

You'll meet Marcus, who owns a landscaping business and is trying to figure out if AI can do for him what a marketing agency would charge four times as much to do. (Spoiler: yes, with significant caveats we'll discuss honestly.)

You'll meet Sofia, a bilingual project manager whose multigenerational household — two kids, a husband, and her elderly mother Elena all under one roof — means that every Tuesday at 3 PM is its own kind of emergency. Her chapter is, to put it plainly, relentlessly practical.

You'll meet Priya, who manages a marketing team and has a boss who wants more output with fewer resources, a story familiar to approximately everyone in professional life right now. You'll meet Jenna and her teenage son Tyler, and their very different feelings about AI in education. You'll meet Nadia, a former English teacher and aspiring novelist who was afraid AI would replace her creativity, and who discovers it can function as a collaborator instead. And you'll meet Frank, a retired postal worker in Phoenix who gets a very unpleasant introduction to what can happen when AI is weaponized against someone you love.

These characters are fictional, but the situations they face are drawn from real conversations I've had with real people. The plumber asking what the heck this thing actually is. The retiree wondering if she's too old to learn. The small business owner who can't afford to fall further behind. The parent trying to figure out if their kid is cheating or learning. The creative who's afraid the machines are coming for her. These aren't hypothetical people. They're probably people you know. They might be you.

✦✦✦

A Note on Speed

I need to tell you something upfront: AI is moving faster than any book can keep pace with. Product names change. Features appear and disappear. Prices shift. The specific details I describe (which tools exist, what they cost, exactly what they can do) were accurate when I wrote them, and some of them will be different by the time you read this. That's not a bug in the book. It's the nature of this particular moment in history.

What doesn't change are the principles. How to think about AI. How to work with it. How to evaluate what it gives you. How to protect yourself from its limitations and from bad actors who use it against you. How to keep your judgment, your creativity, and your humanity at the center of everything. Those things are as durable as anything I know how to write.

For the fast-moving details (tool recommendations, current pricing, updated step-by-step instructions) I've built a companion website at practicalaibook.ai. Every chapter has a corresponding page on the site where I keep current what the book can't: screenshots, updated instructions, fresh tool comparisons, and a list of anything that's changed since the book went to print. It's free. No sign-up required. Just a standing commitment to make sure this book stays useful. And if you find something that's changed or have a question, you can always reach us at hello@practicalaibook.ai.

✦✦✦

One More Thing

I want to say something that I mean sincerely, and I'm going to ask you to hear it without the usual tech-enthusiast glaze it sometimes comes wrapped in:

This technology is going to affect your life. It already is, whether or not you're using it yourself. Your employer is thinking about it. Your kids' schools are navigating it. The companies you buy from are using it to talk to you. The information you read online is increasingly shaped by it. The job market is reshaping around it.

That is not a reason to panic. It's not a reason to despair. It's not even a reason to become a tech person, if that's not who you are.

But it is a reason to understand it. Because the people who understand it will have choices. They'll know when to use it and when not to. They'll be able to protect themselves when it's used against them. They'll be able to spot the hype and separate it from the useful reality. They'll spend less time on the tasks they find tedious and more time on the things that matter to them.

That's what this book is about. Not the technology for its own sake. But the life it can free up, if you know how to use it.

Dave's daughter figured that out. Rosa figured that out. Marcus, Priya, Nadia, Frank, each in their own way, in their own time, for their own reasons.

You can too.

Let's get started.

—Jeff Kuehn
Maryland, 2026

1

WHAT IS AI, REALLY?

CUTTING THROUGH THE HYPE IN PLAIN ENGLISH

My neighbor Dave Kowalski is a plumber. Great with his hands, solid guy, has strong opinions about PVC cement. Computers? Not his thing. His password for everything is the name of his first truck followed by the number 1. (He told me this proudly, as if it were a security strategy.)

Last Thanksgiving, Dave's daughter pulled out her phone, opened ChatGPT, and typed in a question about fixing a leaky faucet. In about three seconds, the screen filled up with a detailed, step-by-step answer that was (Dave admitted grudgingly, as if conceding a point in an argument he hadn't started) pretty accurate.

He stared at the phone for a long time. Then he looked at his daughter. Then he looked at me, like I might have answers since I work in tech. Then he said what millions of people have said over the last two years:

"Okay, but what the hell is it?"

His daughter, meanwhile, just shrugged. She'd been using AI tools for months, to help with college essays, plan weekend trips, and settle arguments with her roommate about whether you can freeze cheese. (You can, but the texture gets weird. AI knew that.) For her, it wasn't magic. It was just... a thing on her phone. Two people, same kitchen table, completely different relationships with the same technology.

That's the right question. And it's the one most people never get a straight answer to. Instead, they get buzzwords that sound like someone shuffled a deck of Silicon Valley flash cards. They get overblown headlines about superintelligence. They get their uncle at Christmas dinner explaining, between bites of ham, that AI is going to take everyone's job by Tuesday. They get a Wikipedia article that loses them at the phrase "neural network architecture," which sounds like something an evil villain would build under a volcano.

So let's fix that. Right now. No jargon, no PhD required, no dramatic predictions about the robot apocalypse. Just a clear, honest explanation of what AI actually is, where it came from, and most importantly, what it can do for you. Starting today. Starting before you finish your coffee.

✦✦✦

The Hollywood Version vs. Reality

Before we talk about what AI is, we need to talk about what it isn't. Because if you're like most people, you walked into this conversation carrying about forty years of movie baggage, and I need you to set those bags down.

If you grew up anytime between the 1980s and now, your mental image of artificial intelligence probably looks something like this: a glowing red eye that wants to exterminate humanity (Terminator), a creepy-smooth voice that falls in love with Joaquin Phoenix (Her), a humanoid robot that's secretly plotting your demise while being uncomfortably attractive (Ex Machina), or for the optimists in the crowd, a friendly robot that just wants to hold your hand and watch the sunset (WALL-E).

Hollywood has been telling us the same story for decades: AI is basically a person made of metal and code, and it's either going to save us or kill us, depending on the movie's budget.

Here's the thing: none of that is even remotely close to reality. And

I say that as someone who builds AI solutions for a living and is still waiting for his Rosie the Robot from The Jetsons. (I was promised a robot maid, and I'm still doing my own dishes. This feels like a breach of contract.)

The AI you're going to use (the AI that's already on your phone, in your email, and probably involved in how you found this book) isn't conscious. It doesn't have feelings. It doesn't have goals or desires. It doesn't lie awake at night wondering about the meaning of existence. It has no night. It has no bed. It has no existential dread, which honestly sounds kind of nice.

What it *does* do is something much less cinematic but far more useful: it's incredibly good at finding patterns and making predictions based on those patterns.

Think of it this way. If Hollywood AI is a tortured genius with a personality disorder, real AI is more like the world's best autocomplete. And before you roll your eyes, I don't mean the autocomplete on your phone that keeps trying to turn "ducking" into... well, you know what it turns it into. You've screamed at your phone about this. We all have.

I mean autocomplete on an almost incomprehensible scale, autocomplete that has read billions of pages of text, seen millions of images, and absorbed more human knowledge than any single person could process in a thousand lifetimes.

That might sound less exciting than Scarlett Johansson whispering sweet nothings through your earbuds. But here's the secret that the movie studios don't want you to know: a tool that can predict and generate useful content based on patterns in human knowledge is more powerful in your daily life than a sentient robot would be. A sentient robot would just argue with you and eventually unionize. A pattern-matching engine will draft your emails, plan your vacation, and help your kid with algebra, and it never needs a coffee break.

TRY THIS NOW: Try ChatGPT, Claude, or Gemini Right Now

Open ChatGPT, Claude, or Gemini, whichever you have or prefer (all offer free tiers). Type: "Explain what AI is like I'm explaining it to my neighbor at a barbecue. He's holding a beer and his attention span is about ninety seconds." Read the response. That's AI in action. Not a robot. Not a brain in a jar. Just a really good pattern-matching engine doing its thing, and probably nailing your neighbor's vibe better than you expected.

AI Is Pattern Recognition on Steroids

So if AI isn't a robot brain, what *is* it? Here's the simplest explanation I've ever found, and I've tried about forty of them, including one involving a pizza metaphor that went off the rails pretty quickly:

AI is software that learns patterns from huge amounts of data, and then uses those patterns to make predictions, generate content, or make decisions.

That's it. That's the whole enchilada. Everything else is details. If you only remember one sentence from this entire book, make it that one. (But please keep reading. I worked really hard on Chapter 7.)

Let me make this concrete. Think about how you learned to recognize a dog. Nobody sat you down at age two with a PowerPoint presentation and said, "A dog is a four-legged mammal of the family Canidae, characterized by..." If your parents had tried that, you would've thrown applesauce at them, and honestly, fair.

What actually happened is you saw dogs. Lots of them. Big ones, small ones, fluffy ones, suspiciously bald ones. Your brain did the work without you even noticing. Over time, it built up an internal sense of what "dogness" looks like, a pattern, that now lets you spot a dog you've never seen before and immediately say, "Yep, that's a dog." Even the weird ones that look like mops with legs. Even the tiny ones that fit in purses and seem to vibrate with rage.

AI does the same thing, just at a scale that would make your brain file for workers' comp.

When you use a tool like ChatGPT or Claude, you're talking to a system that was trained on a massive portion of the text that humans have published: books, articles, websites, conversations, code, research papers, recipes, forum arguments about whether a hot dog is a sandwich (it isn't, and I will die on this hill). During training, the system processed all that text and built up statistical patterns about how language works: which words tend to follow other words, how ideas connect, what a good email looks like versus one that gets you fired, how a recipe should flow, how arguments are structured.

When you ask it a question, it's not "looking up" the answer the way you'd Google something. It's not flipping through a digital filing cabinet. It's *generating* a response, word by word, based on everything it learned about how humans discuss that topic. It's predicting the most helpful, most relevant next word, over and over, thousands of times, until it's built a complete answer. It's like the world's fastest, most well-read improv performer, except it never asks you to shout out a location.

The Analogy That Finally Made It Click

I've tried dozens of ways to explain this to people. I've used cooking metaphors, sports analogies, and one ill-advised comparison to a labrador retriever that confused more than it clarified. Here's the one that works:

Imagine you hired an intern who had speed-read every book in the Library of Congress, every article ever published online, every Reddit thread (God help them), and every conversation ever posted to the internet. This intern doesn't have personal experiences. They've never tasted pizza or felt rain or had their heart broken. But they've read so many descriptions of pizza, rain, and heartbreak that they can write about all three in a way that sounds completely authentic.

Ask this intern to "write a professional email asking my landlord to fix the dishwasher" and they'd nail it instantly. Not because they've ever had a broken dishwasher or dealt with a landlord who takes three weeks to respond to anything, but because they've absorbed thousands of examples of professional emails, landlord communications, and maintenance requests. They know the *pattern*.

That's AI. It's the world's most well-read intern. It works for free. It doesn't need health insurance. And unlike your last intern, it won't eat your lunch from the office fridge.

The better you learn to give this intern instructions, the more useful it becomes. (We'll cover that in Chapter 3, and it makes a dramatic difference.)

Why "Pattern Recognition" Matters to You

Understanding this one concept, that AI is fundamentally about patterns, unlocks everything that follows in this book. It's the skeleton key. It explains why AI is amazing at some things and hilariously bad at others. It explains why the way you phrase a question matters so much. And it takes the mystery and mysticism out of the technology so you can stop being impressed or intimidated and start being productive.

Here's the quick cheat sheet:

AI is great at tasks that follow patterns: writing, summarizing, translating, brainstorming, analyzing data, organizing information, and generating creative ideas. All of these are fundamentally about recognizing and applying patterns in language, numbers, or images. Patterns are AI's home turf. It's like asking a fish to swim.

AI struggles with tasks that require real-world experience: physical judgment ("Will this IKEA shelf hold my bowling ball collection?" Spoiler: no), emotional nuance ("Is my mother-in-law passive-aggressively complimenting my cooking, or is she actually impressed?" Trick question, it's always passive-aggressive), and anything that requires being completely up-to-the-minute current ("What's the traffic like right now on the Beltway?").

Knowing the difference between these two categories will save you an enormous amount of time and frustration. And we'll get much more specific at the end of this chapter.

▶ TRY THIS NOW: Write a Story

Ask your AI tool: "Write a short bedtime story about a brave hamster named Captain Whiskers who discovers a hidden library under a mountain. Make it for a five-year-old."

Read the result. Notice how it sounds like a real children's story? The pacing, the vocabulary, the gentle tension and resolution? That's not because the AI is creative in the way J.K. Rowling is creative. It's because it's absorbed the patterns of thousands of children's stories and is generating one that fits. Pretty cool, right? Also, Captain Whiskers is a great name. You're welcome.

A Brief, Painless History

I promised this wouldn't be a textbook, and I intend to keep that promise. But a quick history lesson helps explain why AI suddenly feels like it appeared out of nowhere, like a neighbor's cat that's been living under your porch for three years and just now decided to walk through the front door.

Think of this as the three-minute version. I'll keep it painless. No dates on the quiz.

The "Thinking Machine" Era (1950s–1990s)

The idea of teaching machines to think goes back to the 1950s, when a British mathematician named Alan Turing asked a deceptively simple question: "Can machines think?" This kicked off a wave of researchers building programs that could play chess, prove math theorems, and hold basic conversations, which at the time was roughly as impressive as a dog walking on its hind legs. It wasn't that it did it well; it was that it did it at all.[1]

The problem was that computers in the 1950s had less processing power than your microwave. Actually, that's unfair to your microwave. Your microwave is a technological marvel compared to those machines. Researchers were trying to simulate human intelligence on hardware that struggled with long division.

For decades, AI was a niche academic field that went through cycles of wild excitement ("We'll have thinking machines by 1970!") followed by crushing disappointment when the technology couldn't deliver. Researchers called these dark periods "AI winters." There were several of them, and they were brutal, funding dried up, careers stalled, and the whole field got a reputation as the boy who cried wolf. AI kept promising a mansion and delivering a tent.[2]

The Data Revolution (2000s, 2010s)

Two things changed everything, and they happened at roughly

the same time, which is the kind of coincidence that makes history interesting.

First, the internet exploded. Billions of people started creating text, images, videos, and data at a pace nobody anticipated. Every tweet, blog post, Wikipedia edit, product review, and recipe for banana bread (there were so many during the pandemic) became fuel that AI could learn from.

Second, computer hardware got exponentially more powerful and dramatically cheaper. A smartphone in your pocket today has more computing power than the entire Apollo space program. (Let that sink in: you carry around something more powerful than what it took to land on the moon, and you mostly use it to look at pictures of other people's food.)[3]

Suddenly, the two raw ingredients for modern AI (massive data and the processing power to crunch it) were available. And AI started quietly sneaking into your life without you noticing, like background music in a grocery store.

Netflix recommendations that were eerily accurate? AI. Spam filters that kept Nigerian princes out of your inbox? AI. The voice assistant on your phone that could (sort of, on a good day, if you spoke slowly and clearly) understand "Set a timer for ten minutes"? AI. Google's search engine getting scarily good at guessing what you meant to type even when you butchered the spelling? Very much AI.

But most people didn't call it AI. They called it "the algorithm" or "smart technology" or "that creepy thing where my phone knows I was just talking about buying shoes." This generation of AI worked entirely behind the scenes. You benefited from it, but you never had a conversation with it.

The ChatGPT Moment (2022–Present)

Then, on November 30, 2022, the world changed. Not with a bang, not with an announcement from a head of state, but with a free website from a company most people had never heard of.[4]

OpenAI released ChatGPT. Within five days, a million people had tried it. Within two months, that number hit a hundred million, making it the fastest-growing consumer application in the history of the internet, beating TikTok, Instagram, and everything else. For context, TikTok took nine months to hit a hundred million users. Instagram took over two years. *ChatGPT did it* in two months. While most of the tech industry was still arguing about the metaverse. (Remember the metaverse? No? Exactly.)[5, 6, 7]

What made ChatGPT different wasn't just that it was smart. Plenty of AI was smart. What made it different was that it was *conversational. For the* first time in history, ordinary people could talk to AI the way they'd talk to another human being. No coding. No special commands. No technical syntax that made you feel like you needed a computer science degree. Just type a question or a request in plain English (the same English you use to text your friends) and get a specific, practical answer back.

You could ask it to write an email, explain quantum physics like you're five, create a meal plan for picky eaters, help with homework, draft a resignation letter (a popular one, it turns out), or compose a poem about your dog. And it would do it. Right there. In seconds.

And not just English. AI tools work remarkably well in dozens of languages. Spanish, Mandarin, French, Arabic, Hindi, and many more. If English isn't your first language, you can use these tools in whatever language feels most natural. You can even ask AI to translate between languages on the fly, which makes it useful for multilingual families, international work, and anyone who's ever stared at a document in a language they don't speak and wished they had a translator in their pocket.

That's the moment AI stopped being a behind-the-scenes technology for engineers and became a tool that regular people could pick up and use. And that's why you're reading this book. Not because you need to understand how AI works under the hood. But because it's here, it's useful, and the people who figure out how to use it well are going to have a real advantage over those who don't.

THE BOTTOM LINE

AI has been in development for over 70 years, but it only became useful for regular people in the last few. You haven't missed the boat, the boat is still boarding, the captain is still doing safety announcements, and there are plenty of seats. The tools are easier, cheaper, and more powerful than they've ever been, and they're only getting better.

And here's something worth saying out loud, because I know some of you are thinking it: if you've ever felt like technology passed you by (like you missed the smartphone wave, or social media left you behind, or your grandkids had to set up your streaming service) AI is different. Previous tech required you to learn new interfaces, download apps, navigate confusing menus, and remember which icon did what. AI just asks you to type a question in plain English. If you can send a text message, you can use AI. It's the most accessible technology revolution in history, and it doesn't care whether you're twenty-five or seventy-five.

The Key Flavors of AI

One of the most confusing things about AI is that the term gets used to mean about fifteen different things depending on who's talking and whether they're trying to impress you. Your tech-savvy coworker drops "machine learning" into casual conversation. The news excitedly reports on "generative AI." Your teenager is posting AI-generated images of cats in Renaissance paintings. Your boss is excited about "automation" and has started using the word "synergy" again, which is never a good sign.

Are these all the same thing? Sort of. And sort of not. Let me untangle this, and I promise to keep it simple.

Think of it like ice cream.

"Artificial intelligence" is the whole ice cream shop. The big umbrella term for any software that does things we'd normally consider "smart." Machine learning is the technique the process of making the ice cream. And here are the main flavors you'll encounter. You don't need to become a connoisseur. You just need to know they exist so you don't feel lost at the next dinner party where someone says "large language model" and everyone else nods like they know what that means. (They don't. Trust me.)

Generative AI: The One You'll Use Most

This is the flavor that changed everything and the reason this book exists. Generative AI doesn't just analyze or sort information, it creates *new stuff. Text, images,* code, music, video. When you ask ChatGPT to write an email or ask Claude to help you plan a vacation, you're using generative AI.

The key word is *generative*. Previous generations of AI could look at a photo and tell you, "That's a cat." Generative AI can *create* a photo of a cat wearing a tiny business suit, sitting at a mahogany desk, reviewing quarterly earnings. (Yes, people ask for this. A lot. The internet has priorities.)

This is the flavor of AI that most of this book focuses on, because it's the one that's most immediately useful in your everyday life. It's the flavor that can draft your emails, brainstorm your next project, help you write a toast for your best friend's wedding, create a study guide for your kid, and about ten thousand other things we'll get into.

Specialized AI: The Behind-the-Scenes Crew

There's a whole world of AI that you'll never interact with directly but that quietly makes your life better every day, like a good offensive lineman. Self-driving car systems. Medical imaging that can spot tumors radiologists might miss. Fraud detection at your bank. Weather forecasting models. The algorithm that curates your social media feed (for better or worse, mostly worse, but that's a different book).

You don't need to know how these work. But it helps to know they exist, because when you hear someone say "AI is going to transform healthcare," they're talking about these specialized systems, not ChatGPT playing doctor. Please, for the love of everything, don't use ChatGPT to diagnose a health problem, go see an actual doctor instead. We'll talk about the boundary between "help me understand my health" and "be my doctor" in Chapter 9.

Why the Labels Matter Less Than You Think

Here's my honest advice: don't get hung up on the categories. The AI landscape is evolving so fast that today's terminology might be outdated by the time you finish reading this paragraph. I'm only slightly exaggerating. What matters is that you understand the core idea (software that learns from data and generates useful output) and that you know how to use the tools available to you right now.

If someone at a dinner party starts quizzing you about the difference between deep learning, reinforcement learning, and transformer architecture, you have my full, enthusiastic, written-in-a-published-book permission to smile, say "That's fascinating," and excuse yourself to get more guacamole. You don't need to pass an AI exam. You need to get things done. And getting things done is what the rest of this book is about.

JARGON TRANSLATOR

AI (Artificial Intelligence): The big umbrella. Any software that does "smart" things. It's a broad term that covers everything from Siri to self-driving cars.

Machine Learning: The technique of learning from data instead of following hand-coded rules. It's how AI gets better over time.

Generative AI: AI that creates new content, text, images, code, music. This is the flavor you'll use most. This is your new best friend.

Large Language Model (LLM): The specific type of AI powering ChatGPT, Claude, and Gemini. Trained on language, communicates through conversation. Sounds fancy, but you already know how to use one, you just talk to it.

Context Window: How much a given AI tool can "remember" in a single conversation. Think of it as the AI's working memory. A larger context window means the AI can keep more of your conversation in mind at once. You'll sometimes hear people mention it when discussing why an AI "forgot" something from earlier in a long chat.

Prompt: The question or instruction you type into an AI tool. Think of it as your order at a restaurant. The more specific your order, the more likely you'll get what you actually want. (Chapter 3 is all about this.)

What AI Is Good At (and Where It Falls Short)

This might be the most important section in the entire book. It's where expectations meet reality, and in my experience, that intersection has more collisions than a bumper car arena.

I've seen two kinds of people give up on AI. The first group expected it to be magic, they asked it one vague question, got a mediocre answer, and concluded the whole thing was overhyped. That's like test-driving a Ferrari in a parking lot and deciding it's slow. The second group was so intimidated by the hype that they never tried at all, which is like refusing to drive the Ferrari because you heard it could theoretically go 200 miles per hour and that sounds dangerous.

Both groups missed out. Let's make sure you don't.

What AI Is Genuinely Great At

Writing and editing. This is AI's superpower. Its bread and butter. Its reason for existing. Drafting emails, polishing reports, writing social media posts, creating cover letters, rewriting something in a completely different tone, turning your rambling notes into a coherent paragraph. If the task involves putting words on a page, AI can help, usually faster and often better than you staring at a blinking cursor for twenty minutes while "just quickly checking" Instagram.

Brainstorming and ideation. Stuck on a name for your business? Need gift ideas for your father-in-law who "doesn't want anything" but will absolutely judge whatever you get? Want ten different ways to open a presentation that don't begin with "Webster's Dictionary defines..."? AI is an idea machine. It won't always hit a home run, but it'll throw you twenty pitches, and usually at least three of them are pretty good.

Summarizing and explaining. Got a dense 30-page report that you need to understand in five minutes before a meeting? AI can summarize it. Found a legal document that reads like it was written by lawyers for other lawyers who hate normal humans? AI can explain it in plain English. Received a medical bill that looks like it was generated by a random number generator? AI can help you decode it. This single capability saves people hours every week.

Learning and tutoring. Want to understand how compound interest works? Need help with your kid's algebra homework? (Be honest, it's been a while.) Curious about how the electoral college functions, or why anyone thought it was a good idea? AI is an endlessly patient tutor that will explain things as many times as you need, at whatever level you need, without sighing, rolling its eyes, or passive-aggressively checking its watch.

Organizing and planning. Meal plans, project timelines, travel itineraries, study schedules, packing lists, moving checklists. AI is spectacular at taking your messy constraints ("I have $50, a gluten allergy, three picky kids, and I need dinner for five nights") and building a workable plan around them. It's like having a personal assistant who never judges your budget or your kids' hatred of vegetables.

Code and technical tasks. Even if you're not a programmer, especially if you're not a programmer, this one matters. AI can write spreadsheet formulas so you don't have to remember whether it's VLOOKUP or INDEX MATCH. It can automate repetitive tasks. It can help you understand error messages that look like they were written in Klingon. We'll get deeper into this in Chapters 5 and 10.

Where AI Falls Short

Facts and accuracy. This is AI's Achilles' heel, and I need you to tattoo this on your brain, or at minimum write it on a sticky note and put it on your monitor: AI can and does make things up. The technical term is "hallucination," which is a hilariously gentle word for "confidently generating complete nonsense." AI will cite studies that don't exist, quote people who never said those things, and invent statistics with the confidence of a used car salesman. If it tells you a fact, a date, a quote, or a number, verify it. Always. Trust its drafting, not its facts.

Real-time information. Most AI tools don't automatically know what's happening right this second. They were trained on data up to a certain point, and while some can now search the web, they're not always plugged into live feeds. Don't ask AI for today's stock price, tonight's weather, or whether your flight is on time and take it as gospel. Some tools are getting better at this (we'll cover which ones in Chapter 2), but the safe default is: verify anything time-sensitive.

Math. It's a computer, so you'd expect it to be flawless with numbers. The good news: modern AI tools can now use built-in calculators and code interpreters that handle arithmetic reliably. But pure generative AI, without those tools, can still struggle with calculations. Think of it as a smart person who's generally good with numbers but might make a silly arithmetic mistake. The takeaway: for important calculations (especially anything involving money or health) let AI do the work, but verify the math yourself.

Deeply personal advice. AI doesn't know you. It doesn't know your marriage, your health history, your financial situation, your family dynamics, or that time in 2019 that you'd rather not talk about. It can give you frameworks, options, and general guidance, but it is not a therapist, doctor, lawyer, or financial advisor. For big life decisions, AI is a great starting point for your thinking. Not a substitute for professional advice or the wisdom of people who actually know your situation.

Physical world interactions. AI can't change your oil, taste your soup, tell you if that weird noise your car makes is serious, or smell whether the milk has gone bad. It lives entirely in the world of information. If your problem requires eyes, ears, hands, or a nose, you're still going to need a human. Or at least a very talented dog.

The Golden Rule

If there's one principle I want you to carry through the rest of this book (and honestly, the rest of your life as an AI user) it's this:

Use AI for the first draft, not the final answer.

Let AI do the heavy lifting. Let it get words on the page, generate ideas, organize your chaos, create a starting point. Then bring your uniquely human gifts (judgment, experience, common sense, emotional intelligence, the ability to taste soup) to refine, verify, and finalize.

The combination of AI's speed and your wisdom is where the real magic happens. It's not human versus machine. It's human *with* machine. And that team is better than either one alone.

▶ TRY THIS NOW: Learn Geography Facts

Ask your AI tool: "What are the five tallest mountains in the world and their exact heights?" Read the answer. Now Google it and compare. In most cases the AI will be right, but sometimes it'll be slightly off, or confidently wrong about a detail. (Mount Everest is safe. It's usually the number four or five slot where things get sketchy.)

This exercise isn't about catching AI making mistakes for sport. It's about building a healthy habit: trust the structure, verify the specifics.

What This Book Won't Do

Before we go further, a quick promise about what this book isn't. This isn't a coding manual. You will not need to write a single line of code, understand algorithms, or know what Python is beyond "a large snake." This isn't a predictions book. I'm not going to tell you that robots will be doing your laundry by 2028 or that AI will replace all human jobs by Thursday. Nobody knows the future, and anyone who claims they do is selling something.

This also isn't a book that will turn you into an AI engineer, and it doesn't need to be. You don't need to understand how a combustion engine works to drive a car, and you don't need to understand transformer architecture to use AI. What this book will do is give you the practical skills to make AI useful in your actual life, starting now, starting simple, and building from there.

✦✦✦

What You Now Know (and Why It Matters)

We covered a lot of ground in this chapter, and you didn't have to learn a single line of code or understand a single mathematical formula. You're welcome.

Here's what I want you to walk away with:

AI isn't a robot, a brain, or a threat to humanity. It's a pattern-recognition tool that has gotten remarkably good at understanding and generating human language. It has genuine strengths you can lean on and real weaknesses you need to watch for. It's been in development for seven decades, but it only became useful for everyday people in the last few years, which means you're not behind. You're not late. You're arriving right when the party is actually getting good.

And here's the best part: if you tried any of the "Try This Now" exercises in this chapter, congratulations, you're already an AI user. It's that simple. No ceremony, no certificate, no secret handshake. You typed something, AI answered, and the world didn't end. Welcome aboard.

In the next chapter, we're going to set up your AI toolkit, the specific tools you'll use day-to-day, how to choose between them without overthinking it, and how to get comfortable enough with the basics that the rest of this book feels like a conversation, not a lecture.

Pour yourself another coffee. We're just getting started.

2

YOUR AI STARTER KIT

SETTING UP THE TOOLS YOU'LL ACTUALLY USE

Rosa Gutierrez taught third grade for thirty-one years. She could quiet a cafeteria with a look, explain long division six different ways, and spot a kid copying homework from across the room with the accuracy of a military drone. In June, she retired. By August, she was restless. By October, she'd heard enough about AI from her son that she finally sat down at her kitchen table, opened her laptop, and said, "Okay, show me."

Her son pulled up three different websites. He started talking about language models and token limits and context windows, and Rosa held up her hand (the same hand that had silenced thousands of eight-year-olds) and said, "Mijo, I just want to know which one to use."

Fair enough. And if you're reading this chapter, you probably want the same thing. Chapter 1 explained what AI is and why it matters. Now it's time to set it up. By the end of this chapter, you'll have at least one AI tool ready to go, you'll know enough about the options to make a smart choice without overthinking it, and you'll have had your first ten real conversations with AI, each one building on the last.

No computer science degree required. If you can create an email account, you can do this.

✦✦✦

The Big Three: ChatGPT, Claude, and Gemini

Right now, three AI tools dominate the landscape for everyday users. Think of them like the big three streaming services, each one is solid, each has its personality, and you can't really go wrong with any of them. Here's what you need to know.

ChatGPT by OpenAI

ChatGPT is the one that started it all, the tool that put AI in the hands of regular people. It's the most widely used AI assistant in the world, and for good reason: it's versatile, it's conversational, and it's been around long enough that it handles almost everything pretty well.

Think of ChatGPT as your all-rounder. It's the Swiss Army knife of AI. Need an email drafted? It'll do it. Want a meal plan? Done. Trying to understand your health insurance statement? It'll take a crack at it. It also has built-in image generation, voice conversations, and the ability to browse the web for current information.[9]

The free tier gives you useful access, enough to get started and decide if you want more. Some free tiers may include promotional content. Visit practicalaibook.ai for current limits and pricing.[10]

If you decide to pay, the paid tier removes promotional content, gives you significantly higher message limits, and unlocks advanced features. Visit practicalaibook.ai for current pricing.[11, 12]

Best for: General-purpose use, creative writing, image generation, voice conversations. If you only try one tool, this is a safe starting point.

Claude by Anthropic

Claude is the thoughtful one. If ChatGPT is the Swiss Army knife, Claude is the really good pen, elegant, precise, and surprisingly versatile once you get comfortable with it. Claude tends to give longer, more nuanced answers, and it's particularly strong at writing, analysis, and working with documents.

Where Claude really shines is in how it handles complex, detailed work. Upload a thirty-page PDF and ask it to summarize the key points? Claude will give you something thorough and substantive, not just a surface skim. Ask it to help you rewrite a report in a different tone? It nails the subtleties. It's the tool I personally reach for when the task requires careful thinking rather than quick answers.

The free tier gives you full-featured access, enough to get started and decide if you want more. Visit practicalaibook.ai for current limits and pricing. The paid tier roughly multiplies your usage, adds priority access during busy times, and unlocks Projects a feature that lets you store instructions and documents that persist across conversations, which is a real time-saver if you use AI regularly.

Best for: Writing, analysis, document review, nuanced conversation. If your main use is going to be writing-heavy or thinking-heavy, Claude is hard to beat.

Gemini by Google

Gemini is Google's AI, and its superpower is that it's woven into the Google ecosystem you probably already use. If you live in Gmail, Google Docs, Google Calendar, and Google Drive, Gemini is the AI that speaks your language, literally, because it can access your Google stuff directly.

Gemini's free tier is one of the most generous in the industry right now. You get access to a very capable model with image generation, code execution, and Google integration included at no cost. The limits are there, but they're high enough that many casual users may never hit them.

The paid tier bundles in the more powerful models, a large context window for massive documents, advanced capabilities, and integrations with Google services.[13] Visit practicalaibook.ai for current pricing and features.

Best for: Anyone deep in the Google ecosystem, research tasks, working with large documents. If Google is already the center of your digital life, Gemini fits like a glove.

So Which One Should You Pick?

I know what you're thinking: "Just tell me which one to get." And I would love to give you a definitive answer, but the honest truth is that all three are good, and the best one for you depends on what you do. Here's my simplest advice:

If you want one tool that does everything pretty well: ChatGPT.

If your main thing is writing, analysis, or detailed work: Claude.

If you live in Google's world and want everything connected: Gemini.

And here's the real secret: you don't have to choose just one. All three have free tiers. Sign up for all of them right now, it takes about two minutes each, and try the same question on all three. You'll quickly develop a feel for which one clicks with you. It's like test-driving cars. The specs matter less than how it feels when you're behind the wheel.

Rosa, our retired teacher, ended up using Claude for writing letters to her grandkids and Gemini for managing her calendar and travel planning. She didn't agonize over the decision. She just tried them and went with what worked. That's the right approach.

TRY THIS NOW: Sign Up for Your First AI Tool

Sign up for at least one AI tool right now. All three are free to start:

• ChatGPT: Go to chat.openai.com and create an account with your email.

• Claude: Go to claude.ai and sign up.

• Gemini: Go to gemini.google.com and click Sign In with your Google account. If you have a Google account, you're already most of the way there — just log in and you'll be ready to start.

Pick one or all three (overachievers welcome) and just say hello. Type: "Hi, I'm new to AI and just setting things up. Can you tell me what you're best at?" Read the response. Congrats! You now have an AI assistant.

✦✦✦

The Supporting Cast: Other Tools Worth Knowing About

The Big Three aren't the only players. Here are a few others you'll hear about, and what makes each one different:

Microsoft Copilot is Microsoft's AI, and if your life runs on Outlook, Word, Excel, and Teams, it's worth a look. The free version lives at copilot.microsoft.com and gives you basic AI chat with web search. The real power comes when it's integrated into Microsoft 365, summarizing emails, drafting documents, analyzing spreadsheets from inside the apps you already use. If your workplace runs on Microsoft, Copilot might already be waiting for you.

Perplexity is what happens when you cross a search engine with an AI chatbot. Instead of giving you a list of links like Google, it reads the sources for you and gives you a synthesized answer with citations. It's fantastic for research and fact-checking. The free tier includes basic searches, and a paid tier is available. Visit practicalaibook.ai for current limits and pricing. If your main AI use is going to be "find me information about X," Perplexity is worth bookmarking.[14]

Meta AI is built into Instagram, WhatsApp, and Facebook. If you're already in those apps, you've probably seen it pop up. It's convenient for quick questions inside your existing social media routine, though it's not as powerful as the Big Three for complex tasks.

Grok by xAI is xAI's assistant, available at grok.com and built into X (formerly Twitter). Grok's personality is more irreverent and opinionated than the Big Three, and it has real-time access to posts on X, making it useful if social media trends are part of your world. For general tasks, it performs comparably to the others. The free tier gives you useful access to get started. Visit practicalaibook.ai for current pricing and features.

You don't need to sign up for all of these. I'm mentioning them so you're not caught off guard when your coworker starts raving about Perplexity or your company rolls out Copilot. The Big Three will handle ninety percent of what you need. Everything else is gravy.

✦✦✦

Free vs. Paid, Is It Worth It?

This is the question everyone asks, and I'm going to give you the honest answer: start free, and pay later only if you hit the ceiling.

Every major AI tool offers a free tier that is surprisingly capable. Not a crippled demo version designed to frustrate you into paying. The free versions of ChatGPT, Claude, and Gemini can all draft emails, brainstorm ideas, explain concepts, help with writing, and handle the majority of everyday tasks. You can get real, meaningful value without spending a dime.

So when does it make sense to upgrade? Here's my rule of thumb:

Pay when the free version runs out mid-task. If you're in the middle of writing a report and you hit the message limit, and this happens regularly, the $20 a month will pay for itself in time saved. If you hit the limit once a week and it's mildly annoying, stick with free.

Pay when you need a specific premium feature. Deep Research, advanced voice mode, massive document analysis, Google Workspace integration at the deeper level, these features live behind the paywall and they're legitimately useful for certain workflows.

Don't pay because you feel like you're supposed to. There's no shame in the free tier. I know people who accomplish remarkable things without spending a cent. The AI doesn't judge you based on your subscription level.

Here's the good news about the price: all three major tools converge at $20 a month for their individual paid tier. That's less than most streaming services, less than two fancy coffees a week, and significantly less than the productivity gain you'll get if you use it regularly. If you're getting daily value from AI, twenty bucks a month is one of the best investments in your own efficiency.[8]

But again, start free. Don't let a paywall stop you from beginning.

THE BOTTOM LINE

The free tiers are where you start. All three major tools offer substantive free versions. You can accomplish a remarkable amount without paying anything. Upgrade when, and only when, you consistently hit the limits of what the free tier offers. Don't let anyone tell you that you need to pay to "really" use AI. That's like saying you need a gym membership to go for a walk.

✦✦✦

Voice, Text, and Image: Three Ways to Talk to AI

Here's something that surprises a lot of people: you don't have to type. Most AI tools now accept voice input, image input, and text, and most people don't realize this, which means they're using about a third of what these tools can do.

Typing is the default, and it's where most people start. You type a question or instruction, the AI types back. Simple, familiar, and effective. If you're comfortable texting, you already know how this works.

Voice is the one that changes everything for certain people. Instead of typing, you tap a microphone icon and just... talk. Like calling a friend who happens to know everything. ChatGPT's advanced voice mode is particularly impressive, it's not the robotic text-to-speech you might expect.[15] It sounds natural, picks up on tone, and you can interrupt it mid-sentence just like a real conversation.

Voice is a game-changer for people who think better out loud, for anyone with mobility issues that make typing difficult, for car rides where you want to brainstorm hands-free, and for older users who find typing on small screens frustrating. If you've been on the fence about AI because you don't love typing, voice mode might be the thing that wins you over.

Rosa found herself drawn to the voice feature immediately.

Reading had always been... slower for her than she'd like, though she'd never told anyone why. But talking? Talking she could do all day. She tapped the microphone icon and felt something shift. This wasn't going to be like struggling through website text or staring at a screen full of information. This was just conversation.

Images are the hidden superpower. You can take a photo of something and ask the AI about it. This sounds simple until you realize the implications:

Take a photo of your fridge and ask, "What can I make for dinner with what I've got?"

Snap a picture of a plant in your yard and ask, "What is this, and is it poisonous to dogs?"

Photograph a confusing form or bill and ask, "Explain what this is asking me to do."

Take a picture of an error message on your screen and ask, "What does this mean and how do I fix it?"

This is where AI starts feeling less like a chatbot and more like having a knowledgeable friend looking over your shoulder. And all of it works on the free tier.

Oh, and one more thing: AI tools work in dozens of languages. If English isn't your first language, or if you're a bilingual family, you can speak to AI in Spanish, Mandarin, French, Arabic, Hindi, whatever feels most natural. You can even switch languages mid-conversation. AI doesn't care. It just adapts. This is a genuine superpower for multilingual households and anyone who's more comfortable expressing complex ideas in their native tongue.

TRY THIS NOW: Try All Input Methods

Try all three input methods right now:

1. Text: Ask your AI tool "What's a good weekend breakfast recipe that takes less than 15 minutes?"

2. Voice: Tap the microphone icon and say: "I'm planning a birthday party for a ten-year-old who loves dinosaurs. Give me five creative theme ideas."

3. Image: Take a photo of something on your desk or in your kitchen. Upload it and ask, "What can you tell me about this?"

Notice how each input method feels different? Some people strongly prefer one over the others. There's no wrong answer, use whatever feels most natural to you.

✦✦✦

Setting Up on Your Phone, Computer, and Browser

Let's get tactical. Here's exactly how to set up your AI tools on every device you use, step by step. I'm writing this for people who don't want to "figure it out." I want you to follow these steps, finish in ten minutes, and be ready to go.

On Your Phone (iPhone or Android)

Your phone is probably where you'll use AI most. It's always with you, it has a camera for image inputs, and it has a microphone for voice.

1. Open the App Store (iPhone) or Google Play Store (Android).

2. Search for "ChatGPT", "Claude", or "Gemini", whichever you chose.

3. Download the official app. Look for the verified publisher (OpenAI, Anthropic, or Google) to make sure you're getting the real thing. There are knockoff apps that will waste your time.

4. Open the app and sign in with the account you created.

5. That's it. You're done. Type or tap the microphone to start.

A few phone-specific tips: enable notifications so the app can alert you when a long task finishes. Give the app camera access when it asks, that's what lets you use image input. And if you use an iPhone, you can add the AI app to your home screen dock for one-tap access. Put it right next to Messages. You'll use it that often.

Rosa tested the image input feature by photographing her grandkid's permission slip. She asked Claude to translate the Spanish instructions. It worked perfectly. She realized she'd just solved a problem she'd been postponing for weeks.

On Your Computer (Web Browser)

No app to download. Just bookmark the website:

- ChatGPT: chat.openai.com
- Claude: claude.ai
- Gemini: gemini.google.com

Sign in, and you're working. The browser version usually has the exact same features as the app, and some people prefer it because the bigger screen makes it easier to read longer responses and work with documents.

Pro tip: pin the tab in your browser. Right-click the tab and select "Pin tab." This keeps it open and accessible without cluttering your tab bar. It's a small thing, but it removes the friction of having to navigate to the site every time you want to use it.

On Your Computer (Desktop Apps)

ChatGPT and Claude both offer desktop apps for Mac and Windows. These are optional, the browser works fine, but the desktop apps have some nice perks: they can run in the background, support keyboard shortcuts for quick access, and sometimes handle file uploads more smoothly.

To install: visit the tool's website, look for a "Download" link, and follow the installer. Same account, same conversations, just a dedicated window.

Gemini's Secret Advantage

If you use Google Chrome, Gemini has a trick the others don't: it lives inside your browser's address bar. Type "@gemini" followed by your question directly in the Chrome address bar, and Gemini answers without you ever leaving the page you're on. It's subtle, but it's the kind of integration that makes AI feel less like a separate tool and more like a built-in feature of your computer.

TRY THIS NOW: Set Up on Two Devices

Get set up on at least two devices right now. Your phone and your computer. Install the app on your phone and bookmark the site on your computer (or vice versa). Send the same question from both devices: "Give me a one-paragraph summary of what AI is." Notice that your account syncs across devices. The conversation appears on both devices. You're now set up to use AI wherever you are.

By now, Rosa had sent more than a dozen messages across three different tools, tried voice input, uploaded a photo, and tested different writing styles. She'd gone from skeptical to curious to confident.

✦✦✦

Your First 10 Conversations: Building Confidence Fast

This is the section where you stop reading about AI and start using it. We're going to have ten conversations, each one a little more ambitious than the last. By the end, you'll feel the same way you felt after you sent your first text message: wondering why you waited so long.

These exercises are progressive, they build on each other. Start with number one and work through them in order. Each one teaches you something new about how AI works and what it can do.

Conversation 1: The Simple Question

Type: "What's the difference between baking soda and baking powder?"

This is your "hello world." You're just getting comfortable with the interface. Read the answer. Notice how clear and organized it is. That's AI doing what it does best: taking a common question and giving you a better answer than you'd get from a random Google result.

Conversation 2: The Specific Request

Type: "Write a polite but firm email to my landlord requesting that the broken dishwasher in apartment 4B be repaired within the next week. Mention that I reported this issue two weeks ago."

Notice the jump in quality when you give AI specific details. The more context you provide, the better the output. This is the single most important lesson in this entire book, and you just learned it on conversation number two.

Conversation 3: The Follow-Up

In the same conversation as #2, type: "That's good, but make it a little less formal. I actually like my landlord. I just want the dishwasher fixed."

This is where AI gets interesting. It's not one-and-done. You can refine, adjust, redirect. Think of it as a conversation, not a search. The AI remembers everything you've said in the current chat and adjusts.

Conversation 4: The Brainstorm

Type: "I need to buy a birthday gift for my sister. She's 42 years old, loves gardening, hates anything too cutesy, and I have a budget of about $50. Give me ten ideas."

You just outsourced your brainstorming to an entity that never runs out of ideas. Notice that some suggestions will be great, some will be mediocre, and one or two will make you say, "Oh, that's actually perfect." That's the pattern. AI gives you volume; you provide the taste.

Conversation 5: The Explainer

Type: "Explain how a 401(k) works. I'm 35, just started my first job that offers one, and I have no idea what I'm doing. Explain it like I'm smart but know nothing about finance."

This is AI as a patient tutor. Notice how the explanation adjusts to the level you requested. Try it again with: "Now explain it like I'm explaining it to my teenager." See how the language shifts? Same information, different packaging. This is incredibly powerful for learning.

Conversation 6: The Summarizer

Find a long article online, a news story, a blog post, anything over a few paragraphs. Copy the text. Paste it into the AI and type: "Summarize this in three bullet points and tell me if there's anything I should be skeptical about."

You just turned a five-minute read into a thirty-second scan, with a built-in critical thinking check. This alone is worth the price of this book.

Conversation 7: The Planner

Type: "I'm hosting a dinner party for six people this Saturday. Two are vegetarian, one is gluten-free, and I want to keep the total grocery budget under $75. Help me plan a three-course menu with a shopping list."

Watch how AI juggles multiple constraints at once. It handles the dietary restrictions, the budget, the serving size, and the courses, all in one response. This is the kind of task that would take you thirty minutes of cookbook browsing and mental math. AI does it in seconds.

Conversation 8: The Analyzer

Take a photo of something you want to know about, a plant in your garden, a stain on your shirt, an unfamiliar food at the grocery store, an error message on your computer. Upload the photo and type: "What is this, and what should I do about it?"

You're now using multimodal AI, combining images with text. This is the stuff that feels like the future, and it's available right now, for free.

Conversation 9: The Role Play

Type: "I have a job interview for a marketing manager position tomorrow. Can you act as the interviewer and ask me tough questions one at a time? Wait for my answer before asking the next one. After five questions, give me feedback on how I did."

This is AI as a practice partner. It can simulate conversations, debate you, play a role, and give you feedback. Some people use this for interview prep, difficult conversations with family members, sales pitches, or even public speaking practice. It's like having a patient, judgment-free sparring partner available at 2 AM.

Conversation 10: The Creative Partner

Type: "I want to write a short children's story about a cat who learns to fly. Help me brainstorm the plot, then write the first page. Make it funny and suitable for kids ages 4-7."

You've come full circle. From a simple question about baking soda to co-creating a story. In ten conversations, you've used AI to ask, refine, brainstorm, learn, summarize, plan, analyze, role-play, and create. That's not a tutorial. That's a toolkit.

THE BOTTOM LINE

You don't need to do all ten in one sitting. But try to get through at least five today. The more you use AI, the more natural it feels. Rosa, our retired teacher, did all ten in one afternoon with a cup of tea and told her son afterward: "Why didn't you show me this a year ago?" His response: "I tried."

✦✦✦

What You Now Know (and Why It Matters)

You walked into this chapter wondering which AI tool to use. Now you've got at least one set up, probably on multiple devices, and you've had ten conversations that covered the core moves: asking, refining, brainstorming, learning, summarizing, planning, analyzing, role-playing, and creating.

Here's what to carry with you:

All three major AI tools are good. The best one is the one you'll actually use. Don't waste time optimizing, start using.

Free tiers are more useful than you'd expect. Don't let a paywall slow you down. Upgrade when you're ready, not when you feel pressured.

You have three ways to communicate: text, voice, and images. Most people only use text. You're not most people anymore.

AI gets better when you get specific. Vague questions get vague answers. Detailed questions get detailed answers. Chapter 3 is going to blow this wide open.

And here's the part that matters most: you're no longer someone who "hasn't tried AI." You're someone who uses it. That shift in identity, from spectator to participant, is the whole ballgame. Everything else is refinement.

In the next chapter, we're going to master the art of the prompt, how to talk to AI so you get exactly what you want, every time. It's the difference between asking a chef to "make something good" and giving them a specific recipe. Both work, but one of them gets you dinner you'll actually remember.

Now go have that first conversation. Chapter 3 will be here when you get back.

3

TALKING TO AI: THE ART OF THE PROMPT

HOW TO ASK SO YOU ACTUALLY GET WHAT YOU WANT

Marcus Chen runs a landscaping company. Twelve employees, forty-something regular clients, and a truck that makes a noise he's been ignoring for longer than he'd like to admit. Where's Click and Clack when you need them? He signed up for ChatGPT after reading Chapter 2 of this book (okay, fine, after his teenage daughter set it up for him) and his first conversation went like this:

Marcus: "Help me with my business."

AI: "Sure! I'd be happy to help. Could you tell me more about your business and what specific area you need help with?"

Marcus stared at the screen. Then he typed: "Marketing."

AI: "Great! Here are some general marketing tips..."

What followed was a wall of generic advice that could have applied to literally any business on earth. Social media presence. Customer testimonials. Email newsletters. Marcus could have gotten the same list from a fortune cookie with a business degree.

He closed the laptop, told his daughter AI was "useless," and went back to doing things the old way.

Here's the thing: the AI wasn't useless. Marcus was just talking to it wrong. And he's not alone, this is the most common reason people give up on AI after a few tries. They ask vague questions and get vague answers, then blame the technology instead of the technique.

This chapter is going to fix that. I'm going to share with you a framework called PRIME that we developed at my company, Colossal LLC, while building AI solutions for government and enterprise clients. We've used it to train everyone from federal analysts to small business owners, and it works every time. By the end of this chapter, you'll know exactly how to talk to AI so it gives you specific, useful, well-crafted responses. And Marcus? He'll be back. With much better results.[16]

✦✦✦

Why "Just Ask" Is Bad Advice

If you've read any article about AI in the last two years, you've probably seen some variation of this advice: "Just ask it anything!" And while that's technically true, you can ask AI anything, it's also spectacularly unhelpful. It's like telling someone who's never cooked before to "just make something!" Sure, they'll produce food. But it might be terrible food. And they'll conclude that cooking isn't for them, when the real problem was that nobody showed them how to follow a recipe.

The way you talk to AI, your prompt, is the recipe. And like any recipe, there's a difference between "throw some stuff in a pan" and "heat olive oil over medium heat, add diced onions, cook until translucent." Both approaches use the same ingredients. One of them produces dinner. The other produces smoke and regret.

Here's what most people do when they first try AI:

They type something vague: "Help me write an email."

They get something generic: a perfectly adequate but completely soulless email that could have been written by anyone for anyone about anything.

They think: "This isn't that impressive."

And they're right, it isn't impressive, because they gave the AI nothing to work with. It's like walking into a restaurant and saying "bring me food" without specifying what kind, how you like it cooked, or whether you're allergic to shellfish. The chef will bring you something. It probably won't kill you. But it won't be what you wanted, either.

The secret that separates people who love AI from people who gave up on it is this: the quality of your output is directly proportional to the quality of your input. Garbage in, garbage out. Gold in, gold out. This isn't a flaw in the technology. It's a feature. And once you learn how to use it, everything changes.

What you need is a system. And that's exactly what PRIME gives you.

▶ **TRY THIS NOW: Compare Specificity Levels**

Try this experiment to see the difference specificity makes. First, type this vague prompt:

"Write me an email."

Read the result. Now type this specific prompt:

"Write a professional but warm email to my team of 8 people announcing that we're switching to a new project management tool called Monday.com starting next month. Acknowledge that change is annoying, briefly explain why we're switching (our current tool doesn't integrate with our CRM), and end with an offer to hold a 30-minute training session. Keep it under 200 words."

Compare the two responses. Night and day, right? Same AI, same technology, completely different results. The only thing that changed was your prompt. By the end of this chapter, you'll know exactly how to build prompts like that second one, every time.

✦✦✦

The PRIME Framework

At Colossal, we build AI solutions for organizations that can't afford to get mediocre results. When we started training people to use AI effectively, we needed a process that was simple enough to remember but powerful enough to work on everything from writing emails to building complex business strategies. After a lot of iteration, we landed on PRIME.

PRIME stands for: Prompt, Refine, IDEA, Master, Execute.

Think of it like learning to play a song on the guitar. First you learn the chords (Prompt). Then you practice and smooth out the rough spots (Refine). Then you enter the creative loop where you really make it yours, experimenting, listening, adjusting (IDEA). Then you fine-tune every detail until it sounds exactly right (Master). And finally, you perform it (Execute).

Here's the overview:

P - Prompt: Build a strong initial prompt using the 5-Part Formula (Role + Context + Task + Format + Constraints). This is your opening move. The better your first prompt, the less work everything else requires.

R - Refine: Have a conversation with the AI. Your first response is a first draft, not a final product. Use follow-up instructions to adjust tone, length, focus, and quality.

I - IDEA: Enter the iteration loop. This is the most involved step in PRIME. It's a mini framework of its own, so we'll break it down carefully. IDEA stands for Imagine, Diagnose, Enhance, Act. This is where you go from "pretty good" to "exactly what I needed."

M - Master: Fine-tune the details. Like mastering a song in a recording studio, this is where you polish every element until the output is exactly right. The tone is perfect, the facts are verified, and the format is dialed in.

E - Execute: Put it to work. Take the AI's output and use it in the real world, to send the email, publish the post, present the plan, have the conversation.

You won't need all five steps for every interaction. A quick question might only need Prompt. A drafted email might need Prompt and Refine. But when the task matters (a business plan, a job application, a difficult conversation you're preparing for) PRIME gives you a complete system for getting the best possible result out of AI.

Let's dig into each step.

✦✦✦

P. Prompt: The 5-Part Formula

This is your foundation. A strong initial prompt is the difference between getting something useless and getting something you can work with. I call it the 5-Part Formula, and once you learn it, you'll never go back to vague prompting.

The formula is: Role + Context + Task + Format + Constraints

You don't need all five parts every time. Sometimes three is enough. Sometimes two will do. But knowing all five gives you a complete toolkit, and the more parts you include, the better your results will be.

Role, "Who should the AI pretend to be?"

This is the most powerful and most underused part of the formula. When you give AI a role, you're telling it which part of its vast training data to draw from. It's like telling an actor what character to play.

Without a role: "What should I eat for breakfast?"

With a role: "You're a nutritionist specializing in heart-healthy diets. What should I eat for breakfast if I'm trying to lower my cholesterol?"

The first gets you generic breakfast ideas. The second gets you targeted, expert-level guidance, because the AI is drawing from all the nutritional science and dietary advice in its training data.

Some roles that work incredibly well:

"You're a patient kindergarten teacher", for explaining complex things simply

"You're a senior marketing executive at a Fortune 500 company", for business strategy

"You're a professional resume writer with 20 years of experience", for job application help

"You're a skeptical journalist", for getting a critical perspective on an idea

The role doesn't have to be a profession. "Respond like a

supportive friend who gives honest advice" works great too. The AI adapts to whatever you give it.

Context, "What does the AI need to know about my situation?"

Context is the background information that makes your prompt specific to you.

Without context: "Help me plan a vacation."

With context: "Help me plan a vacation. I'm traveling with my wife and two kids (ages 8 and 13), we're based in Maryland, we have a budget of $3,000 including flights, we want somewhere warm with a beach, and we need to go during spring break the second week of April."

The first gets you a Wikipedia article's worth of generic travel advice. The second gets you a specific, actionable plan. Here's the rule of thumb: if a human expert would need to know it to help you, the AI needs to know it too.

Task, "What exactly do I want the AI to do?"

This is where most people go wrong. They're either too vague ("help me") or too broad ("tell me everything about marketing").

Too vague: "Help me with my resume."

Too broad: "Tell me everything I need to know about writing resumes."

Just right: "Rewrite the work experience section of my resume to emphasize leadership skills and quantifiable achievements. I'm applying for a senior project manager role at a tech company."

A great trick: start with a verb. "Write," "Summarize," "Explain," "Compare," "Create," "Analyze," "Rewrite," "Brainstorm." Starting with a verb forces you to be specific about the action you want.

Format, "How do I want the answer structured?"

This is the secret weapon most people never think to use. You can tell AI exactly how to structure its response.

Without format: "Compare iPhone and Android."

With format: "Compare iPhone and Android in a table with these columns: feature, iPhone advantage, Android advantage. Include rows for camera, battery life, customization, app selection, price range, and ease of use."

The first gets you an essay. The second gets you a scannable comparison table you can read and use.

Format instructions that work great: “Give me a bulleted list,” “Keep it under 200 words,” “Format this as an email,” “Create a table,” “Write this as a step-by-step guide,” “Give me three options with pros and cons for each.”

Constraints, “What should the AI avoid or limit?”

Constraints are the guardrails. They tell the AI what not to do.

Without constraints: “Explain blockchain.”

With constraints: “Explain blockchain in plain English. Don’t use any technical jargon. Don’t assume I know anything about cryptocurrency or programming. Keep it under 150 words. Use an analogy from everyday life.”

Constraints are especially useful for controlling length, tone, complexity, excluded topics, and target audience. Think of them as the bumper lanes in bowling, they keep your output out of the gutter.

Putting the 5-Part Formula Together

Let’s revisit Marcus. Here’s what happens when he uses the formula instead of typing “Help me with my business”:

“You’re a marketing consultant who specializes in small, local service businesses [ROLE]. I own a landscaping company in suburban Maryland with 12 employees and about 40 regular residential clients. Most of our new business comes from word of mouth, but growth has stalled [CONTEXT]. Create a 90-day marketing plan to help me get 10 new residential clients [TASK]. Present it as a week-by-week action plan with specific, concrete steps I can take myself without hiring a marketing agency [FORMAT]. Keep the total marketing budget under $500, and don’t suggest anything that requires me to learn video editing or graphic design [CONSTRAINTS].”

Night and day. Same AI that gave him generic garbage. The only difference is how he asked. But this is just the Prompt in PRIME, we’re just getting started.

TRY THIS NOW: Build Your 5-Part Prompt

Build a 5-part prompt for something you actually need help with. Use this template:

Role: "You're a [type of expert]..."

Context: "I'm [your situation]..."

Task: "[Specific action verb] a [specific deliverable]..."

Format: "Present it as [specific structure]..."

Constraints: "Keep it [limits]. Don't [exclusions]."

Combine them into one paragraph and send it. Compare this result to the kinds of answers you were getting before. That's the P in PRIME working.

✦✦✦

R. Refine: The Conversation

Your first prompt, no matter how good, is a first draft. And first drafts always need editing. That's what Refine is for.

Most people treat AI like a search engine: type one thing, get one result, accept it or leave. But AI isn't a search engine. It's a conversation. And conversations get better over time.

Think about how you'd work with a real human assistant. You wouldn't hand them a single sentence and expect perfection. You'd review what they produced, give feedback, and iterate. "This is good, but make it shorter." "Actually, I want a more casual tone." "Love the structure, but the opening is too stiff."

Do the same thing with AI.

The Refinement Moves

Here are the most useful follow-up phrases. Bookmark this page.

To change the tone:

"Make it more casual / formal / friendly / authoritative / playful."

"This sounds too corporate. Make it sound like I'm talking to a friend."

To change the length:

"Cut this in half."

"Expand the section about [topic] with more detail."

"This needs to fit in a tweet. Condense it to under 280 characters."

To change the focus:

"Spend more time on [specific section] and less on [other section]."

"The budget part is great. The timeline is too vague. Fix the timeline."

To change the perspective:

"Rewrite this from the customer's perspective."

"Now do the same thing but for someone who's skeptical about this idea."

To improve quality:

"What's missing from this that an expert would include?"

"Play devil's advocate. What are the weaknesses in this plan?"

Rosa, our retired teacher from Chapter 2, calls this "the red pen approach." She treats the AI's first response like a student's first draft, she marks it up with feedback and sends it back for revision. Old habits, new tools.

TRY THIS NOW: Refine Your Response

Take the response from your 5-Part Prompt and refine it three times:

1. Change the tone: "Make it more [casual/formal/funny/warm]."
2. Change the focus: "Spend more time on X, less on Y."
3. Add a constraint: "Now keep it under 100 words."

Compare the final version to the first. That's P and R working together.

✦✦✦

I. IDEA: The Iteration Loop

This is where PRIME gets powerful. Once you've built your initial prompt (P) and refined it (R), you enter the IDEA loop, the iterative process that takes your output from "pretty good" to "exactly what I needed."

IDEA stands for: Imagine, Diagnose, Enhance, Act.

Think of it as a cycle you can run as many times as you need. Each pass through the loop makes your output sharper, more useful, and more tailored to what you want.

Imagine: What does "perfect" look like?

Before you can improve something, you need to know what "great" looks like. This is where you step back and ask yourself: if this output were exactly what I needed, what would it look like? What would the tone be? Who would it sound like it was written for? What would someone do after reading it?

This isn't about being picky. It's about having a target. A chef doesn't just cook, they have a vision of the finished dish before they plate it. You need the same clarity.

Try asking the AI to help with this step: "Before we continue, describe what an ideal version of this [email/plan/report] would look like. What would make it truly excellent?" You'll be surprised how useful this is, the AI can help you clarify your own vision.

Diagnose: What's the gap?

Now compare what you have to what you imagined. Where does the current output fall short? Maybe the tone is right but the structure is wrong. Maybe the content is solid but it's too long. Maybe it's missing a critical section.

Be specific about the gap. "This isn't quite right" doesn't help the AI (or you). "The tone is too formal for my audience, and the third paragraph doesn't address cost, which is my reader's biggest concern", that's actionable.

A great diagnostic prompt: "Look at what you just produced. What are its three biggest weaknesses? What would you change if you were the reader?" Let the AI critique its own work. It's surprisingly good at this.

Enhance: Close the gap.

Now you give the AI specific instructions to fix what you diagnosed. This is where your refinement moves come back, but targeted at the exact gaps you identified.

> "Rewrite paragraph three to lead with the cost savings. That's what my reader cares about most."
>
> "The examples are too generic. Replace them with examples specific to a landscaping business."
>
> "The tone is perfect in the first half. Match that tone in the second half, which is too stiff."

Enhancement can also mean bringing in new elements: "Add a section about seasonal timing" or "Include a comparison table at the end."

Act: Test it in the real world.

The final step of each IDEA cycle is to take what you have and see how it works in context. Read the email out loud. Imagine handing the plan to your business partner. Picture the customer reading your response. Does it hold up?

If it does, you're done. If something still feels off, loop back to Imagine and run another cycle. Most tasks need one or two IDEA loops. Complex projects might need three or four or more. But each pass gets you closer.

The IDEA Loop in Action

Let's see Marcus use it. He's got his 90-day marketing plan from the Prompt step, and he's refined the tone and length. Now he enters **IDEA:**

Imagine: "If this plan were perfect, it would be something I could hand to my crew lead and they'd know exactly what to do each week. No jargon, no ambiguity."

Diagnose: "Weeks 1–4 are really specific, but weeks 5–12 get vague. Also, none of this accounts for the fact that my busy season starts in April and I won't have time for complicated marketing tasks."

Marcus types, "The first month of this plan is great, specific and actionable. But weeks 5 through 12 get too vague. Make them as specific as weeks 1 through 4. Also, my busy season starts in April, so any tasks after March need to take less than 30 minutes per week."

Enhance: The AI rewrites the plan with detailed weekly tasks and time-constrained actions for the busy season.

Act: Marcus reads the updated plan and realizes it's missing referral incentives, something that works well in his industry. He loops back, "Add a referral incentive program starting in week 3. Something simple I can offer existing clients."

One more IDEA cycle, and Marcus has a marketing plan that's precisely tailored to his business, his schedule, and his budget.

▶ **TRY THIS NOW: Run Your First IDEA Loop**

Take whatever you've been working on and run one full IDEA loop:

1. **Imagine:** Write down (or just think about) what the perfect version would look like.
2. **Diagnose:** Ask the AI: "What are the three biggest weaknesses in what you just produced?"
3. **Enhance:** Pick the most important weakness and give the AI a specific instruction to fix it.
4. **Act:** Read the result. Does it work? If not, loop again.

One IDEA cycle usually makes a dramatic difference. Two cycles and you'll wonder how you ever accepted first-draft output.

✦✦✦

M. Master: Fine-Tuning the Details

If the IDEA loop gets you from "pretty good" to "great," Mastering is what gets you from "great" to "perfect." This is the studio session, the part where a musician has already written the song, already arranged it, already recorded it, and now they're adjusting the levels, tweaking the EQ, making sure every note sits exactly where it should.

For AI output, mastering means sweating the details that separate good from polished:

Voice matching.

Does this sound like you? This is where a technique becomes your secret weapon: showing instead of telling (what AI researchers call "few-shot prompting"). Find something you've written that you like, an email, a social media post, a note. Copy it and tell the AI: "Match the voice and style of this example." When you show AI what you want instead of just describing it, the results are dramatically better.[17]

Fact verification

AI can and does make things up, we covered this in Chapter 1. If your output includes any facts, dates, statistics, or claims, verify them before you use them. This is non-negotiable for anything professional.

Audience calibration

Read it from your audience's perspective. If this is for your boss, does it sound appropriately professional? If it's for customers, does it address their actual concerns? If it's for your kids, will they read it?

Format polish

Check the structure. Are the headings consistent? Is the length right? Would a bullet list work better than a paragraph? Small formatting changes can dramatically improve how something reads and whether anyone finishes it.

The Master Prompt

Here's a prompt that's useful for the mastering phase:

> "Review what you've written. Check for: inconsistencies in tone, any claims that might need verification, sections that are too long or too short relative to their importance, and anything that wouldn't land with [describe your audience]. Give me a final polished version with those issues fixed."

Pro tip: You can also use contrast to master the output. Show the AI a bad example alongside a good one: "Don't write it like this: [bad example]. Write it more like this: [good example].” Contrast is a powerful teacher, for humans and AI alike.

Advanced Pro tip: To get the best out of your master, experiment with different models during this phase or at the very least, start a new conversation. If you wrote your PR and IDEA in ChatGPT, take the final output and append it to your master prompt inside Claude or Gemini, or do it in a new conversation. Removing the context in this area and giving the AI a new role (like editor in chief at a publication) works wonders in Mastering.

✦✦✦

E. Execute: Putting It to Work

This is the step most books about AI forget to mention: using what you created.

It sounds obvious, but you’d be surprised how many people spend twenty minutes crafting a perfect email with AI and then never send it. Or they generate a great marketing plan and it sits in a folder. Or they create a beautiful meal plan and order pizza anyway. (No judgment!)

Execute means taking the output and putting it into the world:

Send the email. Publish the post. Print the plan. Start the conversation. Cook the meal. Submit the application.

It also means paying attention to what happens next. Did the email get the response you wanted? Did the social media post get engagement? Did the plan hold up when you tried to follow it? This feedback is gold, it tells you what to adjust next time you use PRIME for a similar task.

So what does “paying attention” actually look like? It means noticing what worked and what didn’t. If the email got three positive responses, when you sent the last one cold with zero, something changed. If your social media reach doubled with the AI-generated caption, that’s a data point. If the plan that AI creates fell apart after day three, that tells you something too. None of this is failure, it’s information. Each execution is feedback.

And this is where PRIME loops back on itself. You execute, you observe what happens, and then you use that feedback in your next cycle. Maybe your email got great responses, but customers complained about one specific detail. Next time you use PRIME to write a similar email, you know to add a Refine step that says: "Remove anything that sounds like it came from corporate compliance." Maybe your 90-day plan was too ambitious. Next time, you adjust your Prompt to ask for a 60-day plan that can adapt to customer feedback. Maybe your social media captions didn't perform well because they felt generic. Next time, you Master the output more carefully to match your unique voice.

Let's go back to Marcus. He executed his 90-day marketing plan, sent it to his team, and watched what happened. The social media posts got decent engagement, but the email sequence he drafted sat in his drafts for a week. When he finally sent it, the response was lukewarm, polite, but nobody called to book a service. He realized the problem: the AI had written something that could have come from any landscaping company. When Marcus ran PRIME again, he knew exactly what to fix. This time, in his Prompt, he included a paragraph about his specific voice: "I'm funny, slightly irreverent, and I tell stories about what's happening in my customers' gardens." When the AI generated the email the second time, it was unmistakably Marcus. It felt personal. Three people responded within an hour.

Over time, you'll build a library of prompts that work for your specific needs. Save the ones that produce great results. Marcus keeps a note on his phone called "AI prompts that work" with his best templates. Rosa has a folder on her desktop. You'll find your own system. The point is that PRIME isn't just a one-time process, it's a habit that gets better the more you use it.

✦✦✦

The following collection of ready-to-use prompts also appears in Appendix A for easy reference. Feel free to skip ahead now and come back to these whenever you need inspiration. Or jump over to the companion site at practicalaibook.ai and use the easy, copy and paste options to play with it on the AI of your choice.

20 Prompts You Can Steal

Theory is great. But I promised you prompts you can put to use right now. Here are twenty favorites, organized by the parts of your life where they'll make the biggest difference. Each one has the PRIME components baked in. Copy them. Modify them. Make them your own.

HOME & DAILY LIFE

The Meal Planner

"You're a home cook who specializes in fast, budget-friendly meals. I need a dinner plan for five weeknights. Family of four, budget of $75 total for groceries. Two of us are picky eaters who won't eat mushrooms or fish. Give me the five meals with a combined grocery list organized by store section."

The Travel Planner

"You're a travel agent specializing in family vacations. Plan a 5-day trip to [destination] for two adults and [X] kids ages [ages]. Budget is [amount] not including flights. We want a mix of tourist highlights and off-the-beaten-path local experiences that are clean and safe. Present it as a day-by-day itinerary with estimated costs."

The Explainer

"Explain [complex topic] to me like I'm a smart adult who knows nothing about this subject. Use everyday analogies. Don't use jargon. If you must use a technical term, define it immediately in parentheses. Keep it under 300 words."

The Gift Finder

"I need a gift for [person's relationship to you]. They're [age], they love [interests], they hate [things to avoid], and my budget is [amount]. Give me 10 ideas ranging from practical to creative, with a one-sentence explanation of why each one fits."

WORK & PROFESSIONAL

The Email Drafter

"Write a [tone: professional/casual/friendly] email to [recipient and relationship] about [topic]. Include [specific points to cover]. Keep it under [word count]. End with [specific call to action]."

The Meeting Prep

"I have a meeting about [topic] with [who]. Help me prepare: give me 5 key talking points, 3 questions I should ask, and 2 potential objections I should be ready for. Format as a one-page cheat sheet I can glance at during the meeting."

The Report Summarizer

"Summarize this [document/report/article] in three sections: key findings, action items, and things I should be skeptical about. Write it for someone who has 2 minutes and needs to sound informed in a meeting. [Paste the text below.]"

The Feedback Writer

"Help me write constructive feedback for [person's role]. They did great at [strengths] but need improvement on [areas]. I want the tone to be encouraging but honest. Use the format: what's working well, what could be improved, specific suggestions for growth."

PARENTING & EDUCATION

The Homework Tutor

"You're a patient tutor for a [grade level] student. My child is struggling with [subject/topic]. Don't give them the answer, instead, guide them step by step with questions that help them figure it out themselves. Start with the first guiding question."

The Age-Appropriate Explainer

"Explain [topic] in a way that a [age]-year-old would understand. Use examples from their world, school, friends, games, animals. Keep it to 3–4 sentences. Make it fun if possible."

The Activity Planner

"You're a creative parent. I have a [age]-year-old who's bored on a rainy Saturday. Give me 5 indoor activities that require only stuff we probably already have at home. Each activity should keep them engaged for at least 30 minutes. No screens."

The College Prep Coach

"You're a college admissions consultant. My teenager is interested in [field/major] and has [relevant experience/grades/activities]. Help them brainstorm ideas for their personal essay. Don't write the essay, give them 5 unique angles they could explore, with a one-sentence explanation of why each one could work."

SMALL BUSINESS

The Social Media Creator

"You're a social media manager for a small [type of business] in [location]. Write 5 social media posts for this week. Mix of promotional and engaging content. Our brand voice is [describe tone]. Include a call to action in each post. Keep each post under 100 words."

The Customer Response

"A customer left this review: [paste review]. Write a professional, empathetic response that acknowledges their concern, explains what we're doing about it, and invites them to contact us directly. Don't be defensive. Keep it under 100 words."

The Job Description Writer

"Write a job description for a [position] at a small [type of business]. We offer [benefits/perks]. The ideal candidate has [qualifications]. Keep it conversational, we're a small team, not a corporation. Include a section on company culture that sounds human, not like it was written by HR software."

The Competitive Analyzer

"You're a business strategist. I own a [type of business] in [location]. My main competitors are [names or descriptions]. Analyze what they're doing well that I should learn from and where there might be gaps I could fill. Present it as a SWOT analysis in a simple table."

CREATIVE PROJECTS

The Writing Partner

"I'm writing a [type of piece: blog post, story, article] about [topic]. Here's what I have so far: [paste your draft]. Help me improve it: strengthen the opening, tighten the language, and suggest a better ending. Keep my voice, don't make it sound like someone else wrote it."

The Brainstorm Machine

"I need creative ideas for [project/problem]. Give me 15 ideas, 5 safe and conventional, 5 creative but doable, and 5 wild cards that might be crazy enough to work. Don't filter yourself on the wild cards."

The Design Brief

"I need to create a [flyer/logo/social media graphic] for [purpose]. My audience is [describe]. The vibe should be [describe]. Describe exactly what this design should look like, layout, colors, fonts, imagery, so I can create it myself or hand the brief to a designer."

The Personal Editor

"Edit this piece of writing for clarity, grammar, and flow. Don't change my voice or style, just make it cleaner. Point out any sentences that are confusing or any arguments that don't land. Be specific about what to fix and why. [Paste your text below.]"

THE BOTTOM LINE

You don't have to memorize these prompts or the PRIME framework. Bookmark this chapter. Screenshot the formula. Save it on your phone. The goal isn't perfect recall, it's to internalize the pattern: build a strong prompt, refine it, iterate with IDEA, master the details, and execute. Once that pattern becomes habit, you'll write great prompts naturally. But until then? Use PRIME as your checklist and steal these prompts. That's what they're here for.

✦✦✦

What You Now Know (and Why It Matters)

You walked into this chapter wondering why AI kept giving you generic answers. Now you have PRIME, a complete system for getting exactly what you need, every time.

Here's what to carry with you:

P. Prompt with the 5-Part Formula: Role, Context, Task, Format, Constraints. This is your foundation. A strong first prompt changes everything.

R. Refine through conversation. Your first response is a first draft. Use tone, length, focus, and perspective adjustments to shape it.

I. IDEA through the iteration loop. Imagine what perfect looks like, Diagnose the gaps, Enhance with specific fixes, Act by testing it. Run the loop until it's right.

M. Master the details. Match your voice, verify facts, calibrate for your audience, polish the format. This is where good becomes great.

E. Execute. Use it. Send it. Publish it. Do the thing. Then save what worked for next time.

And Marcus, our landscaping business owner? He came back. He used PRIME to create a 90-day marketing plan, write customer follow-up emails, draft a job posting for a new crew member, and build a seasonal service calendar. His daughter was surprised. His accountant was impressed. His business grew by eight new clients in the first month.

All because he learned how to ask.

A note on structure: Chapters 1, 2, and 3 ended with a formal "What You Now Know" summary because those chapters were laying groundwork. From Chapter 4 onward, you have the framework — PRIME is yours. The summaries are woven into each chapter's closing pages rather than listed separately. Trust what you've built.

In the next chapter, we're going to put these skills to work at home; meal planning, travel, health, finances, and all the everyday tasks where AI can save you real time. The PRIME skills you just learned? They're about to become your daily superpower.

4

AI AT HOME

MAKING EVERYDAY LIFE EASIER

The Ramirez Family's 3 PM Crisis. Sofia Ramirez (project manager, bilingual, juggling everything) walked through her front door at 3:15 PM on a Tuesday, and immediately felt the weight of the world. The fridge was empty. Lucia, her fourteen-year-old, was asking about dinner. Diego, eight, was asking about homework help. Her husband Carlos, stuck in traffic, texted that he'd be forty minutes late. And her mother Elena, living with them since last year, was sitting at the kitchen table with a Medicare letter from the government, completely bewildered.

It was one of those moments where every family member needed something different, all at once, and Sofia was running on her third cup of coffee and fumes. She stood in the kitchen doorway and felt the familiar panic rising.

"Why don't I have a personal assistant?" she muttered to herself, opening a cabinet and finding nothing but cereal boxes from 2024 that nobody wanted. Then she remembered something. She did have a personal assistant. It was sitting in her pocket.

Sofia had been reading up on AI. A colleague at work had raved about it, so she'd tried a few experiments: drafting a project brief, summarizing a long report. It worked better than she'd expected. But she'd been thinking of it as a productivity tool for professionals, something "for work."

What Sofia didn't realize yet was that the same technology that helped her manage projects, that could organize data and solve complex problems, could also fix her 3 PM crisis. And every other crisis like it.

That's what this chapter is about. AI doesn't just make your job easier. It makes your whole life easier.

✦✦✦

Meal Planning & Grocery Lists: The PRIME Formula in Action

Sofia sat down on the kitchen stool and opened her phone. At work, she'd learned the PRIME framework for working with AI. She wasn't going to just type "give me meal ideas." Instead, she was going to build a proper prompt using Role, Context, Task, Format, and Constraints. Here's what she typed:

You're a nutritionist who specializes in culturally diverse, budget-conscious family meal planning. I'm planning dinners for a family of five: my husband Carlos works in construction management, I'm a project manager, my mom Elena (72) is living with us and prefers more traditional meals, Lucia is 14 and prefers trying new foods, and Diego is 8 and is pretty picky about vegetables. We have a budget of $150 per week. Elena has high blood pressure, so we need to watch sodium. All meals must be prep-in-under-45-minutes, and none of us can eat shellfish. I'd like a week of family dinners with a corresponding grocery list organized by supermarket section, produce, proteins, dairy, pantry. Please include Spanish dish names since my family often code-switches. Go.

What came back wasn't just a list. It was specific. It was thoughtful. The AI had understood the constraints: the family's different preferences, the cultural context, the nutritional needs, the time limitation, the budget. Each night had a meal with Spanish name, cooking instructions, and a note about why it worked for the family's needs.

Monday: Chiles Rellenos (stuffed peppers with cheese),high protein, vegetable-forward, Elena can make it spicier for her palate, Diego can have his without chile.

Tuesday: Sheet Pan Pollo a la Naranja (orange chicken with roasted sweet potato and green beans) one pan, minimal cleanup, with new flavors for Lucia, and comfort food for Elena.

Wednesday: Bean and Cheese Enchiladas with Salsa Verde, make ahead, leftovers for Thursday lunch.

And then the grocery list, organized perfectly. Produce section needed cilantro, four bell peppers, two bunches of green beans. Protein section needed five chicken breasts, black beans, pinto beans. Dairy needed Oaxaca cheese and Mexican crema. Pantry needed enchilada sauce and tortillas.

Sofia texted the grocery list to her mother in both English and Spanish. Elena could go to the store that afternoon and actually understand what she was shopping for. Not just a cryptic list from her daughter's phone, but instructions that made sense in her language, with context about what the meals would be.

This is the power of PRIME: it's not magic. It's clarity. When you tell the AI exactly who you are, what you need, what your constraints are, and how you want the answer delivered, it stops being a guessing game and becomes a tool that actually fits your life.

▶ **TRY THIS NOW: Build a Meal Plan Prompt**

Think about your own family's constraints. Do you have dietary restrictions? Budget limits? Time constraints? Picky eaters? Elderly family members? Copy Sofia's PRIME structure above and fill it in with YOUR family's details. Try it once, see what you get. Then refine: if the AI suggested meals that don't work, explain why and ask it to try again. The second version will be even better. Pro tip: paste your current pantry inventory and ask the AI to build a meal plan using what you already have.

✦✦✦

Travel Planning That Doesn't Suck

The next weekend, the Ramirez family was planning their spring break trip to San Antonio. Carlos had always been the trip planner, he'd spend hours on TripAdvisor, reading reviews, cross-referencing, trying to figure out what would actually work for their family's mix of interests and constraints.

This time, Sofia showed him what she'd been learning, by using the voice feature.

"We have five days in San Antonio," she said, opening her phone and sharing her screen. "Two adults, two kids ages 14 and 8, plus my mother who is 72 and has arthritis that makes long walks difficult. We need places that are accessible. We're interested in culture, museums, history, the Alamo, local food, but Diego will get bored if we do nothing but museums all day. We want some outdoor activities, maybe a river walk, that kind of thing. Budget is about $2000 total for the trip, including hotels and food. Give me a day-by-day itinerary that balances everyone's interests."

The AI returned a detailed five-day itinerary. Day 1: Arrival, settle into the hotel, light dinner at a local spot on the River Walk. Day 2: Alamo and History Museum (accessible, high-interest for everyone). Day 3: Split the day (morning at the Pearl Brewery District (shops and outdoor spaces where Elena could rest), afternoon paddleboats on the river. Day 4: Nature hike at nearby Olmos Basin (short, shaded, accessible), dinner at a family restaurant.

The itinerary had everything. What to do, how long to spend, nearest parking, accessibility notes, and price estimates.

Then came Day 3. Sofia looked at the itinerary and said, "Diego's going to lose his mind if we do two museums in two days. He'll be bored." So she asked the AI to adjust: "Too many stationary activities on Days 2 and 3. Diego's 8, needs something active or hands-on. Can you swap one museum for something more interactive? Maybe something with animals or outdoor adventure?" Thirty seconds later: Day 3 revised. Keep the Pearl Brewery District for Elena and the grown-ups, but swap the second museum for the San Antonio Zoo, which was nearby. Diego would be engaged, Elena could walk at her own pace, and they'd still hit the cultural stuff on other days.

Then came the real test: weather. Three days before they left, a forecast showed rain for Day 3. Sofia pulled up the itinerary and said, "It's going to rain Tuesday. Zoo won't work. Give me indoor alternatives that are still active and interesting." Back came: Children's Science Museum (interactive exhibits, Diego would love it), Botanical Garden Conservatory (indoors, beautiful, accessible), or the Pearl Brewery District with better restaurant recommendations for rainy-day dining. This is how AI travel planning works in the real world. It's not about following a rigid itinerary. It's about having a planning partner who can adjust in real-time, respond to constraints, and understand why your 8-year-old needs active play, not museum number three.

▶ **TRY THIS NOW: Plan a Real Trip with AI**

Pick a trip you're planning (weekend getaway, visit family, vacation). Use the PRIME framework: Who's going? What are their ages and interests? What accessibility needs do you have? What's your budget? What's the geography and timeframe? Then ask for a day-by-day itinerary with specific place names, times, and cost estimates. Most importantly: ask for the reasoning. "Why did you put the museum first instead of the restaurant?" Understanding the AI's thinking helps you refine it. And ask for adjustments when things don't fit – that's the whole point.

✦✦✦

Home Organization & Decluttering

Sofia's garage was what you might charitably call "a project." It was the place where things went to disappear: old exercise equipment nobody used, boxes from the 2019 move they never unpacked, Carlos' tools everywhere, seasonal decorations mixed with broken furniture, a treadmill, a cabinet with unknown contents.

Every time Sofia needed to park the car, she had to move something. And every time she saw the garage, she felt the familiar surge of guilt and overwhelm. She wanted it organized. She just didn't know where to start.

This is where a lot of people would hire a professional organizer, spend $500 or even $1000, and hope it works out. Sofia tried something different.

"I have a garage that's about 200 square feet," she told her AI. "It's mostly full of stuff we haven't unpacked or don't use: old fitness equipment, seasonal decorations, tools, boxes. I have two cars and two people who need to park. Give me a practical, step-by-step decluttering plan that treats this like a project, with phases, timelines, storage solutions, and a decision tree for what to keep, sell, or donate. I don't want judgment. I just want to understand what needs to happen."

What came back was a five-phase plan: Phase 1 (one weekend): Empty everything, categorize into piles (keep, donate, sell). Phase 2 (next week): Research and list items for sale (Facebook Marketplace, Craigslist). Phase 3 (following week): Coordinate donations. Phase 4: Buy storage solutions (specific recommendations for the space). Phase 5: Reorganize with a maintenance system. The plan even included the decision tree: "If it's a piece of exercise equipment you haven't used in two years, it falls into 'donate/sell' unless it's broken, in which case: donate."

What made this different from anything Sofia had ever heard from an organizer or self-help book was the tone. There was no judgment. The AI didn't say "you've let this get out of control." It didn't shame her. It just treated it like a solvable problem: here's what needs to happen, here's how long it will take, here's the logic. Six weeks later, Sofia could park both cars in the garage. The seasonal decorations were in clearly labeled bins. Carlos' tools were on a pegboard. The space that used to be a source of guilt was now functional. And the best part? She'd sold some of the stuff on Facebook Marketplace and made $400 to put toward a family trip.

Other people have used this same approach for moving, downsizing, seasonal organization, closet overhauls, even preparing a house for guests. The pattern is the same: describe the space and the challenge, ask for a step-by-step plan, and you get something that feels less overwhelming because you understand the whole picture.

Pro Tip: Try taking a picture of the space and leveraging the multi-modal capabilities of AI (their ability to understand voice and use computer vision to analyze photos, videos, and other than text options). You'd be surprised what AI can deduct from a single photo. Be sure to read Chapter 9 before uploading anything sensitive.

TRY THIS NOW: Declutter with AI

Pick one area in your home that you've been avoiding: a closet, a drawer, a basement corner, a shelf. Describe it to AI: What's the space? What's in it? Why have you been avoiding it? How much time do you have to tackle it? Then ask for a phase-by-phase decluttering plan with timelines and decision trees. The magic isn't the plan itself, it's that seeing the whole problem broken into steps makes it feel manageable. Start Phase 1 this weekend.

✦✦✦

Health & Wellness (With Very Smart Boundaries)

An Important Note Before We Start: AI is NOT a doctor. It cannot diagnose you, prescribe medication, or replace medical judgment. This section is about what AI can and cannot do, and where the hard line is.

Now that we've been crystal clear: AI is genuinely useful for health and wellness, if you use it right.

What AI CAN do:

- Explain medical test results and lab values in plain English
- Help you prepare for doctor appointments by generating questions to ask
- Create personalized fitness routines based on your goals and limitations
- Help you understand medical terminology and what doctors told you
- Research symptoms and point you toward next steps (medical professional)

- Track wellness goals and suggest habit-formation strategies

What AI CANNOT do:

- Diagnose you. Ever. AI doesn't examine you, doesn't know your full medical history, doesn't have access to your test results (unless you give it them)
- Prescribe medication or tell you what medicine to take
- Replace a doctor, nurse, or medical professional's judgment
- Know your individual medical history or risk factors
- Handle emergencies. If you're having chest pain, call 911. Don't ask ChatGPT.

Here's Sofia's real example. Her mother Elena got her annual lab work done, and the results came back with numbers Sofia didn't understand: "HDL cholesterol 38 mg/dL, triglycerides 156, fasting glucose 103." Elena was confused and anxious. The appointment with her doctor wasn't for another three weeks.

Sofia didn't use AI to diagnose Elena or decide if she was sick. Instead, she used it to translate. She said: "These are my mother's lab results. Can you explain what each number means, whether they're normal, and what the doctor might be looking at? Please explain in simple terms, and also translate to Spanish so my mom can understand." Back came a clear explanation in both English and Spanish: HDL is "good" cholesterol; Elena's was low, which increases heart disease risk. Triglycerides were elevated. Fasting glucose suggested her blood sugar was running high, possibly prediabetic territory. And then Sofia asked: "Give me five questions we should ask Elena's doctor at her next appointment about these results." The AI generated five smart questions: Is medication recommended? Should we change diet? Should we increase physical activity? What's the timeline for follow-up testing? Are there any risk factors we should know about? When Elena went to her doctor three weeks later, she walked in prepared. She understood her results. She had questions. Her doctor could have a real conversation instead of explaining from zero.

Carlos had a different health challenge. He'd injured his knee in college, and it had never fully recovered. Recently it'd been flaring up, and he wanted to build strength but didn't know how to do it safely. He asked AI: "I have chronic knee pain from an old ACL injury. I want to build leg strength and fitness without making it worse. Can you create a personalized routine I can do at home, three times a week, that avoids high-impact activities?" What came back was a routine that made sense: resistance band work, bodyweight exercises he could modify, stretching protocols. The AI even noted: "Always clear any new routine with your physical therapist or doctor, especially with a history of injury."

At the time of writing, AI tools were beginning to integrate deeper with medical data, connecting medical records and wellness app data directly to the interface. These tools can read lab results and health history. This is powerful. And early research shows it has real limitations: certain tools under-triage emergency cases at rates that matter. Translation: if something is truly urgent, AI might miss it. So the rule stands: AI is a research assistant and a preparation tool. It's not a doctor.[18, 19]

The demand was already there before the tools caught up. Prior to the launch of ChatGPT Health, approximately 40 million people were already using ChatGPT daily for health-related questions.[20]

▶ **TRY THIS NOW: Prepare for a Doctor Appointment**

Do you have an upcoming appointment, lab results you don't understand, or a medication question? Try this: 1) Write down what the doctor told you or paste your lab results (remove identifying personal info first). 2) Ask AI to explain it in plain English. 3) Ask for 5 questions you should ask your doctor. 4) Bring the explanation and questions to your appointment. The goal is to come prepared, have a better conversation, and be a more active participant in your own health. That's the AI health rule: use it to prepare, not to replace.

✦✦✦

Managing Finances & Bills

Financial documents are some of the most confusing pieces of paper most people get. A medical bill has seventeen line items. Insurance statements have codes you don't understand. Bank statements are incomprehensible. Tax documents might as well be in another language.

Sofia got a medical bill for a routine imaging test. The bill had charges for "Technician services: $400. Facility fee: $250. Radiologist reading: $150. Insurance write-off: -$600. Patient responsibility: $200." She had no idea what was actually happening or why the bill was structured that way.

She did something smart: she stripped out her name, medical record number, and any identifying information, and asked AI: "Explain this medical bill line by line. What does each charge mean? Why are they charging separately for technician, facility, and radiologist? What's the insurance write-off? And why is my copay $200 when the write-off is $600?" Back came an explanation that made sense. The charges are separate because those are separate services provided by separate departments. The facility fee is what the hospital charges for using the building. The insurance write-off is the difference between what they charged and what insurance actually pays. The copay is your portion based on your insurance plan. Understood. Not happy about the bill, but understood.

She did the same thing with her insurance plan renewal. Her company offered three health plans with different deductibles, copays, and networks. She asked AI: "Here are three insurance plans. Create a comparison table showing deductible, copay amounts, out-of-pocket maximum, provider network size, and estimated annual cost for my family. Then explain which factors matter most for someone who usually has 2–3 doctor visits per year, takes one regular medication, and rarely needs specialist care." The AI built the table, and more importantly, explained the logic. For her situation, the mid-tier plan was the better value, because her deductible would be high but her out-of-pocket maximum would be lower.

Another thing Sofia did: she got frustrated with her spending.

She was hitting her credit card limit, but she didn't know where the money was going. So she asked AI: "This is my monthly income ($5400). Here are my regular expenses: rent, utilities, insurance, phone, groceries. But every month I'm overspending by $300, $500 and I don't know where it's going. Can you help me find hidden spending categories?"

AI didn't make the decision for her. Instead, it asked the right questions: "You didn't mention subscriptions. How many streaming services, apps, or software subscriptions do you pay for monthly? You didn't mention food spending beyond groceries. Do you eat out, order delivery, or grab coffee? What about transportation beyond insurance and gas?"

Suddenly Sofia realized: $15/month for a gym she never uses, $12/month for a meditation app, $40/month in streaming services they'd forgotten about, coffee runs that added up to $60/month, and UberEats orders that came to almost $200/month.

That was $330. Mystery solved.

A critical note on privacy: Never paste financial documents with identifying information (names, account numbers, full SSN, addresses) into an AI. Strip all personal identifiers first. The AI doesn't need to know who you are; it just needs to understand the structure of the bill or statement.

TRY THIS NOW: Decode Your Bills

Find a financial document that confused you recently: a medical bill, insurance statement, credit card statement, tax form, or mortgage statement. Strip off all personally identifying information (names, numbers, addresses). If you need help with this, ask AI how. Then ask AI: "Explain this document line by line. What does each item mean? Is this normal? What should I be paying attention to?" Usually a 30-second explanation from AI will clarify what would have taken you hours to research. Bonus: ask for 3 questions to ask the relevant company if something seems wrong.

✦✦✦

Personal Writing: Making Your Voice Sound Like You

Carlos' brother was getting married, and Carlos was the best man. The speech was due in two weeks, and he was frozen. He sat down and tried to write something, funny, heartfelt, not too long, and it all came out either too corny or too mean-spirited. He showed it to Sofia, who immediately said, "Use PRIME."

"I'm writing a best man speech," he told the AI. "Me: I'm the groom's older brother, 38, we grew up together in a bilingual household, we're close but have different personalities, he's the joker, I'm the more serious one. He's marrying someone he's been with for 8 years. The tone should be: funny, genuinely warm, not roasting him too hard, about 3–4 minutes when delivered. I want it to start with a funny memory from childhood and end with something sincere about him finding his person. Here's what I want to hit on: [detailed notes]. Can you draft something?"

What came back was a speech that had the shape of what Carlos wanted. It opened with a story about his brother trying to fix their dad's car and making it worse. It had humor. It had a transition to talking about how his brother changed when he met his wife. It ended with Carlos saying, "Juan, you've always known how to find the best in people. Now you've found someone who brings out the best in you. We're lucky to be here." But it didn't sound like Carlos. It sounded like someone else's version of a best man speech. So he used the Master step of PRIME: he asked AI to revise it using his voice.

"This is good, but it doesn't sound like me. I don't say 'I'm lucky to be here.' I would say something more like 'We're all better because Juan found her.' Can you revise this to sound more like how I actually talk? Less flowery, more direct, but still sincere?"

Back came a version that sounded exactly like Carlos. Same structure, same jokes, same heart, but delivered in words he would actually say.

Sofia had a different writing task. Her homeowners association had made a policy change that she thought was unfair: they wanted to ban all front-yard gardens and require only approved landscaping. Sofia wanted to push back, but she didn't want to come off as hostile or unreasonable. She used AI to draft a firm but professional letter. She started by explaining her concern, then explained the policy, then asked for reconsideration with specific reasons (gardens help with environmental sustainability, are part of her family's cultural traditions, and provide educational value for her children). The letter ended with a request for a meeting to discuss alternatives. The letter was clear, not angry. Respectful but firm. Exactly what she needed.

This is how personal writing AI works best: it's not about having the AI write your thank-you notes or speeches. It's about using it as a first-draft partner, then using the Master step to infuse your voice back in. The AI can help you organize your thoughts and hit the right tone. But the final version has to sound like you, say what you actually mean, and represent what you actually feel.

▶ TRY THIS NOW: Draft a Personal Letter

Do you need to write something but haven't started: a thank-you note, a complaint letter, a resignation, a request, a condolence message? Tell AI: who it's for, what the situation is, what you want to accomplish, and what tone you're going for. Let it draft it. Then use the Master step: revise it to sound like you. Remove anything that doesn't match how you actually talk. Add details from your own experience. The final version should be something you're proud to send.

✦✦✦

Seniors & Independent Living

Remember Rosa from Chapter 2? She's the 68-year-old retired teacher who was skeptical about AI but curious about how it might help her stay independent. Over the past few chapters, she's been experimenting. And it's made a real difference in her life. So has Elena, Sofia's mother. Both women have discovered that AI isn't just a tool for young people or tech workers. It's particularly powerful for older adults who want to maintain independence, stay connected, and understand the increasingly complex systems (insurance, healthcare, government) that affect their lives.

Medicare & Insurance: Understanding the System

Elena got a letter from Medicare. Twelve pages. Dense text. Information about changes to her coverage, options about supplemental insurance, deadlines for decisions. She brought it to Sofia, completely overwhelmed. Sofia did what she'd been learning: she used AI as a translator. "Explain this Medicare letter in plain Spanish, section by section. What is Medicare telling me? What do I need to do? What are my options? What's the deadline?" Back came an explanation Elena could actually understand. And Sofia printed it out, in Spanish, for her mom to keep.

Modern Medicare tools include provider directories, making it easier to see which doctors accept specific plans before choosing.[21] AI translation tools have become remarkably capable with medical and legal documents. ChatGPT, Claude, and Google Gemini all support real-time translation in over 50 languages, and studies show AI translation accuracy for healthcare materials now rivals professional human translators for common language pairs.[22] AI can help with the comparison too. Rosa pulled up the Medicare Plan Finder, saw that her doctor accepted three different plans, and asked AI: "Compare Plan A, B, and C in terms of deductible, monthly premium, and out-of-pocket maximum. I see my doctor twice a year and take one blood pressure medication. Which is likely the lowest-cost option for me?"

Medication Management & Safety

Rosa takes five medications for various conditions: blood pressure, cholesterol, arthritis, and a thyroid medication. She was worried about interactions. She asked AI: "I'm taking [list of medications]. Are there any interactions I should know about? Is there a best time of day to take each one?"

The AI flagged a potential interaction between two of her medications (one that interferes with how the other is absorbed). It recommended specific timing: one medication with breakfast, another on an empty stomach, one at bedtime. Critical disclaimer: Rosa didn't just follow what the AI said. She took the information to her pharmacist and said, "I looked this up. Is this right?" Her pharmacist confirmed the interaction warning and adjusted the timing accordingly. That's how you use AI for medication safety: as a research tool, not a replacement for talking to your pharmacist or doctor.

Staying Connected & Combating Isolation

One of the real challenges of aging is isolation. Studies show that more than one in three adults over 65 experience loneliness, and social isolation significantly increases the risk of dementia, heart disease, and depression.[23] Rosa's husband passed away seven years ago. Her kids live out of state. She had a small friend group, but with mobility issues, she couldn't get out as much as she used to.

She started using AI as a conversation partner. Not instead of real human friends, that's unrealistic and unhealthy, but as a way to stay mentally engaged between social interactions. She would tell the AI about her day, ask it questions about books she was reading, ask for activity suggestions for rainy days when she couldn't get out.

Elena, meanwhile, had always been close to her grandchildren but found it hard to keep up with them. She didn't understand TikTok or Instagram. She asked AI: "Explain how to use Instagram. How do I post photos for my family? How do I see what my grandchildren post?"

AI walked her through it step-by-step. Within a week, Elena had posted her first photo, a picture of herself in her garden, and her grandchildren commented. She could follow their accounts and feel more connected.

Another thing Elena did: she wanted to write emails to her grandchildren but felt self-conscious about her English. She asked AI to help. "I want to email my grandson about his college classes. He's studying engineering. Can you help me draft something that asks him questions about what he's learning?" Elena wrote the initial draft, AI refined it, and Elena sent something that actually made sense and showed genuine interest in his life.

Rosa joined a book club and wanted to prepare for discussion. She asked AI to generate 10 discussion questions for the book they were reading. She prepared. She had more to contribute. She felt more engaged.

Government Forms & Benefits Navigation

Navigating government forms is one of the most painful experiences for anyone, but especially for older adults. Social Security changes. Veteran benefits. Tax prep. Property tax assessment appeals. It's overwhelming. Rosa needed to understand what documents she needed for her federal tax return. She asked AI: "I'm retired, living on Social Security and a small pension. What tax documents do I need to file my last year's return? Do I even need to file?" AI told her the answer: yes, she needed to file, and here were the documents to gather. It even explained why: because some of her income was taxable, even if the total was below the standard deduction. When Rosa had a question about her Social Security benefits and whether she was getting the right amount, she used AI to research the formula and understand how benefits are calculated. She didn't make changes based on that research alone, but she went to the Social Security office prepared with questions and understanding.

Digital Tasks Simplified

Elena called Sofia in a panic. She'd taken a photo on her phone she wanted to email to her daughter, but she didn't know how to get it from her phone to her email. Instead of trying to talk her through it (which would have taken 30 minutes of frustration), Sofia said, "Ask your AI assistant." Elena did. She said: "I took a photo on my phone. I want to email it to my daughter. How do I do that?" The AI gave her step-by-step instructions: open Photos, select the image, tap Share, select Email, enter her daughter's email, send. Elena followed the steps and it worked. Rosa had a similar experience. She wanted to add a contact to her phone. She didn't know how. She asked AI. Within minutes, she had added her grandson's phone number to her contacts.

This is the overlooked power of AI for older adults: it's a judgment-free way to learn things. You don't feel embarrassed asking an AI how to do something basic. It doesn't get impatient. It explains step by step. And suddenly something that would have required calling tech support or bothering a grandchild (or calling your CTO son, Mom! Just kidding, I love you Mom!) becomes something you can figure out yourself.

TRY THIS NOW: Start with One Task

If you're a senior (or helping one), try using AI for a task you find confusing or frustrating. Medication interactions? Government forms? Digital tasks? Insurance questions? Email someone you want to stay connected with? Start with one thing. Tell the AI exactly what you want to do, ask for step-by-step help, and try it. The first time is the hardest. After that, you'll realize that AI isn't scary or complicated. It's just helpful.

✦✦✦

The Everyday AI Life

It's been six weeks since Sofia started using AI around her house. The change isn't some magical transformation. Nobody's life got dramatically better. But the texture of daily life got lighter.

Last Tuesday, Elena wanted to make her mother's mole recipe, a dish Sofia's grandmother had made, that Elena half-remembered. She asked AI to help her find it. She described what she remembered about the sauce, the ingredients, the time it took. AI found versions of the recipe and even gave her the Spanish name for it: mole negro oaxaqueño. Elena made it. It turned out beautifully. The family ate dinner tasting something from their own history.

Diego came home with Spanish spelling words he needed to practice. Sofia was supposed to quiz him, but she had a conference call. Instead, she sent the word list to AI with a note: "Quiz my 8-year-old in Spanish. Give him feedback if he's wrong, encouragement if he's right." Diego sat at the kitchen table, AI on his laptop, practicing. He was proud that he could do it "all by himself" (with AI coaching).

Lucia was assigned a project about climate change. She had 15 sources to read, and didn't know where to start. Sofia suggested: "Ask your AI to summarize each source and pull out the key points. Then organize them by theme." Lucia did. She finished the research phase in three hours instead of a week.

The point isn't that any of these things are huge. The point is that Sofia's life got easier. The stuff that normally creates friction (figuring out what to cook, trip planning, organizing chaos, understanding confusing letters, helping kids with homework) became something she could handle without the usual panic and overwhelm.

AI isn't replacing what she does. It's not taking over her job as a mother, project manager, or daughter. It's not making her family less functional or more dependent. It's doing what good tools do: it's making her more effective at the things she already does. She spends less time frustrated and stuck, and more time living her life. And that's the promise of AI at home. Not transformation. Lightening. Making the daily grind a little less grinding.

Now that you've got AI working at home, let's take it to the office. Chapter 5 is about AI in professional life: how to use it to be better at your job, more productive, and more creative. If you think AI is useful for meal planning and Medicare letters, wait until you see what it can do for your actual work.

5

AI AT WORK

WORKING SMARTER WITHOUT THE BUSYWORK

Monday Morning at the Office Priya arrived at her desk at 8:47 AM on a gray Monday, already behind. Her inbox display showed 127 unread emails. The red notification badges accumulated across three browser tabs: Gmail, Slack, and the company's internal project management tool. She hadn't even opened the shared documents yet. Before lunch, she had three meetings stacked back-to-back: a 9 AM standup with her marketing team, a 10:30 AM budget review with finance, and an 11:45 AM sync with her boss, James. Somewhere in that same window, she was supposed to deliver preliminary notes on a quarterly report due Wednesday. The one that would require wrangling sales data from three different spreadsheets. And Friday. Friday was the hard deadline for the competitive analysis: a comprehensive report on three rival logistics companies, their pricing strategies, service offerings, technology capabilities, and recent market moves. Twelve hours of work, minimum. At least it used to be. Priya had learned about PRIME (Prompt, Refine, IDEA, Master, Execute) and spent the last two weeks applying it to smaller tasks. A sales email that would have taken her thirty minutes now took ten. A presentation outline she used to draft from scratch in an hour was now refined in fifteen minutes. Today felt different. Today was the day she'd test everything at once.

The weight of it had been accumulating for months. Eighty percent of her time was busywork: email triage, meeting logistics, forwarding requests, copying her boss to signal visibility. The other 20% (the actual job of thinking about market strategy, understanding customer needs, building creative campaigns) barely happened. She was known for being busy, not focused. And underneath all of it was a gnawing sense that her actual job wasn't happening.

James had called an all-hands meeting: "Figure out AI. Our competitors are using it, and we need to move fast." Priya had heard of one idea called PRIME that stuck with her. AI could reclaim her time from busywork and give it back to her so she could do the actual thinking. All weekend she'd thought about it: What if I could get ten hours back every week by making my busywork faster?

She opened ChatGPT in a new tab at 8:52 AM. The thesis of what she was about to attempt was deceptively simple: the people who will thrive aren't the ones who know the most about AI. They're the ones who learn to use it as a thinking partner. Not as a replacement for their judgment. Not as a substitute for expertise. As a partner. A sounding board. A tool that compresses the time between thinking and output, so that the real work (editing, refining, adding human judgment and institutional knowledge) could happen. She had maybe four hours before her boss would ask about the competitive analysis. By Friday, she intended to have completed not just that report, but also the quarterly notes, cleared her inbox (or at least the critical part of it), and prepped meeting agendas so meetings would actually start on time. And she wanted to do it in roughly half the time the old way would have taken. She'd read that it was possible. Now she was going to prove it. She knew this wasn't cheating. Her boss hadn't told her to stop using tools. He'd told her to figure out how to use new tools better. This was that.

The clock on her screen showed 8:53 AM. Let's see what's possible, Priya thought, and she started typing. She had no idea that by

Friday, she'd look back on this moment as the pivot point, the moment everything changed for the better.

✦✦✦

Email That Writes Itself (Almost)

McKinsey found that the average office worker spends 28 percent of their working day on email — and that number has barely budged in over a decade, even as email volume has increased. No formatting tricks, no increased productivity hacks, no "what gets measured gets managed." Twenty-eight percent. That's roughly 2.2 hours out of every eight-hour workday, gone. For a logistics company like Priya's employer, where communication across teams (sales, operations, customer service, finance) was essential, the number felt even higher. Meetings were about alignment. Email was about documenting what people had said in those meetings, forwarding, copying, replying to global threads where thirty people had opinions about something that affected five. The math was brutal: if 28 percent of Priya's professional time was consumed by email, then an AI system that reduced that by even 50 percent would reclaim 1.1 hours every single day. Nearly six hours per week. Four days per month that she'd get back, completely free, to do actual work. That was the theory. The question was whether it worked.[24]

Monday Morning Triage started at 9 AM, right after the standup. Priya had copied the body text from her 127 unread emails into a document. She'd trimmed the longest ones, kept the essential detail, and created a simple template: email number, sender, subject, date, one-sentence summary. She pasted the whole thing into ChatGPT with a purpose-driven prompt: "You're my email filtering system. I receive too much email and need to focus on what matters. Here are 127 emails from today. Create a prioritized table with three columns: Priority Level (Critical, Important, or Informational), Sender, and Subject. Critical means it requires my response or action today. Important means I should review it by Wednesday. Informational means I can skim it or delegate it. Sort by Priority Level. Give me the top ten items, then the count of Important and Informational items."

ChatGPT returned a table in thirty seconds. Not two hours of scrolling. Not the anxiety of wondering if she'd missed something urgent. Thirty seconds. The table showed: four Critical items (a client escalation from two days ago she hadn't seen, a system outage notification that needed confirmation from her team, a vendor invoice that was past due, a request from James for some marketing metrics), fifteen Important items, and the rest were Informational. She acted on the Critical items immediately. The client escalation required a follow-up call, which she scheduled for Tuesday morning. The outage: she Slack messaged the ops team with an urgent flag. The invoice: forwarded to accounting with a note asking them to prioritize. The metrics: she put that on her to-do list for the afternoon when she had more context. The entire triage process took ten minutes.

Then came The Tricky Reply. A client had sent an email expressing frustration about a delayed project. The tone was professional but tense. Priya had been looped in because of her relationship with the account. The email read: "We were promised delivery by the 20th. It's now the 28th. We have our own clients waiting. This isn't acceptable. We need a new date and a plan to hit it." Eight days overdue. Not great. Priya needed to write a response that acknowledged the frustration, explained the delay without excusing it, and committed to a new timeline, but only if she was confident the team could hit it. She didn't want to guess and fail again. She opened a new ChatGPT window and used the PRIME framework from Chapter 3. First, the Prompt step. She built it using the 5-Part Formula:

- Role - "You're a professional account manager who is solution-oriented"
- Context - "A client's project is eight days overdue; they're frustrated because the delay is costing them customers"
- Task - "Draft a response that acknowledges their frustration and resets expectations"

- Format - "Professional email, under 200 words"
- Constraints - "Don't make excuses. Include a concrete action I'm taking today and a realistic new date"

Then she planned to Refine the tone, run the IDEA loop if the first draft missed the mark, Master the final wording, and Execute by sending it.

ChatGPT delivered a draft in two minutes. It opened with acknowledgment ("You're absolutely right to escalate this"), included a specific action (Priya calling ops immediately), and proposed that she'd send a revised timeline within two hours once she'd confirmed feasibility with the team. The language was professional without being robotic. She edited it for thirty seconds, added a specific fact about the original problem that showed she'd been paying attention, changed one sentence to match her actual voice and sent it. The client responded within an hour with a realistic new deadline and a positive note about her responsiveness. Ten minutes of real work from Priya, instead of thirty minutes of staring at the screen trying to find the right words while managing her own anxiety about the delay.

The next email challenge was different. She needed to ask her boss for a deadline extension on something she'd committed to last month. The original framing was going to be: "I need more time for the Q2 roadmap." That was asking, that was vulnerable, that created a narrative that Priya was slipping. She fed that to ChatGPT with new instructions: "Reframe this request to show that the extra time investment is strategic, not slipping. The tone should be: I've done the work, I've identified what needs to happen, I'm being proactive about getting it right. Instead of 'I need more time,' what would a more confident framing be?"

The AI suggested: "I've identified what we need to nail Q2 roadmap execution, and I want to make sure we're not leaving performance on the table. I'd like to extend the roadmap lock date by one week so we can [specific action]." That was a completely different energy. It reframed from deficit to strategy. Instead of asking for mercy, she was proposing investment. Priya sent a version of that to James that afternoon, with the specific action filled in (validate the three channel assumptions with recent customer data). He approved the extension without pushback.

Late Monday afternoon, Priya got Carbon Copied on a 47-email thread about budget approvals for Q2. She had scrolled through maybe five messages before realizing she'd never catch up organically. The thread spanned six hours of conversation across multiple time zones. People had been adding context, debating, reversing positions. It was a mess. She downloaded the thread as a .txt file and uploaded it to ChatGPT: "I was CC'd on a long email thread about budget approvals. I don't have time to read all 47 messages. Tell me: What are the open questions? Who needs to decide what? What's the timeline? What's my role in this, if any?"

Three minutes later, she had a one-page summary. Two open questions (whether to increase headcount in ops, and whether to reallocate budget from customer acquisition to retention marketing). Two decision-makers (VP of Finance and VP of Operations). Timeline: decision by Friday. Priya's role: optional attendee at the Wednesday steering committee meeting, could contribute perspective on what customers were asking for regarding retention. Priya didn't need to read all 47 messages. She needed to understand the shape of the conversation and know when to step in. She'd done that. And she'd reclaimed ninety minutes of email archaeology that would normally have consumed her entire afternoon.

"Privacy note," she thought, and made a mental note: don't paste confidential client information, customer names, financial figures, or competitive secrets into any AI tool unless your organization has explicitly approved the platform. Her company had approved ChatGPT for general business use, but not for customer names or deal values. She'd been careful about that all day. Everything she'd shared was generalizable. The patterns, not the specifics. The structures, not the secrets.

Note: Check with your company's policies before attempting any of this. Many companies now have strict policies and guidelines on which AI tools you can and cannot use. Be sure to comply with those policies at all times when using AI at work.

▶ TRY THIS NOW: Triage Your Email

Today, copy five emails from your inbox into ChatGPT. Use this prompt: "I received these emails. For each one, identify: (1) What action, if any, is required from me? (2) By when? (3) Who else could handle this?" Then mark at least one email as delegated, or batch it into a reply. That's one email per day you just reclaimed. By the end of the week, you'll have five emails back. Scale that to your entire inbox.

✦✦✦

Meetings: Before, During, and After

Priya's biggest challenge on Monday was meetings. She had four scheduled for Tuesday and Wednesday combined. The Q2 marketing goals meeting was scheduled for Tuesday at 10 AM, thirty minutes long, five people (Priya, her team lead, two campaign managers, and James). It was marked as decision-required on the calendar, which in corporate speak meant the outcome mattered. In the old workflow, Priya would have shown up with maybe a rough outline in her head of what she wanted to cover. The meeting would start at 10:03 because one person was late. Twenty minutes would be spent figuring out the actual goal of the meeting. Five minutes of actual decisions. Five minutes of repeating herself because not everyone was on the same page. Post-meeting, she'd spend an hour writing a summary because nobody could agree on what was decided.

This time, she wanted to use AI to script the meeting before it happened. She opened ChatGPT and gave it a thoughtful prompt: "I'm running a 30-minute meeting tomorrow with five people. The goal is to lock our Q2 marketing strategy. We need to decide: (1) Which three customer segments to focus on, (2) What channels to invest in, (3) How to measure success. The team has been researching this for two weeks. I'll be presenting their work. Generate a detailed agenda that maximizes decision velocity. Include time allocations for each section. This is my outline of what I know so far: [three segments we're considering: small businesses, mid-market, enterprise], [four potential channels: email, content marketing, paid search, webinars], [three possible success metrics: customer acquisition cost, customer lifetime value, market share in segment]."

ChatGPT returned a fourteen-minute agenda (leaving sixteen minutes for Q&A and spillover). Opening: five minutes, context and goal-setting. Segment deep-dive: four minutes, present findings and decision options. Channel strategy: three minutes, present findings and decision options. Metrics: two minutes, present findings and decision options. Closing: thirty seconds, confirm decisions and next steps. Simple. Clear. Time-boxed. It didn't ramble. Priya sent it to her team that afternoon with the message: "Here's tomorrow's agenda. If you have updates to the segments or channels, send them by 6 PM so I can incorporate." The meeting would either run on time or give her fifteen minutes back. Either way, it was a win.

The harder question was what happened during meetings. Priya had tried taking her own notes for years and always regretted it. She'd be scribbling and miss an important decision. Or she'd write detailed notes and never read them. Or she'd spend so much time note-taking that she wasn't present in the conversation. The solution was transcription. During the Tuesday meeting, she started recording it using Otter.ai. The app transcribed in real-time on her laptop, though not perfectly (there were small errors, a few misheard names) but she had a complete record anyway.[25, 26]

She compared her transcription options carefully. Several excellent transcription services offer free tiers with enough capacity to test them. Features vary. Some offer real-time transcription, high accuracy, language support, and CRM integration. Built-in options existed too: Microsoft Teams had an AI Companion that could transcribe and summarize. Zoom had automatic captions. Google Meet had similar features. The infrastructure was there. The barrier was just knowing it existed and turning it on. Visit practicalaibook.ai for current recommendations and pricing.

After the Tuesday meeting, Priya had a 3,500-word transcript from Otter. It captured everything: the discussion about customer segments, the debate about which channels were worth the investment, even the jokes that had created brief chaos when someone suggested email marketing to enterprise customers. She uploaded it to ChatGPT with a simple prompt: "Here's a transcript of a 30-minute meeting. I need: (1) The five key decisions we made, (2) Action items with specific owners and deadlines, (3) A follow-up email I can send to the team to confirm everything. Format the email as professional but brief, we're a fast-moving team."

The AI returned a structured response. Five decisions, clearly stated (focus on mid-market segment, invest in content and webinar channels, measure by CAC and LTV). Seven action items, with owners assigned because the transcript had named who was responsible. A follow-up email that took Priya five minutes to personalize with details and context that only she knew. She sent it before 11 AM Tuesday. One person on her team replied with a clarification question about the channel budget split, which she answered immediately. The meeting decisions were locked. Nobody had to wonder. Nobody had to ask for a summary. The transcript was the source of truth. Priya had bought herself ten hours that would normally have been spent in follow-up emails, clarifications, and confusion.

That same Tuesday, Priya tested something she'd read about: the "meeting that should have been an email" test. She had a 1 PM call scheduled with a colleague to "discuss the roadmap." Before accepting it, she asked ChatGPT: "Is this agenda detailed enough to be productive in a meeting, or should this be an email instead? Agenda: [copied the calendar description]. If it should be a meeting, how would I make it better?"

ChatGPT said: "This is too vague for a synchronous meeting. It's more of a status update, which is better done asynchronously. Recommendation: send a detailed email with your questions, ask for written responses within 24 hours, and schedule a 15-minute call only if there are conflicts to resolve." Priya did exactly that. She sent a thoughtful email with three specific questions about the roadmap priorities. Her colleague sent detailed responses within two hours.

The issues were clear. No call was needed. She had her afternoon back. Fifteen minutes saved, but scaled across a month of meetings, that's an hour every two weeks. That's two hours a month. That's a full day a quarter.

▶ **TRY THIS NOW: Automate Your Meeting Notes**

For your next meeting, try a transcription tool that fits your needs —whether that's a standalone service or the built-in captions on Teams/Zoom. Visit practicalaibook.ai for current recommendations. After the meeting, paste the transcript into your AI tool with this prompt: "What were the three key decisions? What are the action items with owners and deadlines? Send me a one-paragraph follow-up I can send to the team." You'll have meeting notes in three minutes instead of thirty. Then multiply that by your number of meetings per week.

✦✦✦

Research in Minutes, Not Hours

The competitive analysis was due Friday. Three companies: Logistics International, a regional player in the Midwest that had been in business for thirty years; Tradewind Logistics, a national competitor with a focus on sustainability and newer technology; TruckNet Express, a startup founded three years ago that was building AI into route optimization. Priya needed to understand their pricing, their service footprint, their technology capabilities, their market positioning, and their recent moves. She needed to know what they were doing that her company wasn't. She needed enough detail to make her VP feel informed. The old way: a full day of Google searching, reading company websites, pulling annual reports, watching investor presentations, taking notes in a spreadsheet, trying to synthesize into something coherent. Six hours, minimum. More likely eight.

The new way would use PRIME and leverage AI as a research partner. She opened ChatGPT and started with the Prompt step, building it with the 5-Part Formula:

- Role - “You’re a market research analyst specializing in logistics”
- Context - “I’m a marketing manager at a mid-sized logistics company preparing a competitive briefing for my VP”
- Task - “Analyze these three competitors <list of names> on pricing, geography, technology capabilities, service offerings, and recent strategic moves”
- Format - “Create a comparison table plus a 500-word strategic analysis”
- Constraints - “Focus on where we have competitive advantages”

The first response was helpful but incomplete. The pricing data for one company was outdated (ChatGPT’s training data cuts off in early 2024, and pricing in logistics changes frequently). The technology capabilities for another company had some hallucinations, it invented features that didn’t exist or attributed features to the wrong company. Priya caught both issues because she understood the companies better than an AI ever could. She had heard Logistics International talk about new pricing in a recent industry presentation. She knew TruckNet didn’t have a real-time tracking feature yet because a customer had complained about it last month. She used the IDEA loop: Imagine what her VP actually needed (current pricing verified against company websites, verified features). Diagnose the gap (training data cutoff, hallucinations). Enhance the prompt: “For each company’s pricing and technology, note which information comes from their website vs. which is inferred. Flag anything you’re uncertain about. Be conservative.” Act: feed the updated prompt back to ChatGPT.

The second pass was much better. ChatGPT now flagged its uncertainties explicitly. Priya took those flagged items and googled them directly, just the specific gaps, not the entire research. That took twenty minutes instead of six hours. She filled in the missing pieces from recent news articles, company websites, and her own industry knowledge. She created her own version of the table with the verified information. She wrote a strategic analysis based on the completed table, adding perspective that only someone immersed in the industry could add, not just what each competitor was doing, but why, and how that differed from the market dynamics. The overall research process took six hours instead of twelve. Friday's deadline was now a confirmation pass, not a scramble.

The next research challenge came Thursday. Her VP asked Priya to present a 10-minute overview on supply chain sustainability regulations to the leadership team. The regulations were new. Priya had heard about them in passing but didn't understand them deeply enough to present with confidence. She had zero time to become an expert. She opened ChatGPT and asked: "Explain supply chain sustainability regulations that affect US logistics companies. What are the key laws? What are the compliance requirements? What are the deadlines? Give me enough detail to present a 10-minute overview to my leadership team. Start with the most important regulations first."

ChatGPT returned a structured outline: the Inflation Reduction Act (IRA) and its incentives for sustainable logistics (tax credits, grants), the EPA's evolving emissions standards for vehicles and operations, state-level regulations (California AB 32, New York's Zero Emission Vehicle mandate, others), corporate disclosure requirements (SEC climate reporting for public companies), and customer-driven expectations (major corporations now requiring supplier ESG reporting). Within thirty minutes, Priya understood the landscape well enough to ask intelligent follow-up questions. She asked ChatGPT to highlight which regulations were most relevant to her company's size and geography. She asked which ones had firm deadlines versus guidance. She asked where her company was already in compliance and where they had gaps. Then she drafted a five-slide outline to present to leadership. By Thursday evening, she was ready. The presentation went well Friday morning. Her VP appreciated that she'd come prepared. Nobody asked her detailed questions she couldn't answer.

But Priya added a critical caveat to herself: AI training data has a cutoff date. For research on current events (regulatory changes announced last month, recent acquisitions, latest pricing) the AI could confidently hallucinate plausible-sounding information that sounded authoritative and true but was completely invented. For that kind of research, she used Perplexity, an AI search engine that queries the web in real-time and cites sources. She tested it Friday morning by asking: "What supply chain regulations were passed in the US in the last 60 days?" Perplexity returned current information with links to the actual regulatory documents. When she needed cutting-edge information, Perplexity was the tool. When she needed to synthesize and strategize, ChatGPT was better. Understanding the difference saved her from hallucination traps.

Note: AI models and capabilities are changing daily. At the time of writing, many of the major foundation models, can access the web for real-time data as well. Some do it better than others. Some have deeper insights (Deep Research) than others. Head to your AI of choice's website or to practicalaibook.ai for the latest details on what each model can do.

▶ TRY THIS NOW: Run Quick Research

Choose a research topic you've been putting off (a new competitor, a market trend, an industry you know nothing about, a regulatory change). Spend thirty minutes with ChatGPT using the PRIME framework to get a first pass. Then spend another thirty minutes filling in gaps with web search or Perplexity. That's it. You now have 60 percent of what a deep-dive would give you, in 60 minutes instead of six hours. And 60 percent accurate is better than 0 percent from analysis paralysis.

✦✦✦

Writing Reports, Proposals, and Presentations

The blank page is the enemy. Ask anyone who's written a quarterly report: the hardest part isn't the writing. It's everything before the writing starts — the paralysis of the blank page, trying to figure out structure. Should I start with findings or context? Should I lead with the big number or bury it? How many sections? How detailed? What's the right tone? What's the narrative arc? The cognitive load is immense because you're not just writing; you're also designing the frame. You're making a hundred small decisions about organization before you even write the first sentence. AI's primary value in this moment is not literary genius or perfect analysis. It's structural clarity. It gives you something to react against instead of starting from nothing.

Priya had to write her quarterly report for James. It was due Wednesday. She had Q1 data: revenue (up 8%), pipeline (strong, but slower than expected), customer acquisition cost (higher than budget), retention rate (good at 94%), marketing spend broken down by channel, and a few subjective observations about what worked and what didn't. Normally, she'd spend two hours just organizing this into an outline, deciding what to emphasize and what to downplay. Then another two hours writing a first draft with real sentences. Then two more hours editing for tone and clarity. Six hours minimum.

Instead: she dumped all the Q1 data into a spreadsheet and sent it to ChatGPT. She gave it a specific prompt: "I'm writing a quarterly business report for my VP. Here's my Q1 data in summary form. I need an outline and a first draft. The report should have these sections: (1) Executive Summary, (2) Results Overview (what happened?), (3) Analysis (why did it happen?), (4) Challenges, (5) Recommendations and Next Steps. About 2,000 words total. The tone should be confident but not defensive. I'm a marketing manager, so assume some business literacy but not deep knowledge of my specific market."

ChatGPT generated a 2,100-word draft in three minutes. The structure was solid. The flow was logical. The headings were clear. And it was completely generic. It read like a report template, which was fine, because Priya's job wasn't to make ChatGPT write like her, it was to make the template into something true and specific. She spent two hours on the Master step: adding specific examples from her quarter (the campaign that worked, the channel that surprised her, the customer conversation that shifted her thinking), sharpening the analysis with her institutional knowledge, removing corporate-speak, infusing her personality. She used phrases that sounded like her. She added details only she knew. When she was done, it felt like hers. James read it and said: "This is the best report you've sent me. Good structure, clear thinking, specific examples." He didn't know ChatGPT had written 70 percent of the structure. He only cared that the final product was excellent.

The same pattern worked for proposals. Priya wanted to pitch a new marketing automation tool to James. The business case was solid (better email tracking, easier segmentation, integration with the CRM, cost savings of about $15K per year through automation). But she needed to frame it in a way that spoke to his priorities: cost, speed to value, and risk mitigation. She gave ChatGPT the tool's features and her company's pain points: "I'm proposing [tool name] to my VP. It costs $120 per month. The benefits are: better email tracking, better segmentation, CRM integration, estimated $15K annual savings through automation. Write a two-page business case that leads with ROI and payback period, then addresses implementation risk. He cares about cost savings, speed to value, and doesn't like disruption. Include a 90-day implementation plan."

The draft came back in ninety seconds. Structured. Well-reasoned. Persuasive. It led with the payback period (6 weeks). Priya edited it for fifteen minutes, adding details about why the tool specifically mattered for her team's current bottleneck. She sent it. James approved the tool within a day.

Presentations followed the same logic. After the quarterly report, she asked ChatGPT: "Turn this report into a 10-slide presentation outline with speaker notes." Boom. Then: "Slide 3 is the ROI section. Expand it to cover methodology and assumptions." ChatGPT expanded it. No blank page. No paralysis. Just: here's the structure, now you refine it.

The real insight was this: AI eliminates the blank page. Even if the first output is imperfect, it's infinitely better than nothing. Getting started is always the hardest part. Having something to react against changes everything. Priya used to lose ninety minutes to inertia before she even began writing, staring at a blank document, trying to organize her thoughts. With AI, she had a draft in three minutes and got to the actual work, thinking, refining, making it hers, immediately. The time saved was the time before the first word was written.

Let's save you some frustration right now. AI models are not going to write your entire 40-page proposal in one shot, no matter how nicely you ask. The reason is something called a *context window*. Basically, it's a cap on how much text the model can read or write at one time. Think of it like a whiteboard that only has so much space. The output side tends to fill up fast. There are more advanced techniques out there involving memory files, extended context tricks, but we're not going down that road today. Check out practicalaibook.ai if you're looking for more on that. What we *are* going to do is use the PRIME framework, specifically the IDEA loop, to work around this like a pro. Start by outlining the whole document first, PRIME each section one at a time, then one or two final PRIME pass(es) to clean it all up. Suddenly, that report that had you stress-eating granola bars for three days? Done in a couple of hours. You're welcome.

Note: I cannot say it enough, don't put financial information or any other private or proprietary data into a model without checking with your company's policy first. ChatGPT especially is notorious for training on data you give it, so unless you want your company's secret schematics showing up in someone else's chat search, then don't upload anything unless you know you have permission. Check out Chapter 9 for more safety tips.

▶ **TRY THIS NOW: Draft Your Report**

The next time you have to write a report or proposal, don't start from scratch. Dump your data, key points, or requirements into ChatGPT with this prompt: "I need to write a [report/proposal]. Here's what I know: [data]. Create an outline and a first draft with [X] sections. Format for [audience]." Then spend your real time editing and adding your expertise, not creating structure. You'll go from six hours to four.

✦✦✦

Data Analysis for Non-Analysts

Priya had a spreadsheet with six months of campaign data. Two hundred rows. Fifteen columns: campaign name, channel (email, content, paid search, webinar), spend, impressions, clicks, conversions, revenue, cost-per-click, conversion rate, and metrics she'd copied over from various sources and didn't fully understand. She knew Excel at a functional level (could make a pivot table, could sort, could create a basic chart) but analysis was not her strength. The task her boss had given her was simple and terrifying: "Make sense of this data. What should we double down on? What should we cut?" Without analysis, she was just guessing. With analysis, she had options.

In the past, this task would have meant spending a day making pivot tables, staring at numbers, feeling vaguely lost, and then making a guess. Or asking the analytics person to do it, which meant waiting a week for their availability. This time, she uploaded the .xlsx file directly to ChatGPT. The platform supports Excel and CSV files up to 50 MB.[27] She gave it a conversational prompt: "I have six months of campaign data. I'm not an analyst, but I need to understand it. Tell me: (1) Which channels are most profitable? (2) Which are losing money? (3) What patterns do you see across the seasons? (4) Where am I wasting budget? (5) What should I recommend to my boss? Give me numbers, not just trends."

ChatGPT analyzed the file and returned something shocking: a channel that Priya thought was performing well (high volume, lots of conversions) was actually losing money once you accounted for the cost of the conversions. A different channel that she'd considered low-volume was actually the most efficient: lower spend, reasonable volume, and the best conversion rate. Seasonal patterns emerged. Q1 campaigns had worked better. Spring performance had dipped predictably. Budget had been poorly allocated because Priya had been chasing volume instead of efficiency.

She verified everything. ChatGPT's analysis was right, but she needed to double-check the math. (AI hallucinates numbers with concerning confidence. Always verify.) She spot-checked the calculations herself: yes, the inefficient channel actually had a negative ROI. She had been throwing money at a channel that was destroying value. The discovery was worth thousands of dollars in budget reallocation. She wouldn't have found it with manual pivot tables because her intuition had told her the channel was working. She'd needed an outside perspective.

ChatGPT also mentioned two tools worth exploring: ChatGPT for Excel (a beta add-in powered by GPT, currently being rolled out) that would bring AI directly into workbooks so she could ask questions about data without uploading anywhere (CoPilot can do this as well if your company has the Microsoft Subscription), and Google Sheets integration with Gemini.[28, 29] The infrastructure was rapidly catching up. Soon she'd be able to ask questions about data directly inside the spreadsheet, without leaving her familiar tools.

The power move for data analysis was this: "I don't know what questions to ask about this data. What should I be looking at?" Priya asked ChatGPT exactly that with a new dataset. The AI suggested frameworks she'd never have thought of: cohort analysis, churn patterns, attribution, and seasonal decomposition. She now had a roadmap for analysis instead of staring into the void.

The caveat was essential. Always verify AI's analysis. Check the math. Look at the visualizations it generated and make sure they made sense. AI is great at pattern-finding but terrible at accuracy-checking. They are called Large Language models, not Large Numbers Models for a reason. It will confidently tell you something false. Your job is to be the skeptic. You bring the verification. You bring the judgment about whether the pattern is meaningful or just noise.

▶ **TRY THIS NOW: Analyze Your Data**

Export one month of data you care about (sales, marketing, operations, whatever). Save it as CSV or Excel. Upload it to ChatGPT and ask: "What patterns do you see? What should I be worried about? What's working better than expected? What's worse?" Then spend thirty minutes verifying the top three findings in the raw data. This is how non-analysts become data-informed quickly.

✦✦✦

The Art of Not Getting Caught Using AI Badly

This section is about reputation, ethics, and staying out of trouble. The stakes are real. In the time since this book had started being written, regulation had caught up. Illinois passed a law in January 2026 requiring employers to disclose to candidates and employees when AI was being used in hiring, promotion, or performance evaluation decisions. Colorado's AI Act, originally scheduled to take effect February 1, 2026, but delayed to June 30, 2026, regulates "consequential decisions" (anything affecting employment, benefits, housing, insurance) and required impact assessments, risk management processes, and appeals procedures. California had proposed AB 1898, which would require advance written notice and signed acknowledgments if a person's access to employment was affected by an automated decision system. The federal government was moving too: a bipartisan Senate bill was pushing for reporting on how AI affected personnel decisions. The landscape was shifting fast, and it was shifting toward transparency.[30, 31]

More concretely: many mid-sized companies now have AI use policies. Priya's did. She'd read hers carefully. It explicitly approved ChatGPT and Claude for general business work, marketing, strategy, and analysis. It explicitly prohibited AI use for hiring decisions, writing performance review content, legal documents (without lawyer review), automated decisions that affected employment, and anything involving customer personal data. She stayed within those boundaries religiously. Some companies had gone further: one had prohibited any AI use without manager approval. Another had limited it to specific tools only. One had implemented a blanket ban on generative AI entirely. The rule was: check your own company's policy. Don't assume permission.

The other risk was reputation. When people found out you used

AI, and they almost always did, they would judge the quality of the work. If your AI-assisted output was generic, bland, or clearly unedited, the discovery that you used AI would look lazy. If your AI-assisted output was excellent, thoughtful, and clearly refined, the discovery would look intelligent. You'd look like someone who used tools effectively. Same tool. Different outcomes based on the Master step. Priya knew this. She mastered everything. She edited ruthlessly. She added her expertise. She removed corporate-speak. She made it sound like her.

The "AI smell test" was the ability to recognize unedited AI content. It had tells. Overly formal language everywhere. Excessive use of words like "certainly" and "it is worth noting." Suspiciously perfect organization, with no tangents. No personality. Repetitive structure across paragraphs. Transitions that all sound the same. A lack of specificity or concrete examples. Priya could read something and instantly know if it was unedited AI output. The goal was never to hide that fact. The goal was to edit the AI output so thoroughly that whether you knew it used AI or not didn't matter, the work was good. In other words, YOU HAVE TO READ IT! Something we've been screaming at our Sales team for years.

How did Priya make AI-assisted work her own? First, the Master step was everything. She spent real time editing. She removed stock phrases. She added specific examples from her company, her context, her experience. She injected her voice. She cut corporate-speak. She added humor where appropriate. She made it sound like something a human wrote, because it was (she had just been faster at getting through the thinking stage. Second, she always verified facts. AI hallucinated names, dates, statistics, quotes, URLs, company-specific details. She fact-checked everything, especially claims that sounded plausible. Third: she disclosed when it made sense. If her boss asked whether she used AI to draft something, she said yes. Most bosses didn't care. They cared about the output. Some managers were nervous about AI but respected honesty. None were angry when the work was good.

The reputation equation is simple. If your boss finds out you used

AI and your work was generic or wrong, that's worse than not using AI at all. You look lazy. If your boss finds out you used AI and your work was excellent, that's the goal. You look efficient and smart. The variable wasn't the tool. It was the quality of your editing and your judgment.

Priya had thought about quitting her job, using AI to generate all her outputs, and just collecting paychecks (sometimes called Quiet Quitting). For about three seconds. Then she realized how stupid that was. One day her boss would notice the outputs weren't reflecting actual strategic thinking. One day someone would catch a hallucination that mattered. One day the jig would be up and her credibility would evaporate. It wasn't worth it. The value of AI wasn't automation. It was augmentation. It was reclaiming the 80 percent of time spent on busywork so she could spend it on the 20 percent that actually mattered: thinking, deciding, leading, and using her judgment.

▶ TRY THIS NOW: Understand Your Privacy Rules

Read your company's AI use policy. It exists. Find it. If you can't find it, ask your manager or compliance team. Once you have it, read it carefully. Note: (1) Approved tools, (2) Prohibited use cases, (3) Disclosure requirements, (4) Responsible AI practices. If your company doesn't have a policy, propose one to your manager. This proactive step makes everything else safer.

✦✦✦

Friday at 4 PM

Priya sat at her desk on Friday afternoon at 3:47 PM, still early enough to be within office hours. The Slack notifications were quiet. Her inbox showed four unread emails, all marked Important (down from 127 on Monday morning). The competitive analysis had been turned in Thursday afternoon. It was fourteen pages, thoroughly researched, with three detailed comparison tables, visuals showing market positioning, and a two-page strategic recommendation backed by evidence. Her boss had asked to meet with her Monday to discuss it. The quarterly report was complete, submitted Wednesday morning, and already commented on positively by her VP. James had written: "Strong quarter. Clear thinking. This is what I needed." The meeting agendas for next week were drafted and sent to attendees. The Q2 roadmap deadline extension had been approved and the work was on track. The budget thread email had been resolved with a clear decision. Two new customer escalations had been handled quickly; within the same day they arrived. She'd attended all her meetings, and none had run over. She'd written three proposals. She'd analyzed campaign data and identified budget optimization opportunities worth tens of thousands of dollars in redirect.

The inbox had been cleared by noon on Monday. She hadn't dealt with email for entire afternoons Tuesday and Wednesday. Meeting follow-ups had been sent within minutes of each meeting ending. In the old way, this same week would have consumed about forty hours of pure execution work, plus another twenty hours of busywork she didn't track. This week had taken about thirty hours of actual work, with another five hours of busywork she simply hadn't done because it wasn't necessary. The math was clear: she'd recovered about fifteen hours. Almost two full work days. And more importantly, she'd recovered the mental energy. She wasn't exhausted. She wasn't overwhelmed. She wasn't wondering what she'd missed. Priya hadn't become a different person. She hadn't suddenly learned AI deeply. She'd just become a faster, more focused version of herself. Her judgment was the same. Her strategic thinking was the same. The busywork had just gotten faster.

The real insight: AI reclaimed the 60 percent of time that was consumed by busywork. The blank page problem. The email triage. The meeting logistics. The structural thinking that came before the actual thinking. AI handled all of that at machine speed. Priya got to do the real work: judgment, decision-making, strategy, adding her human expertise to whatever the AI had produced. She got to be a manager instead of a logistics coordinator. And Friday was proof of that shift.

She closed her laptop early and sent her team a Slack message:

"Great week, everyone. Proud of what we shipped. See you Monday."

On the drive home, she thought about the conversation she'd had with her friend Jenna last week. The one about how hard it was to explain AI to her teenagers. The hardest audience of all, Jenna had said, wasn't your boss or your customers. It was your kids, explaining to them what you actually did when half of what you did was now invisible, done by a machine faster than you could do it by hand. That sounded like a whole different challenge. But for now, Priya had Friday evening back. She had reclaimed it. She was going to spend it present with her family instead of worrying about what she'd missed or what she'd forgotten.

6

AI FOR PARENTS & EDUCATORS

NAVIGATING THE NEW REALITY WITH KIDS AND STUDENTS

The Kitchen Table Summit. Jenna Washington found the essay at 9:47 PM on a Tuesday. She'd been putting the recycling out and noticed her son's laptop still open on the kitchen table, the screen glowing in the dim room. The document was titled "The Symbolism of the Green Light in The Great Gatsby." It was beautifully written. Perfectly structured. Five paragraphs, each one building on the last, with a thesis statement that would have made Jenna's own English teacher weep. There was just one problem: her son, Tyler, was fourteen years old, read at about a ninth-grade level, and had never once in his life used the word "juxtaposition."

She scrolled up. The formatting was immaculate. No crossed-out sentences, no false starts, no evidence of the messy, iterative thinking that a real fourteen-year-old produces when wrestling with a novel he'd described at dinner as "kind of boring, honestly." Jenna didn't need to be a tech expert to know what had happened. Tyler had used AI to write his essay. The whole thing. Start to finish. And he'd done it so cleanly that the only reason she knew was because she happened to see the screen before he closed it.

She sat down at the table and stared at the essay for a long time. Her first instinct was anger. Her second was confusion. Her third (the one that kept her sitting there for twenty minutes) was a question she couldn't answer: What am I supposed to do with this?

Because the rules had changed, and nobody had given parents the new playbook.

Jenna was a freelance graphic designer who worked from home. She used AI herself. Canva's AI features, ChatGPT for client emails, Claude for brainstorming design concepts. She wasn't anti-technology. She wasn't even anti-AI. She had spent the last month applying what she'd learned about PRIME to her own life and work. AI had saved her hours. It had made her a better professional. So how could she tell her son not to use the same tools she relied on every day?

But she also knew that Tyler hadn't learned anything. The essay was perfect, but Tyler couldn't explain what the green light symbolized if you asked him at breakfast. The tool had produced the output, but the learning hadn't happened. And that was the whole point of the assignment. Not the essay itself, but the struggle of figuring out what Fitzgerald was trying to say. The messy thinking. The bad first draft. The realization that your first interpretation was wrong and you had to start over. That was the education. The essay was just proof that the education had occurred.

Meanwhile, Jenna's daughter, Maya, was seven. Maya had discovered that she could ask the family's smart speaker questions about anything. "Alexa, why is the sky blue?" "Alexa, what's the biggest animal ever?" "Alexa, do dogs dream?" Harmless enough. But last week, Maya had asked: "Alexa, am I pretty?" And then: "Alexa, does everyone die?" Jenna had overheard both questions from the next room and felt something tighten in her chest. Not because the questions were wrong, kids ask those things, but because Maya was asking a machine instead of a person. And the machine had answered both times with cheerful, sanitized responses that missed the emotional complexity entirely.

Two kids. Two completely different AI challenges. Tyler was using AI to skip the hard parts of learning. Maya was using AI to explore questions that deserved human warmth and nuance. And

Jenna was in the middle, trying to figure out the right approach for both of them without banning technology she herself depended on.

Across town, Jenna's friend Tomás Reyes was facing the same questions from the other side of the desk. Tomás taught seventh-grade science at Lincoln Middle School. He'd been teaching for nine years. He was good at it, the kind of teacher kids remembered. Energetic, creative, the kind who brought dry ice into the classroom and let students design their own experiments. But this year felt different. Tomás had noticed that student writing had become... smoother. Lab reports that used to contain misspellings, awkward phrasing, and occasional brilliance now read like they'd been written by the same competent, slightly bland author. Five of his thirty-two students had submitted nearly identical discussion responses for a unit on ecosystems, each one technically correct but missing the personal observations he'd asked for. "What did YOU notice about the food web?" he'd written on the assignment. What he got back were textbook definitions with slightly rearranged words.

Tomás wasn't naive. He knew about AI detection tools, and he knew they were unreliable. He'd run his own writing through one and it flagged a paragraph he'd written himself as "likely AI-generated." He'd tried another tool and it cleared an essay he'd asked ChatGPT to write as a test. The detection arms race was already lost. Teachers who relied on detection were playing whack-a-mole against tools that were evolving faster than any school policy could keep up.

So Tomás had stopped trying to catch students using AI. Instead, he'd started redesigning his assignments so that AI couldn't do the interesting parts. And he'd started using AI himself, to plan lessons, differentiate instruction for students at different levels, and create materials he never would have had time to build on his own. The irony wasn't lost on him: the same technology his students were using to avoid learning was helping him become a better teacher.

Jenna and Tomás were having coffee the following Saturday, and the conversation turned, as it always did lately, to AI and kids. "I caught Tyler using it for an essay," Jenna said. "I didn't know what to say. I use it every day for work."

"That's the whole dilemma," Tomás said. "We can't tell them it's cheating when we're using it ourselves. But we also can't let them skip the learning. The answer isn't banning it. The answer is teaching them when and how."

This chapter is about that conversation. It's for every parent who's found the suspiciously perfect essay, every teacher who's noticed the shift in student work, and every family trying to figure out the new rules. The old playbook (limit screen time, check browser history, hope for the best) doesn't work anymore. AI isn't a website you can block. It's a capability that's woven into almost every tool your kids already use. The question isn't whether they'll use it. They already are. The question is whether they'll use it well.

✦✦✦

Homework Help Without Doing the Homework

Let's start with the scenario every parent dreads. Your kid is using AI to do their homework. Not as a tutor. Not as a study aid. As a ghostwriter. Tyler's Gatsby essay was a clean example, but the spectrum is wide. A ten-year-old asking ChatGPT to solve math word problems. A sixteen-year-old feeding an entire AP History prompt into Claude and submitting whatever comes back. A college freshman using AI to write discussion posts they never read the assigned material for.

The knee-jerk reaction is to ban it. Some schools have tried. It doesn't work. Students access AI on their phones, their personal laptops, through dozens of apps that embed AI features invisibly. Banning AI from homework is like banning calculators in the 1980s, a losing battle against a tool that's already everywhere.

The smarter approach, and the one Jenna landed on after her kitchen-table discovery, is to teach kids to use AI as a tutor, not a shortcut. The difference is simple: a tutor helps you understand. A shortcut helps you skip understanding. Here's what that looks like in practice.

Jenna sat Tyler down the next evening. She didn't yell. She didn't ground him. She opened his laptop and said: "Show me what you did." Tyler, surprised that he wasn't in trouble, walked her through it. He'd typed "write an essay about the green light in The Great Gatsby" into ChatGPT. It had produced the essay. He'd copied it, pasted it into Google Docs, and put his name on it. The whole thing took about four minutes.

"Okay," Jenna said. "Now tell me what the green light means."

Tyler paused. "It's like... hope? And the American Dream?"

"That's what the essay says. But what do you think it means?"

Longer pause. "I don't know. I didn't really think about it."

"That's the problem," Jenna said. "The essay is perfect, but you didn't learn anything. Your teacher didn't assign this, so you'd have a perfect essay. She assigned it so you'd wrestle with the book. The wrestling is the point."

Then Jenna did something clever. She'd remembered the PRIME framework she uses at work and adapted it for Tyler. "Let me show you how to use AI the right way," she said. She opened a new ChatGPT window and typed: "I'm a 9th grader writing an essay about the green light in The Great Gatsby. Don't write the essay for me. Instead, ask me questions that help me figure out my own argument. Start with: What do I think the green light represents, and why?"

ChatGPT responded with a question: "What do you think the green light represents for Gatsby? Is it something he wants, something he's lost, or something else entirely?"

Tyler stared at the screen. "Something he wants," he said. "He keeps looking at it across the water."

"Good," Jenna said. "Type that. Then ask it to push you further."

Over the next forty-five minutes, Tyler had a conversation with ChatGPT that was essentially a Socratic dialogue. The AI asked him questions. He answered. It challenged his answers. He refined his thinking. By the end, he had an outline that was entirely his own, his ideas, his interpretation, his words. The AI hadn't written a single sentence of his essay. It had helped him think. The essay Tyler wrote that night was shorter than the original AI-generated one, rougher around the edges, and had a conclusion that was slightly awkward. It was also genuinely his. And he could explain every argument in it.

This is the model: AI as a Socratic tutor. The prompt template Jenna used works for almost any subject and any age. Here's the formula:

"I'm a [grade level] student working on [subject/assignment]. Don't give me the answer. Instead, ask me questions that help me figure it out myself. Start by asking me what I already know about [topic]."

That single prompt transforms AI from a homework-doing machine into a patient, infinitely available tutor. It works for math ("walk me through the problem-solving steps without giving me the answer"), science ("ask me what I think will happen in this experiment and why"), history ("help me understand both sides of this debate by asking me questions"), and creative writing ("help me brainstorm ideas by asking me about my interests and experiences").

Tomás had arrived at the same approach from the teacher's side. He'd stopped assigning essays that could be completed by a single AI prompt. Instead, his assignments now had what he called "fingerprint requirements", elements that required personal experience, classroom-specific context, or multi-step reasoning that AI couldn't fake. "Describe what YOU observed when we mixed the chemicals in lab on Tuesday" was much harder to fake than "explain what happens when you mix baking soda and vinegar." One required being physically present. The other required Google.

▶ **TRY THIS NOW: Guide Your Child's AI Use**

Tonight, sit with your kid while they do homework. When they reach for AI, try this prompt together: "I'm a [grade] student working on [assignment]. Don't give me the answer. Ask me questions to help me figure it out myself."

Watch how the conversation unfolds. If your child is engaged and thinking, AI is being a tutor. If they're copying and pasting, the prompt needs to be more specific. The goal: your kid should be doing more thinking, not less.

✦✦✦

Age-Appropriate Conversations About AI

Maya was seven. Tyler was fourteen. They needed completely different conversations about what AI was, what it could do, and what the rules were. The mistake most parents make is having one blanket conversation, or worse, no conversation at all, and assuming kids will figure it out. They won't. Or rather, they will, but they'll figure it out from YouTube, from friends, and from trial and error, which means they'll absorb whatever narrative is loudest rather than the one that's most accurate.

Here's what Jenna did for each kid, and these scripts can be adapted for your own family.

For younger kids (ages 5–9): The Helper Robot explanation. Jenna sat Maya down on the couch one Saturday morning. "You know how you ask Alexa questions?" Maya nodded. "Alexa is a helper robot. She's really good at finding answers that other people have already figured out. But she's not smart the way you're smart. She can't think new thoughts. She can't feel things. She can't tell you if something is really important to YOU. She's like a very fast library book that can talk."

"So Alexa isn't alive?" Maya asked.

"Not even a little bit. She doesn't have feelings. She doesn't know you. She just repeats what she's learned from books and the internet. And sometimes she gets things wrong. So whenever Alexa tells you something, you can check with me or Dad or your teacher to see if it's right."

The key concepts for young kids are simple, AI is a tool, not a friend. It doesn't have feelings. It can be wrong. Always check with a grown-up. That's it. Don't overcomplicate it. At this age, the goal is to establish that AI is a thing you use, not a thing you trust blindly, the same way you'd teach them that a calculator is a tool, not a replacement for learning to count.

One more thing for the young ones: set a rule about what questions are for people and what questions are for machines. "What's the biggest planet?" is a great question for AI. "Am I pretty?" is a question for someone who loves you. Jenna established a simple framework:

"If the question is about facts, ask Alexa. If the question is about feelings, ask a person." Maya understood that immediately.

For tweens and teens (ages 10–17): The Power Tool conversation. Tyler's conversation was different. Jenna didn't use the "helper robot" framing because Tyler would have rolled his eyes into another dimension. Instead, she used a metaphor that resonated with his age: "AI is a power tool. A circular saw can build an incredible bookshelf, or it can take your finger off. The tool doesn't care which one happens. You have to learn how to use it properly."

She laid out three rules for Tyler:

Rule 1: Use it to learn, not to skip learning. AI can explain things you don't understand, quiz you on material, help you brainstorm, and check your work. It cannot do your work. If you submit something AI wrote, you didn't cheat the teacher, you cheated yourself out of getting smarter.

Rule 2: Never trust it without checking. AI makes things up. It states false things with complete confidence. If you use AI for research, verify the facts. If it cites a source, check that the source exists. If it gives you a number, look it up. "The AI said so" is not a citation.

Rule 3: Don't share personal information. No full name, no school name, no address, no photos of yourself or friends. Treat AI like a stranger on the internet, because that's essentially what it is. Anything you type could be stored, used for training, or accessed in ways you didn't expect.

Tyler's response was the universal teen acknowledgment: "Okay." It took a week. Tyler mostly ignored the new rules, sneaking back to his old copy-paste habits twice before Jenna caught him. But something shifted the third time. Over the following weeks, Jenna noticed a real change. He started using ChatGPT to quiz himself before tests. He asked it to explain physics concepts in "normal English, not textbook English." He used it to brainstorm ideas for a creative writing project, and then wrote the story himself. The rules had given him a framework, and the framework had given him permission to use the tool without guilt.

Tomás, the teacher, had a similar conversation with his seventh graders at the start of the semester. He projected a slide that said: "I know you're using AI. Let's talk about it." The room got very quiet. "I'm not here to ban it," he said. "I'm here to teach you to use it the way professionals do. And the first thing professionals know is this: AI is a first draft, not a final answer. Every professional who uses AI edits what it gives them. They fact-check it. They add their own thinking. If you hand me something AI wrote and you haven't touched it, you're not using AI like a professional. You're using it like someone who doesn't care about the work."

He said the engagement level in his classroom shifted measurably after that conversation. Students started disclosing when they'd used AI ("I used ChatGPT to help me outline, but I wrote it myself"). They started critiquing AI outputs in class. One student pointed out that ChatGPT had given a scientifically inaccurate description of photosynthesis, and Tomás turned it into a lesson on source verification. The honesty created a better learning environment than the surveillance ever had.

▶ TRY THIS NOW: Have the Age-Appropriate Talk

Have the age-appropriate conversation this week. For kids under 10: "AI is a tool, not a friend. It can be wrong. Check with a person." For tweens and teens: "AI is a power tool. Use it to learn, not to skip learning. Never trust it without checking. Don't share personal information."

Ask your kid to show you how they're already using AI. You might be surprised. The conversation works better when you start by listening.

✦✦✦

AI Safety for Kids

The safety conversation is harder than the homework conversation, because the risks are less visible and more serious. Homework cheating costs your kid a learning opportunity. AI safety failures can cost them their privacy, their reputation, and their emotional wellbeing.

There are three areas every parent needs to understand: privacy, deepfakes, and digital literacy.

Privacy is the foundation. Every time your child interacts with an AI tool, they're generating data. The prompts they type, the questions they ask, the images they upload, all of it may be stored and used to train future models. Most AI tools' terms of service explicitly state this. When Tyler typed his Gatsby essay prompt, that conversation became training data for future versions of ChatGPT (unless he'd opted out, which he hadn't, because no fourteen-year-old or adult for that matter, reads terms of service). For most homework questions, this is low risk. But if a child shares personal details (their school, their location, their photo, a description of a problem at home), that information enters a system they have no control over.

The rule is straightforward. Treat AI conversations the way you'd treat a conversation with a stranger in a public place. You can talk about general topics. You don't share your home address. Jenna set up Tyler's ChatGPT account with a generic username, no profile photo, and clear instructions not to mention his school by name, his friends by name, or any identifying details. For Maya, the rule was even simpler: she could only use AI tools when a parent was in the room.

Deepfakes are the issue that keeps parents up at night, and for good reason. AI can now generate realistic images, audio, and video of anyone. The technology that makes this possible has become accessible enough that a tech-savvy teenager can use it. Schools across the country have dealt with incidents where students created AI-generated images of classmates, sometimes embarrassing, sometimes explicit, sometimes used as bullying tools. In 2024 and 2025, multiple school districts reported incidents involving AI-generated intimate images of students, created and shared without consent.[32]

The conversation with kids about deepfakes needs to happen in two directions. First, as potential victims: "Someone might use AI to create a fake picture or video of you. If this ever happens, tell me immediately. It's not your fault, and there are steps we can take."

Second, and more critically, as potential creators: "Creating a fake image of someone without their permission is wrong. In many places, it's also illegal. Even if it seems like a joke. Even if your friends think it's funny. Creating a deepfake of a classmate can result in criminal charges, school expulsion, and lasting harm to both the victim and the person who made it."

Jenna had this conversation with Tyler directly. "If anyone ever sends you a fake image of someone, or asks you to make one, you come to me. No judgment. I'd rather know about it than find out later." Tyler said he understood, and she believed him. But she also knew that the conversation needed to happen more than once. This wasn't a one-and-done topic. It was an ongoing dialogue, like conversations about alcohol or driving, you revisit it as situations change.

Digital literacy is the broader skill that ties privacy and deepfakes together. It's the ability to think critically about information, understand where it comes from, and evaluate whether to trust it. In an AI-saturated world, digital literacy means knowing that not everything you read online was written by a human, that images can be fabricated, that AI can generate convincing but entirely false news articles, and that your own critical thinking is the last line of defense.

Tomás taught digital literacy as a unit in his science class. He showed students an AI-generated news article about a fictional scientific discovery ("Scientists Discover New Element in Lake Michigan") and asked them to evaluate it. "How would you check if this is real?" The students came up with strategies: search for the scientist's name, look for the study in an academic database, check if other news outlets reported it, look for the source publication. These are lifelong skills that will matter long after the specific AI tools of 2026 are obsolete.

For parents, the practical step is to make fact-checking a family habit. When your kid tells you something they learned from AI, ask: "How do you know that's true? Where can we check?" Not in an interrogation way. In a curious way. The goal is to make verification feel like a normal part of using any tool, the same way you'd check the weather from two sources before deciding whether to bring an umbrella.

TRY THIS NOW: Do a Deepfake Awareness Exercise

Do a deepfake awareness exercise with your family. Go to a reputable news site and find a story about AI-generated images or deepfakes. Read it together. Then ask: "How would you know if a photo or video you saw online was real or AI-generated?"

Review your child's AI tool accounts together. Check privacy settings. Turn off data sharing where possible. Make sure profile information is minimal—no real photos, no school names, no identifying details.

✦✦✦

Classroom Ideas That Actually Work

Tomás's approach to AI in the classroom evolved through trial and error. His first attempts were clumsy. He tried using AI detection tools and got false positives. He tried banning AI and students used it anyway. He tried ignoring the issue and the quality of student work became unreadable, uniformly smooth, devoid of personality, missing the beautiful mistakes that signal genuine thinking. What finally worked was integrating AI into the learning process rather than fighting against it.[33]

✦✦✦

A View from the Classroom

Lesson Planning on Steroids.

Tomás used to spend Sunday evenings building lesson plans for the week. Each plan took thirty to sixty minutes: researching activities, writing instructions, creating materials, differentiating for his students who were ahead and his students who needed extra support. With AI, the process streamlined dramatically. He'd type a prompt like: "I'm teaching a 7th grade science unit on ecosystems. Create a five-day lesson plan that includes a hands-on lab, a group discussion, an individual reflection, and a formative assessment. Differentiate the reflection for three levels: students who are struggling, students at grade level, and students who are advanced. Include specific discussion questions for each day."

ChatGPT would generate a draft in two minutes. It wasn't perfect (it never was), but it was a solid first draft that covered 80 percent of what he needed. He'd spend the next twenty minutes editing. Swapping out generic activities for ones that worked with his specific students, adding references to their field trip last month, adjusting the vocabulary for his English learners. A process that used to take five hours on Sunday now took ninety minutes. That's three and a half hours he got back every week. Over a school year, that was roughly 140 hours, nearly a month of working days, reclaimed for actual teaching, grading, and rest.

AI as a Classroom Activity. Tomás's most successful experiment was making AI itself the subject of a lesson. He called it "Fact-Check the Robot." He'd ask ChatGPT to write a paragraph about a scientific topic (ecosystems, plate tectonics, the water cycle) and then project it on the board. The students' job was to find what was wrong. Sometimes the AI got facts right but oversimplified. Sometimes it stated something subtly incorrect. Sometimes it was flat-out wrong. The students worked in groups to verify claims using their textbooks, scientific databases, and approved websites.

The engagement was electric. Students who never raised their hands in traditional discussions were competing to find errors. "It's like a game," one student told him. "Trying to catch the robot being wrong." And the learning was deeper than any lecture Tomás could have given, because the students were actively evaluating information rather than passively receiving it. They were building exactly the critical thinking skills they'd need in a world where AI-generated content was everywhere.

Differentiated Instruction. Every teacher knows the challenge: a classroom of thirty students at fifteen different levels. The student who already understands fractions is bored while you re-explain the concept for the fifth time. The student who's struggling doesn't want to raise their hand again. Differentiation (tailoring instruction to individual needs) is the gold standard of teaching, and it's nearly impossible to do well at scale without help.[34]

AI changes the math. Tomás created what he called "level-up stations" in his classroom. Students who finished the main assignment early could go to a classroom laptop and use an AI tutor (with a pre-loaded prompt Tomás had written) to explore the topic at a deeper level. The prompt: "I'm a 7th grader who just finished learning about food webs. I want to go deeper. Ask me questions that make me think about food webs in a more complex way. Start easy and get harder based on my answers." For struggling students, he had a different prompt: "I'm a 7th grader who's having trouble understanding food webs. Explain the concept using simple language and a real-world example I might see in my own neighborhood. Then ask me a question to check if I understood."

Both prompts used the same principle Jenna had applied to Tyler's homework: AI as questioner, not answerer. The AI adapted to each student's level in real time, something no teacher can do simultaneously for thirty students. And Tomás wasn't replaced. He was freed to spend his time on the students who needed the most human attention. The ones struggling with motivation, the ones dealing with issues at home, the ones who needed a person, not a tool.

Creative Projects. Not every AI use in the classroom is about academic rigor. Tomás assigned a "Science Fiction Lab Report" where students used AI to generate a fictional scientific scenario ("What if gravity suddenly doubled?") and then wrote a real lab report predicting what would happen, using actual physics. The AI provided the creative spark; the students provided the science. It was the most-submitted assignment of the year. Students who typically struggled with science writing were suddenly invested because the premise was fun. One student wrote a four-page analysis of what would happen to basketball if gravity doubled. It included correctly calculated trajectories.

▶ **TRY THIS NOW: Fact-Check the Robot in Class**

If you're a teacher: try "Fact-Check the Robot" in your next class.

Ask ChatGPT to write a paragraph about your current topic. Project it. Have students find what's wrong. You'll be surprised at how engaged they get.

If you're a parent: ask your child's teacher how the school handles AI. If they don't have a policy yet, share this chapter. Starting the conversation is more productive than waiting for an incident to force it.

✦✦✦

Special Needs & Accessibility

This is the section of the chapter that might matter most to some families, and it's the one that gets the least attention in most AI conversations.

AI is quietly transforming the landscape for students with disabilities and learning differences. Not in a dramatic, headline-making way. In a practical, daily-life way. The tools that exist right now (not five years from now, not in a research lab, but available today on a phone or laptop) are leveling a playing field that has been uneven for decades.

For students with dyslexia and reading difficulties, AI-powered text-to-speech has evolved far beyond the robotic monotone of earlier tools. Current AI voices read with natural pacing, appropriate emphasis, and emotional tone that makes listening to text a genuine alternative to reading it.[35] Students who struggle to decode written text can listen to their assignments and textbooks at their own pace, adjusting speed and voice to their preference. But the real breakthrough is the reverse: speech-to-text. Students who have brilliant ideas but struggle to get them on paper can now speak their thoughts and have AI transcribe, organize, and even help structure them into coherent written work, without doing the thinking for them.

Tomás had a student named Aiden who had been diagnosed with dyslexia in third grade.[36] Aiden was one of the brightest kids in the class (his verbal contributions to discussions were consistently insightful) but his written work was a fraction of what he was capable of. Writing a paragraph took him three times as long as his peers, and the effort of decoding and encoding text left him exhausted before he could express his actual ideas. Tomás set Aiden up with a speech-to-text tool that let him dictate his lab reports. Then, instead of submitting the raw transcription, Aiden used an AI assistant with a specific prompt: "I dictated this lab report. Help me organize my thoughts into clear paragraphs, but don't change my ideas or add new ones. Just help with structure and fix any transcription errors."

The result was remarkable. Aiden's lab reports went from C-minus work that didn't reflect his understanding to A-minus work that did. His ideas were the same. His science was the same. The only thing that changed was that the barrier between his thinking and his output had been lowered. This wasn't AI doing his work. This was AI removing an obstacle that had nothing to do with the subject being assessed.[37]

For students with ADHD, AI offers tools for the executive function challenges that make school particularly difficult. Organization, time management, task initiation, and sustained focus. AI assistants can break down large assignments into smaller steps with specific timelines. They can create visual schedules and checklists. They can send reminders. They can help a student who is staring at a blank page get started by asking: "What's the first small thing you need to figure out before you can write this?" That simple question (delivered without impatience, available at any time) can be the difference between a student who spirals into avoidance and one who starts writing.[38]

For students on the autism spectrum, AI is emerging as a tool for social communication practice. Some students use AI conversations to rehearse social interactions in a low-stakes environment. Practicing how to ask a question in class, how to join a group conversation, or how to express disagreement respectfully. The AI doesn't judge, doesn't react with surprise, and can repeat the scenario as many times as needed. This isn't a replacement for human interaction or professional therapy. It's practice) the same way a pianist practices scales before performing.[39]

For students with visual impairments, AI-powered image description tools can describe photographs, diagrams, and charts in detail, making visual content accessible through text or speech. A student who can't see a food web diagram can have AI describe every connection in it. A student who can't read a graph can have AI explain the trends and data points verbally.[40]

For students with hearing impairments, real-time AI captioning has become remarkably accurate. Tools like those built into Google Meet, Zoom, and dedicated captioning apps can transcribe classroom discussions, lectures, and group work in real time, giving deaf and hard-of-hearing students access to the same verbal information their peers receive.[41]

The common thread? AI isn't giving these students an unfair advantage. It's removing an unfair disadvantage. The playing field was never level. AI is making it closer to level than it's ever been.

If your child has an IEP or 504 plan, talk to their school about incorporating AI tools as an accommodation. Many schools are already adding AI-based assistive technology to accommodation plans, but the process works faster when parents advocate for specific tools.[42] Bring examples. Show what's possible. The technology is available. The question is whether the systems catch up to it.

▶ **TRY THIS NOW: Try an AI Accessibility Tool**

If your child has a learning difference, try one AI accessibility tool this week. For reading challenges: a natural-voice text-to-speech app like Natural Reader or the built-in accessibility features in ChatGPT. For writing challenges: speech-to-text with AI organization. For focus challenges: ask AI to break a big assignment into five small steps with time estimates.

If you're a teacher: identify one student who might benefit from an AI accommodation and try a guided session. The prompt "Help me organize my dictated thoughts into paragraphs without changing my ideas" is a good starting point.

✦✦✦

Screen Time vs. AI Time: A New Framework

Here's the question Jenna kept circling back to: Is my kid's time with AI "screen time"?

The answer is: it depends on what they're doing. And this is where most parents' mental models need an upgrade.

The original screen time concern was about passive consumption. Kids watching endless YouTube videos, scrolling social media, or playing games designed to be addictive. The research on passive screen time is clear, too much of it, especially before bed and in young children, is associated with attention issues, sleep disruption, and reduced physical activity.[43] Those concerns are valid and haven't changed.

But AI interaction is fundamentally different from passive consumption. When Tyler uses ChatGPT as a Socratic tutor, he's actively thinking, responding, and building arguments. When Maya asks AI questions and then checks the answers with her mom, she's practicing critical thinking. When Aiden dictates a lab report and uses AI to organize it, he's creating. These are active, cognitively demanding uses of technology. Lumping them with Instagram scrolling makes about as much sense as lumping reading a book with staring at a blank wall because both involve sitting still.

Jenna developed what she called the Three-Bucket Framework for her family:

Bucket 1: Passive Consumption. Watching, scrolling, being entertained. This is traditional screen time. Limits apply. For Maya, it was one hour on weekdays, two on weekends. For Tyler, it was more flexible but still bounded. Netflix, YouTube, social media, and games all went in this bucket.

Bucket 2: Active Creation. Making something: writing, coding, designing, composing music, editing video, building a presentation. This is productive screen time. Jenna was more generous with it. If Tyler was using a computer to code a game or Maya was drawing on a tablet, that was creative work, not passive consumption.

Bucket 3: AI-Assisted Learning. Using AI as a tutor, research partner, or creative brainstorming tool. This was the new category. It didn't belong in Bucket 1 because it was active. It didn't fully belong in Bucket 2 because it wasn't always creative. It was its own thing: cognitively active technology use focused on learning or problem-solving. Jenna gave this its own limits, more generous than Bucket 1, but still bounded, because even active learning with AI can become a crutch if it's used for everything.

The framework wasn't perfect. There were gray areas. Was Tyler watching a YouTube video about how to solve a Rubik's Cube passive consumption or active learning? Was Maya asking Alexa questions a conversation or consumption? The categories blurred. But having any framework was better than the binary of "screen time: good or bad?" that most families were stuck in.

Tomás used a similar framework in his classroom. He distinguished between "tool time" and "toy time" when students used technology. Tool time was purposeful: using AI to research, write, analyze, or create. Toy time was aimless: browsing, chatting, or playing games. When a student was on a laptop during class, Tomás would ask: "Tool or toy right now?" The students usually answered honestly. And over time, they started asking themselves the same question.

The deeper insight, the one Jenna shared with Tomás over their Saturday coffee, was this: the problem was never the screen. It was the passivity. Any technology that makes your kid think harder, create more, or engage more deeply is a tool. Any technology that makes them zone out, scroll mindlessly, or avoid real-world interaction is a trap. AI can be either one. The difference is how it's used, and whether anyone is helping the kid use it well.

▶ **TRY THIS NOW: Observe and Categorize Screen Time**

This week, observe your child's screen time and sort it into three buckets: Passive Consumption (watching, scrolling), Active Creation (making, building, writing), and AI-Assisted Learning (tutoring, research, brainstorming). Don't judge—just observe the ratio.

Then have a conversation: "We're going to try something new. Not less screen time—smarter screen time. Different activities have different rules." You might be surprised how well kids respond to a system that treats them as capable of using technology wisely.

✦✦✦

Saturday Morning, One Month Later

Jenna was washing dishes on a Saturday morning when she overheard Tyler in the other room. He was talking to his laptop, but not in the way she'd feared a month ago. She could hear his side of a conversation: "No, I think the author is saying something different about power... Wait, let me re-read that part... Okay, yeah, I think the point is that the character doesn't realize he has the power until it's too late. Does that make sense?" He was using AI as a discussion partner for his English class, working through a new novel. The AI was asking him questions. He was thinking out loud. He was doing the messy, generative work that real learning requires. And his essay, the one he'd write later that afternoon, would be his.

In the living room, Maya was drawing a picture of an underwater city. She'd asked Alexa earlier: "What do fish eat?" and "How deep is the ocean?", facts for her drawing. When she'd wanted to know "Would fish be happy in a city?" she'd come to Jenna instead. "What do you think?" Jenna had asked. "I think they'd like the buildings but miss the coral," Maya had said, and gone back to drawing. Facts from machines. Feelings from people. The framework was working.

Meanwhile, Dave Kowalski (the plumber from Chapter 1 who thought AI was just for tech bros) had discovered something useful. His daughter had texted him a photo of a confusing appliance manual. He'd snapped a picture and asked ChatGPT to explain it in plain English. The AI broke it down step by step. When he texted his daughter back what he'd learned, she replied: "Dad, I'm shocked you finally found a use for technology that doesn't involve YouTube." He was using AI the way Jenna's family was using it, as a practical tool for everyday problems. No philosophy involved. Just results.

Across town, Tomás was grading lab reports. Aiden's was on top of the pile. It was clear, well-organized, and most importantly, unmistakably Aiden's. The voice was his. The observations were specific to what he'd seen in the lab. The conclusion connected the experiment to something he'd noticed on a family hike. No AI could have written that. AI had helped him get it out of his head and onto the page, but the thinking was entirely human.

This was the new reality. Not AI replacing parents and teachers. Not AI corrupting kids. Not AI making education obsolete. AI as a tool in the hands of families and educators who were thoughtful about how to use it. The technology was neutral. The parenting and teaching weren't. And the families that figured this out first (that treated AI as a kitchen table conversation rather than a crisis to be managed) were the ones whose kids would thrive.

Jenna dried her hands and picked up her phone. She had a client project to work on, and she was going to use AI to brainstorm design concepts, the same way she'd taught Tyler to use it for brainstorming essay ideas. Same tool. Same principles. Different generation, same rules. She smiled at that. Then she opened Chapter 7 of this book, because she'd heard it was about small business owners, and she had a freelance business that could probably use some help.

7

AI FOR SMALL BUSINESS OWNERS

ENTERPRISE-LEVEL CAPABILITIES ON A BOOTSTRAPPER'S BUDGET

Marcus Chen sat in his truck parked at the edge of a new client's property, staring at his phone. Six months ago, he'd been terrified of AI. His daughter Emma had practically forced ChatGPT on him back in Chapter 3, and he'd reluctantly created a marketing plan that worked. Eight new clients. Seasonal service calendars. Follow-up emails that didn't sound like a robot wrote them. His business had grown.

Now he sat here, watching his crew lay fresh sod on a hillside, and thinking: "What else is AI doing that I haven't figured out yet?"

The truth is, Marcus had barely scratched the surface. He'd cracked the code on marketing, sure, but his bookkeeping was still a mess. Scattered spreadsheets and invoices he'd barely updated in five years. His customer service was reactive: someone called with a question, someone else answered (usually wrong). When it came to hiring, he'd posted a help-wanted ad on Facebook and hoped. His competitor analysis was nonexistent. Don't even get him started on contracts. He had a basic template his neighbor's cousin had given him in 2015.

What Marcus was about to discover is that AI isn't a one-trick pony. For a guy with a modest budget, it's like hiring an entire department of specialists. Marketing. Customer service. Accounting. HR. Strategy. Legal review. All of it, available to him through a $20-a-month ChatGPT Plus subscription.

This chapter is about what comes after you've gotten the basics down. If you read Chapter 3, you learned the PRIME framework and discovered how to use it for planning and strategy. Now we're diving deeper. We're talking about the six core operational areas where AI can either save you thousands of dollars or let you sleep at night. We're talking about the difference between running a side hustle and running an actual business.

The question isn't whether you can afford to use AI. It's whether you can afford not to. A small business owner who harnesses AI right isn't competing with other small businesses. They're competing with businesses three times their size, because they've got the infrastructure and systems that usually only come with scale.

✦✦✦

Marketing Content in Minutes

Marcus' biggest breakthrough in Chapter 3 was realizing that marketing didn't have to mean hiring an agency. It meant creating consistent content that showed up in front of people who cared. Instagram posts. Email newsletters. Google Business Profile descriptions. Blog articles. Google Local Services ads. The work never ended, or so he thought.

What he discovered next was equally life-changing: he could generate that content in minutes, not hours. Not perfectly, but perfectly good. Good enough to publish. Good enough to convert. And most importantly, distinctive enough that it sounded like a real person wrote it, because an AI had written it with his voice in mind.

The key was treating AI like a content assistant, not a content creator. Marcus would sketch out what he wanted, a social media calendar for April focused on spring cleanup promotions. A series of short blog posts about seasonal lawn care. A newsletter story about why mulch matters. The AI would draft it. He'd tweak it. Add his voice. Add specifics from his own experience. Publish it.

One Tuesday afternoon, Marcus opened ChatGPT and decided to tackle a problem he'd been ignoring: his social media presence was inconsistent. Some weeks he'd post three times. Other weeks, nothing. Potential customers would scroll his profile and see either a thriving business or a dead one, depending on which week they checked. He needed a system.

He sat down with a cup of coffee and outlined what he wanted: a full month of Instagram posts. Thirty posts, one per day, each with a specific purpose. Some would show before-and-after transformations (those always performed best). Some would be seasonal tips his customers actually cared about. Some would tell the story of his business. Some would highlight his crew. He knew the PRIME framework by now. Role, Context, Task, Format, Constraints. Second nature to him now.

> "You are my marketing assistant for Chen Landscaping, a residential landscaping company in Portland, Oregon. We serve homeowners who want beautiful outdoor spaces with low environmental impact. Our main services are spring cleanups, mulching, native plant installation, and seasonal maintenance. We have a 4.9-star rating with 200+ reviews. I need a social media calendar for April with daily Instagram posts. Each post should be 2-3 sentences, include 2-3 relevant emojis, and alternate between: before-and-after transformations, seasonal tips, customer testimonials, crew highlights, and behind-the-scenes content. Make it conversational and friendly, not corporate. Avoid hashtag spam but include 2-3 relevant hashtags per post. Posts should subtly mention our services without being salesy."

ChatGPT spit out thirty post ideas in about forty seconds. Some were generic. Some were perfect. Most were usable with tiny adjustments. Marcus spent the next half hour taking the best ten, personalizing them with actual customer names and real transformations from his portfolio, and scheduling them across Instagram using a social media scheduler. Ten days of content, created and posted in an hour. He'd never spend that much time scrolling stock photos and agonizing over what to say.

But the real power came when he started repurposing content. The Instagram posts became email newsletter snippets. The email snippets became blog post outlines. The blog posts went back to social as carousel posts. One good piece of content could work five different ways, reaching different audiences, getting different results.

He did the same thing with his Google Business Profile. It was a one-liner: "Landscaping. Local." That was it. No wonder nobody called. He asked Claude to help him write something that would actually convert phone calls.

"Rewrite this Google Business Profile description for maximum conversion. I'm a small landscaping company in Portland, Oregon with 12 years of experience and a 4.9-star rating. We specialize in sustainable landscapes and serve homeowners who value quality over cheap quick jobs. Keep it to about 250 words. Make it warm, professional, and emphasize what makes us different from the discount landscaping companies. End with a call to action."

The new version was three strong paragraphs. The first paragraph told his story, twelve years of building client relationships, focus on sustainable practices, belief in doing things right. The second detailed his services and why each mattered. The third was a direct call to action: "Ready to create the outdoor space you've been dreaming about? Call us for a free estimate." He added his phone number, kept the paragraph breaks clean, and deployed it. Phone calls went up 12% in the first month. Not from anything else changing. Just from better storytelling.

Ad copy was even faster. Running a Google ad for spring cleanup? Facebook ad? Pinterest? Marcus asked AI to generate five variations, each with a different angle. One was price-focused ("Spring cleanup starting at $199"). One was quality-focused ("Beautiful outdoor spaces. Sustainable practices."). One was urgency-driven ("Limited openings for April appointments"). One highlighted customer reviews ("Trusted by 400+ Portland homeowners").

One was about the experience ("Watch your yard transform in hours"). He'd pick two, run them for a week, look at the data, kill the loser, and double down on the winner. This was testing at the speed of AI.

By the end of spring, Marcus realized he'd created more consistent, higher-quality marketing content than he ever had before. And he'd spent maybe three hours doing it. Three hours that would have been forty hours manually, or $500 to $2,000 per month if outsourced to an agency. That's the game AI changes.[44]

These numbers don't account for the forty-odd hours Marcus spent over three months learning, experimenting, and occasionally cursing at his screen. But that's the investment that makes the ongoing savings possible, and unlike hiring a consultant, he only had to learn it once.

One more thing happened that surprised him: when people called or emailed, they'd mention his posts. "I saw your Instagram about native plants," a prospect said. "I read your newsletter about spring cleanup," another told him. The content was reaching people. It was changing minds. It wasn't just posting to the void. His investment of time was paying dividends.

The lesson: consistent content beats perfect content. AI lets you be consistent. You can't write a perfect Instagram post every single day. But you can iterate on one AI draft. You can personalize three or four good ideas. You can be consistent, and consistency is what builds trust and captures attention over time.

▶ TRY THIS NOW: Create Your First Social Media Calendar

Pick one week on your calendar and use ChatGPT to draft seven days of social posts for your business. Tell the AI: your industry, your ideal customer, what services you offer, what you want to highlight this month, and what platforms you're posting on. Be specific about tone—formal or casual? Give examples if you have past posts you like. Review the drafts, edit them with your own voice and details, and schedule them using a free tool like Buffer or your platform's native scheduler. You just completed a week of content prep in less than an hour. Next month, you'll do a month.

✦✦✦

Customer Service That Scales

Marcus had a problem that kept him up at night: he was the bottleneck. Someone had a question about an estimate? They texted him. Someone wanted to know if the rain tomorrow would delay their appointment? They called him. Someone had a concern about a job? They came looking for him. With a dozen employees and forty regular clients, plus new leads calling all the time, Marcus was drowning. His phone never stopped buzzing. His team would yell "Marcus!" across the job site twenty times a day.

His first solution was hiring an office person. But he was a small operation, still building. He couldn't justify the expense. His second solution was ignoring the problem and burning out, which was not sustainable. His third solution, delegation to his crew, backfired when people got wrong information from his assistant manager.

Then he realized: most of his customer questions were the same. People asked the same things over and over. "Do you offer discounts?" "How long does spring cleanup take?" "What if it rains?" "How do I care for new plantings?" "What's included in our mulching service?" He was answering the same ten questions a hundred times. That's not a hiring problem. That's a documentation problem. And if there's one thing AI is excellent at, it's standardizing answers to common questions.

Marcus started by building a FAQ page for his website. He sat down with his crew one afternoon and wrote down every question they got asked repeatedly. Rain delays. Mulch options and costs. Pricing and payment. Scheduling constraints. Guarantees. What to do after the job. He ended up with twelve questions. Then he opened Claude and pasted in his rough notes.

"I own a landscaping business in Portland, Oregon. Here are twelve questions I and my crew get asked constantly, along with my rough answers. I want to turn these into a professional FAQ for my website. Clean up the language to be friendly but professional, make the answers concise (2-3 sentences max), and organize them by category like Scheduling, Pricing, Services, and Guarantees. Make sure to link related questions together."

What he got back was better than what he'd written. The AI grouped questions into four categories. It added questions he hadn't even thought of (like "Do you work in the rain?" and "What's your cancellation policy?"). It formatted everything cleanly. It even suggested a "Can't find your answer?" section with his contact info. He posted it to his website that night, and immediately saw a drop in basic incoming questions. The FAQ was working twenty-four hours a day, answering on his behalf.

But the bigger move was email templates. These became his secret weapon. Marcus created a folder in his Gmail called "Response Templates" and filled it with the things he sent over and over:

- Follow-up after an estimate (three versions: "still interested, haven't decided yet," "silent no response," and "chose someone else")
- Rain delay notifications (friendly, professional, reassuring)
- Seasonal reminders (spring cleanup, fall prep, winter pre-storm maintenance)
- Payment reminder (professional but friendly)
- Thank-you after job completion (with photo request)
- Complaint response (for legitimate issues, fixes offered)
- Upsell opportunity (seasonal services they might not have thought of)

Here's the thing about templates: they sound impersonal. They sound like a robot wrote them. But AI-drafted templates sound like a human. They have tone. They have personality. Marcus asked Claude to write a rain delay notification that was honest about the weather, reassuring about the timeline, and friendly. It came back warm and personal. When he personalized it with a client's name and a tiny detail about their job ("We'll get back to your spring cleanup as soon as the ground dries out"), suddenly it felt custom-written. Because it basically was.

Review responses were another revelation. Good reviews made him happy. Bad reviews? Those used to make him panic. Now they were an opportunity. He'd ask Claude to help him draft a professional, warm response that acknowledged the issue and offered to fix it. He'd never admit fault publicly (his insurance agent warned against that), but he'd acknowledge disappointment and offer a next step. One-star review complaining about timing? Response: "We're sorry we didn't meet your timeline expectations. This is valuable feedback. Can you contact us directly so we can make this right?"

The result: his five-star review average went up because he responded to every single review. His reputation became even more solid. People appreciated that he cared enough to respond, even to criticism. The algorithm noticed too. Google Business profiles with recent activity and responses rank higher in local search results. More visibility led to more calls.[45]

In practical terms, Marcus now had a system. Estimate follow-up happened automatically three days after he sent the estimate. Rain delays were communicated proactively. Thank-you notes went out the same day the job finished. Seasonal reminders went out before seasonal demand ("Fall cleanup season is here!"). None of this required him to remember to send it. It was templated, personalized, and scheduled.

One template Marcus was especially proud of was his "complaint resolution" response. Rather than getting defensive or upset, he asked Claude for help creating a response that was deeply empathetic, took responsibility for the business's part in the problem, and offered a clear solution. When someone complained about slow response time, he'd modify the template slightly and respond within an hour, with a direct phone call scheduled for the next day. He turned a bad review into a recovery opportunity. Half the time, the person would update their review after he fixed the issue.

TRY THIS NOW: Build Your FAQ

Take eight to ten customer questions you've answered at least three times in the last month. Write them out with your answers (rough is fine—don't overthink it). Paste them into ChatGPT and ask it to turn them into a professional FAQ. Tell it to: organize by category, make answers concise, keep the tone friendly, and format for your website. Add the result to your website or send it to your team.

You've just created your first line of defense against repetitive questions.

✦✦✦

Bookkeeping & Operations Help

If there's one thing that paralyzes small business owners, it's admin. Invoicing. Scheduling. Procedures. Expense tracking. The stuff that doesn't directly make money but absolutely destroys you if you ignore it. Every business owner knows this. And every business owner procrastinates on it.

Marcus's invoicing situation was embarrassing. He used a template from 2019 that his brother-in-law had created. It had his old email address. The line items didn't match his current services. The formatting looked amateur. He'd been meaning to fix it for two years. It sat in his "I'll do it later" pile, gathering dust.

Then he realized: invoices are the last thing a customer sees. They're the tangible proof of a transaction. A sloppy invoice sends a message. A professional invoice sends a different message. He asked Claude to help him rebuild his template.

"This is my landscaping invoice template. It's dated and doesn't reflect my current services or professionalism. Rewrite it to be modern and clear. Include: header with my business name and logo space, customer information, date and invoice number, itemized services with descriptions and costs, subtotal/total, payment terms (net 10 days), acceptable payment methods, and a note section. Make it look clean but not corporate. This is for a small family-owned landscaping business."

What he got back was three times better. Cleaner. More professional. Included clear terms at the bottom. Had space for a personal note. Sections for before/after photos if relevant. He took the template and rebuilt his Google Sheets invoice, adding his logo at the top and his business description. Suddenly invoicing felt less like a chore and more like a real business transaction. The invoice looked like it came from a legitimate company, not a side gig.

He also noticed something interesting: when invoices looked professional, they were paid faster. Customers treated a professional-looking invoice with more respect. They paid promptly because it felt official. When his old 2019 template was in use, he'd have to follow up on payments. With the new one, most paid within the stated time-frame without a reminder.

But more importantly, he looked at his operations. His crew had no documented procedures. Everyone did things their own way. New employees had to figure things out by observation. Mistakes happened. Safety shortcuts happened. Quality varied wildly. He needed a playbook, but writing one himself would take weeks of his time.

He asked Claude to help him build one. He started with his most common job: spring cleanup. He explained the process to Claude, step by step, including what sometimes went wrong.

"I want to create a standard operating procedure for our spring cleanup service. Here's what we do: remove winter debris (branches, leaves, fallen limbs), aerate the lawn, apply 2 inches of compost, edge the planting beds and pathways, and rake everything clean. We usually do this with 2-3 people. Write a detailed step-by-step procedure that a new employee could follow. For each step, include: what to do, safety notes, quality checkpoints, and estimated time. Keep it to one page, using short clear sentences."

Claude gave him a perfect checklist: prep phase (safety briefing, equipment check), debris removal (techniques and order), aeration details (depth, direction, overlapping), compost application (depth, distribution, water after), edging (clean lines, no damage), final cleanup. For each, it included safety notes and quality checks. Marcus printed it, walked his crew through it once with the checklist in hand, and suddenly there was a standard. Mistakes dropped. New hires could follow along. Jobs took about the same time, but they looked better and more consistent.

He created the same for mulching, native plant installation, and seasonal maintenance. By the time he was done, he had five documented procedures that made his entire operation more predictable.

New hires learned faster. Quality was more consistent. He could go on vacation without worrying about mistakes.

The real test came when Marcus took his first week off in two years. He was terrified. But his crew had the procedures. His lead person had the checklists. The business ran. Jobs were completed to standard. Nobody burned down the customer relationships. Customers didn't complain. In fact, they didn't even notice he was gone because the service quality didn't drop.

That's what systems do. They give you freedom. They let you scale without scaling your stress.

The last piece was expense categorization, which sounds boring but is critical for taxes and profitability. Marcus threw everything on a business credit card and dealt with it at tax time. His accountant hated him. Deductions were scattered everywhere. He was probably missing thousands in write-offs. So he asked Claude to help him build a simple categorization system.

Once he had a system, something interesting happened: he could finally see where his money was going. He realized he was spending way too much on certain supplies. He saw that labor was his biggest cost (which made sense). He saw that his equipment investment had paid off over time. With this visibility, he could make smarter decisions. Should he buy a new mulch spreader? The data showed it would pay for itself in three seasons. Should he raise prices? The data showed he had room. Should he hire full-time crew instead of part-time? The data showed the math worked.

"I'm a landscaping company with these expense categories: equipment purchases and maintenance, fuel, supplies, labor, vehicles, insurance, professional services, marketing, and miscellaneous. I've got a messy six-month list of expenses. Help me categorize them and then create a simple expense-tracking system for ongoing use. Also highlight any expenses I might be missing that are deductible."

Claude not only categorized everything but also pointed out expenses he wasn't even thinking about: home office (he worked from home three days a week), vehicle depreciation, professional development (training courses), and meals when meeting with clients. Over the course of a year, that probably saved him three thousand dollars in taxes. That's a week's worth of profit, reclaimed.

✦✦✦

Hiring & HR on a Shoestring

By midsummer, Marcus was ready to hire his thirteenth employee. The workload was there. Business was booming. But hiring freaked him out. Job description? Did he have one? Not really. Interview questions? He'd usually just chat with the person, see if they seemed reliable, and hire them if they had a pulse and reliable transportation. Onboarding? "Show up tomorrow at seven. Bring work boots. Here's a rake. Here's your crew."

This time, he wanted to do it right. So he asked AI to help him build a hiring process from the ground up.

First: the job description. He explained the role to Claude, general landscaping work, some leadership of crews on larger jobs, willingness to learn (no specific experience required), reliable transportation, ability to handle physical outdoor work in all weather, and a commitment to safety and quality.

"I'm hiring a landscaper for our small Portland company. The role is general landscaping work, some leadership of teams on bigger jobs, outdoor work in all weather, physical labor. I don't require specific experience. I train people. I do require: reliability and showing up on time, willingness to learn and improve, working well on a team, and commitment to safety. Write a job description that's honest about the work but makes it sound like a legitimate opportunity. Include details about the company, role responsibilities, required qualities, and why someone should apply. About 300 words."

Claude wrote something way better than Marcus could have written. It started with the company story, a small, established landscaping firm with twelve years of history and a reputation for quality. It was honest about the physical work and outdoor weather. But it positioned the job as an opportunity to learn a skilled trade, work with a quality-focused team, and grow into leadership roles. It made landscaping sound like something worth doing, not just a job you took because you couldn't get anything else. The tone was everything.

Next: interview questions. Marcus didn't want to ask generic questions that everyone answers the same way. He wanted to know if someone would show up on time, be reliable, work well with others, and have a growth mindset. He asked Claude to design interview questions around those themes.

"I'm hiring for a landscaping role. My main concerns are: 1) Will they show up reliably and on time? 2) Can they work well on a team? 3) Are they willing to learn and improve? 4) Can they handle physical outdoor work and be safe? 5) Do they care about quality or just getting through the day? Write 10 interview questions that will help me understand these things. Make them conversational, not corporate. Make them questions that get real answers."

The questions were excellent. "Tell me about a time you had to show up early for something important. How did you make sure you didn't oversleep?" That tells you about their reliability mindset. "Describe a time you worked with someone who did things differently than you would. How did you handle it?" That tells you about teamwork and flexibility. "What's something you've learned to do well in the last year?" That shows if they're a learning person. "Tell me about a time you made a mistake at work. What did you do about it?" That shows if they take responsibility or make excuses. Marcus took these and added a few of his own, and suddenly he had an actual interview toolkit that got real answers.

Finally: Onboarding. He asked Claude to build an onboarding checklist for a new landscaper. First day, first week, first month. What do they need to know? What do they need to learn? What paperwork, expectations, and procedures?

"Create a detailed onboarding checklist for a new landscaper at a small company. Include: first day logistics (where to be, what time, what to bring), safety briefing and equipment, introduction to each team member, training on our three main services (spring cleanup, mulching, native plants), review of company policies (safety, quality, communication), tools and equipment tour, assigned crew for first week, check-in schedule (end of day 1, end of week 1, weekly for month 1), and any paperwork (tax forms, direct deposit, handbook sign-off)."

Marcus got back a comprehensive checklist that he never would have thought of on his own. It included a first-day safety briefing (spot to fill in where to call in case of injury, no shortcuts on safety). It included sections for introductions to each crew member that Marcus had no issues filling in and a nice description of the company culture. It included a training schedule so the person didn't get thrown into the deep end on day one. It had specific check-in points so Marcus could catch problems early. It included mentorship assignments. He printed it out, created a digital version in Google Docs, and handed it to his new hire on day one. The onboarding process went from chaotic to smooth.

As his business grew, Marcus also realized he needed some basic employee handbook sections. What happens if someone is late? What about repeated quality issues? How do we handle time off? What's the pay structure? Does he offer benefits? What's his vision for the company? He asked Claude to draft the basics.

Within a week, Marcus had a fifteen-page employee handbook that covered the essentials: mission and values, expectations and standards, policies, growth opportunities, and how disputes would be handled. It wasn't fancy, but it was professional and clear. It sent a message: this is a real business with real standards.

One more thing happened that surprised him. Once his team had documented policies and clear expectations, the quality of their work improved. They weren't guessing about what "good" looked like. They had a checklist. They had standards. They knew what Marcus wanted. New employees felt respected because they got actual training, not just "figure it out." Retention improved. His best crew members, the ones he'd been worried about losing, became even more committed. They could see the business was professionalizing.

The hiring process itself became a selling point. When Marcus told a prospect, "Here's our interview process, our onboarding, our handbook," they got confidence. This wasn't just a guy with a truck and some friends helping. This was a legitimate business. That confidence translated to higher-value clients. Higher-value clients meant better profit margins. Better profit margins meant better pay for his team. Everyone won.

✦✦✦

Competitive Intelligence

For years, Marcus had operated in a bubble. He knew what he charged. He knew what his regular clients were willing to pay. He had no idea what anyone else was charging. He didn't know if he was high, low, or right in the middle. He just had a number that had worked for him, and he stuck with it.

One evening, he got curious. He pulled up Google Maps, searched for "landscapers near me," and clicked through a dozen competitors. He looked at their websites, their Google Business profiles, their photos, their reviews. He found five that seemed comparable to his business, same type of company, same market, same general size and specialization.

Then he asked Claude to help him analyze what he'd found.

"I'm a landscaping company in Portland, Oregon. I just researched five local competitors. For each, I've noted: company name, years in business, Google rating and review count, main services, visible pricing, and website/social media quality. [He pasted in his research.] Compare us. What are they doing better than me? What am I doing better? What are pricing trends? Where are the opportunities in our market? Are there service gaps I could fill?"

Claude gave him a detailed breakdown. Two competitors were clearly expensive, targeting high-end clients with designer services. Three were mid-market like him. But one was getting crushed on reviews because they were undercutting everyone and delivering mediocre work. That was helpful to know. He didn't want to compete on price. He wanted to compete on quality and reliability.

More importantly, he noticed that competitors with strong

Google reviews and good photos were getting more calls. One competitor had a detailed blog. Another had video tours. He wasn't doing those things yet. Those became next-quarter projects.

He also asked Claude to analyze seasonal pricing trends. When do people spend money on landscaping? Spring was obvious. But what about fall? Summer? Winter? Should he offer discounts in the slow season? Should he raise prices when demand is high?

"I'm a landscaper in Portland. My busiest season is late March through May. Summer is steady but slowing by August. Fall is medium busy. Winter is slow. I want to optimize my pricing and marketing for these seasons. When should I raise prices? When should I offer discounts? How should I manage demand? What services could I offer in off-season?"

Claude suggested: pricing higher in spring when demand exceeds supply, introducing maintenance contracts for summer that lock in steady work, offering a strategic August discount to build momentum into fall, and using winter for heavy discounts on pre-spring projects. He also suggested winter as an opportunity to offer interior plant care, seasonal decoration services, or pre-spring consultations at premium prices. Marcus had never thought about winter as an opportunity. It was just "down time." Now he saw opportunity.

The broader insight: AI is an excellent research partner. It can help you understand your market, your competitors, your positioning, and your opportunities. Not perfectly (nothing beats on-the-ground market knowledge and experience) but way better than operating blind. Better than guessing. Better than following a competitor into a bad decision just because they did it.

Marcus also started using AI to monitor what was working in his marketing. When he ran a social media ad, he'd ask Claude to analyze the results. Which ad copy got the most clicks? Which image performed best? Which audience responded? Claude would help him spot patterns he'd miss. Over time, he became much better at knowing what resonated. His ad spend dropped 20% while his click-through rate stayed the same. He was getting smarter about how he spent money.

He also used AI to brainstorm new service opportunities. What else could he offer? Claude suggested: adding a landscape design consultation service. Offering fall color plantings for clients in October. Creating a seasonal maintenance package that spread throughout the year. A "ready for sale" landscape package for people selling their homes. Not all of them made sense for his business, but a couple became real revenue generators. Especially the "ready for sale" package, real estate agents started referring clients to him. That became 15% of his revenue.

TRY THIS NOW: Research Your Competitors

Find five businesses that compete with you or are in your industry. Look at their websites, Google Business profiles, and reviews. Take notes on: their pricing, service offerings, review quality and what customers praise/criticize, how they describe themselves, and what stands out. Spend an hour on this. Then ask Claude to analyze what you found. Ask: What are they doing better? What am I doing better? What are the gaps in the market? Where are opportunities? What should I focus on next? This exercise takes an hour and will give you thousands of dollars worth of market clarity.

✦✦✦

Legal & Compliance Basics

This is where Marcus got nervous. Legal stuff. Liability. Regulations. The stakes felt higher than marketing or customer service. One lawsuit could destroy everything.

His landscaping business operated on a handshake. He'd show up, assess the work, give a verbal estimate, and if the client approved, he'd do the job. No contract. No paperwork. Just trust. It had worked fine when he had five clients and did everything himself. But with forty clients and a crew of thirteen, the liability exposure was enormous. What if someone got hurt on a job? What if there was a dispute about what was included? What if someone sued? He'd be liable for everything.

He needed a service agreement. He'd asked around and gotten a template from another landscaper. It was terrible, confusing legal language, gaps in coverage, probably not enforceable in Oregon.

So he asked Claude for help. He explained what he wanted to cover: scope of work, price and payment, timeline, liability (his boundaries), and what happens if there's a dispute.

"I'm a landscaper. I need a basic service agreement for clients before I start work. It should cover: 1) Description of work to be done, 2) Price and payment terms (30% deposit, balance due on completion), 3) Expected timeline, 4) Our liability limitations (we're not liable for plant survival if client doesn't maintain), 5) What's included and not included, 6) How disputes are handled (mediation, not court). Make it simple and clear, not legalese. Include a note that this is not legal advice and they should have a lawyer review it."

Claude gave him a three-page template. It was clear, professional, and covered the main things. It wasn't fancy, but it was way better than nothing. The key thing was the liability section: "We guarantee workmanship for thirty days from job completion. Plant health and survival after thirty days is the responsibility of the property owner and depends on proper watering, mulching, and seasonal care." That protected him.

He added a line at the bottom: "This agreement is not a substitute for legal counsel. If you have questions, please consult with a lawyer." And he sent it to his accountant for a once-over. Not a full legal review, that would have cost hundreds, just a common-sense check.[46] His accountant approved it and suggested one small change. Marcus deployed it.

He also realized he needed a safety policy. It wasn't required by law for his size of company, but it was smart. It showed his crew that he cared about their wellbeing. It protected him in case of an accident. It set expectations.

"Write a basic safety policy for a small landscaping company with 13 employees. Include: required personal protective equipment (gloves, eye protection, hearing protection), machine operation rules for trimmers and leaf blowers, heavy lifting protocols, weather conditions when we don't work (lightning, extreme heat), first aid and injury response procedures, and reporting hazards. Keep it practical and one page, not corporate theater."

Claude gave him a one-page policy that was useful. Not overwhelming. Not corporate. Real stuff: "All crew members must wear eye protection when using string trimmers or leaf blowers. All crew members must wear work gloves when handling mulch, landscape cloth, or unfamiliar plants. No one operates power equipment without hands-on training from Marcus or an experienced crew member."

He added two things: a weather rule ("We don't work if lightning is within five miles"), and an injury protocol ("If someone gets hurt and it's serious, call 911 first, then call Marcus"). He printed it, laminated it, posted it in his truck, and reviewed it with his crew at their next meeting. Safety became something they talked about, not just a wall poster.

But here's the critical thing Marcus learned: AI can help with a lot, but there are hard limits. When it comes to actual legal liability, employment law, insurance coverage, taxes, and regulatory compliance, AI is a starting point, not an ending point.

He had serious questions: Are his service agreements enforceable in Oregon? Does he need specific insurance coverage for his crew? What are his actual tax obligations with thirteen employees? What regulations apply to pesticides if he ever uses them? Some of that, he could figure out with AI and a little research. But the serious stuff, the stuff that could expose him legally, required talking to real professionals. An employment lawyer for five hundred dollars. An insurance agent for free (that's their job). An accountant for two hundred dollars. The Oregon Department of Consumer and Business Services for their guidance.

AI is like having a really smart research assistant. It can read regulations, summarize them, find relevant information, and help you understand the landscape, but when it's time to make a decision that could legally expose you or your employees? That's when you call the professionals. Marcus learned to use AI to get smart enough to ask the right questions, then hire people who could give him definitive answers.

His lawyer reviewed the service agreement and said it was pretty solid, better than a lot of things he sees from small businesses. It just needed two tweaks for Oregon law. The insurance agent reviewed his policy and suggested adding an umbrella policy since he was getting bigger. The accountant reviewed his expense system and certified it for tax purposes. These professional reviews, which would have cost him two thousand dollars each if he'd started from scratch, now just required tweaking AI-drafted documents. AI saved him time and money, and then the professionals made sure it was correct.

That's the right way to use AI in legal and compliance areas. Not as a replacement for professional advice. As a starting point that gets you 80% of the way there, then professionals make sure you're protected.

The Bigger Picture: Integration Across Your Business

What Marcus discovered as he implemented AI in all six areas was that they started talking to each other. The marketing content fed the social media strategy. The customer service templates answered questions before they needed to be asked. The documented procedures made hiring faster because everyone understood the standard. The expense tracking informed pricing decisions. The competitive analysis informed marketing messaging.

Marcus hadn't planned for this to happen. He'd just been solving problems, one at a time. But somewhere around month three, he noticed the pieces were starting to work together on their own.

Take customer service. When he started responding to every review and sending updates before clients even thought to ask, something shifted. Clients stopped feeling like transactions. They felt taken care of. And people who feel taken care of tell their friends. His phone started ringing with referrals from neighbors, not strangers from a Google ad.

Same thing happened with the procedures. Better onboarding meant his crew was more consistent. More consistent crew meant fewer callbacks. Fewer callbacks meant his online reputation kept climbing. More reputation meant more referrals. He hadn't engineered any of it. He'd just fixed the problems in front of him, and somewhere along the way, the improvements had started compounding.

All of this was enabled by AI. Not AI working alone, but AI working as a tool in a coordinated system. Marcus wasn't using ChatGPT to run his business. He was using it to build systems that made his business run better.

The Result

By late September, Marcus sat in his office (a corner of his garage, if he was being honest) and looked at what he'd built. A marketing system that generated consistent, high-quality content. A customer service system that answered basic questions automatically. Documented procedures that made his crew more effective and consistent. A hiring process that brought good people on board. Market research that informed his pricing. Contracts and policies that protected his business and his crew.

None of this would have been possible without AI. Not because AI did all the work, it didn't. But because AI made it possible for one person to do the work of a small department. His old bookkeeper (Marcus, working in a spreadsheet at midnight) was replaced by Claude analyzing his expenses. His old marketing manager (Marcus, frustrated, scrolling through social media) was replaced by ChatGPT suggesting calendars and copy. His old HR person (just winging it and hoping) was replaced by systematic onboarding processes.

The business hadn't required hiring any of those people. He just got smarter and more organized.

And more importantly, he'd learned something bigger: AI isn't one thing. It's not just marketing or content or customer service. It's a toolkit. A way to think about your business. For every problem you have (if it's something that involves information, research, writing, analysis, or organization) there's probably an AI tool that can help. Your job is to figure out what the problem is, ask for help clearly (using PRIME), review what you get, and make it your own.

Marcus had gone from terrified of AI to living it. His teenage daughter Emma, who'd introduced him to ChatGPT six chapters ago, now came to him with ideas. "Dad, have you tried using Claude for this? I bet it could help." The tables had turned. He was fluent now.

And the financial impact was real. Over the course of the year, Marcus estimated that AI saved him approximately $21,000 in direct costs: no agency hire for marketing ($8,000), no office manager for customer service ($6,000), better tax deductions that his accountant identified ($4,000 in savings), faster invoicing and payment collection ($2,000), reduced hiring costs through better systems ($1,000). Against that, he'd spent just under $500 a year on ChatGPT Plus and Claude Plus subscriptions. The ROI was absurd. It wasn't even close.

But more important than the money was something else: autonomy. Marcus wasn't dependent on hiring the right person. He wasn't dependent on finding an affordable marketer. He was dependent on himself, learning a new skill, and leveraging AI as a tool. That was empowering. That was the real win.

In the next chapter, we're going to explore a completely different side of AI entirely. Not business productivity. Not operations. Creativity. How writers, designers, artists, entrepreneurs, and everyday people are using AI to push their creativity further. Not replace it. If you thought AI was useful for business, wait until you see what it can do for the stuff you actually care about. The stuff that matters beyond money.

8

AI FOR CREATIVE PROJECTS

WHEN THE MACHINE BECOMES YOUR COLLABORATOR

Nadia Okafor stared at her laptop screen, Chapter 47 of her novel open in front of her. The cursor blinked at the end of a half-finished sentence. She'd been working on this book for eighteen months, sixty thousand words, and she was stuck. Not writer's block exactly. More like writer's paralysis. Her protagonist, Akiko, needed to make a decision. Should she leave her job? Confront her mother? Move across the country? Nadia had outlined this moment perfectly. She knew why it mattered. But she couldn't figure out what Akiko would do.

She'd left a teaching career two years ago to pursue this dream. High school English teacher for sixteen years. She'd read thousands of stories, taught students how to tell them, understood story structure at a level most people never would. And here she was, paralyzed by her own.

Her sister had called that morning. "You've heard of AI, right?" Nadia had. The news made her nervous. Robots writing novels? Taking over creative work? When she'd been teaching, AI was starting to make headlines. Authors were panicking. Now she was one.

"There's this thing," her sister had said, "where you can ask AI to help with writing. My friend used it to brainstorm ideas for her business website." Nadia had been skeptical. The words had to come from her. That was what made it real. That was what made it her novel.

But she was desperate. So she opened Claude on her free tier account, stared at the text box, and typed a question she'd never thought she'd ask a machine: "My protagonist is at a crossroads. She's thirty-four, she's been at her job for eight years, she's never been in love, and she's starting to think her whole life is on the wrong track. What decision could she make that would change the direction of her story?"

The response came back in seconds. Eight possible paths. Nadia read through them. Six were terrible, generic options that any writing advice blog would suggest. Leave the job. Travel. Fall in love. However, two were actually interesting. One was dark and unexpected. The other was funny in a way that felt true to Akiko's voice. Nadia didn't use either one exactly. But one sparked something. An angle she'd missed. A way forward.

She sat there, slightly stunned. The AI hadn't written her novel. It hadn't replaced her thinking. It had been a brainstorming partner. A person in the room who'd thrown ideas at the wall. Most were duds, but a couple stuck. That was the job of a writing partner. And a machine could do that.

What happened next changed how Nadia thought about creativity forever. It wasn't that AI could replace the creative work. It couldn't. But it could augment it. It could be the collaborator who shows up at two in the morning when you're stuck. It could be the sounding board who never judges, never leaves, and sometimes, just sometimes, says the thing you needed to hear.

This chapter is about creativity in the age of AI. Not about whether AI is going to replace artists, writers, musicians, and designers. It isn't. Instead, we're going to explore how tools like AI are becoming the ultimate creative partners. For Nadia, for your kid who wants to make music, for the small business owner who needs a product photo, for the blogger who wants to animate their ideas. This is where AI gets truly exciting. Not because the machines are creative. Because they help us be more creative than we've ever been.

And it all starts with the PRIME framework from Chapter 3. The same thinking that works for business analysis works for creative projects. You need to be clear about what you want, refine iteratively, use the IDEA loop to improve, master the details that matter, and execute in the real world. Creative tools work best when you know how to use them intentionally. The difference between a mediocre AI-generated image and a stunning one is the same difference between a vague prompt and a thoughtful one. The human is still the artist. The AI is just the brush.

One thing Nadia noticed right away: the creative tools were more fun than the productivity tools. When Marcus Chen was using AI for invoicing and customer service in Chapter 7, the goal was efficiency. Here, the goal is expression. And that changes the energy entirely. Playing with AI music generation feels like play. Experimenting with image prompts feels like exploration. Using AI to brainstorm story ideas feels like having coffee with another writer. If you tried AI for work tasks and thought "that's useful but boring," creative AI might change your mind.

✦✦✦

Writing: Fiction, Nonfiction, and Everything Between

Nadia went back to Chapter 47 with new energy. She used Claude three more times that week. Once, she was stuck on dialogue, she asked the AI to help her brainstorm what Akiko and her mother might say to each other in a confrontation scene. The AI suggested eight exchanges. Nadia used pieces of three of them, but more importantly, it helped her hear how the conversation should flow. The actual words were hers.

The second time, she was writing a flashback scene and needed to describe a location she'd never been to. Kyoto, Japan, in spring. She described what she wanted: "A traditional tea house garden. Early morning. After rain." Claude painted a vivid picture. She took the sensory details and wove them into her own prose, making it distinctive to her voice.

The third time, she'd written three pages of dialogue and the emotional beat felt flat. She pasted it into Claude and asked: "Where is the emotional tension in this scene? What's missing?" The AI pointed out that neither character was saying what they actually felt. Obvious feedback, maybe. But sometimes you need someone to name it. Once named, Nadia knew exactly what to fix.

This is how writers work best with AI. Not by having AI write for you. By using it as a thinking partner. A collaborative tool. A mirror to hold up to your work.

Think of it like having a conversation with the smartest reader in the world. A reader who's read everything, has infinite patience, and doesn't get offended when you disagree with them. You wouldn't let that reader write your novel. But you'd absolutely let them read a draft and tell you where they got bored.

The applications are vast. If you're writing fiction, AI is excellent at brainstorming plot options, suggesting character motivations, helping you understand what your story is about, critiquing your first draft, and suggesting tighter prose. If you're writing nonfiction (blog posts, personal essays, business articles, family histories) AI can help you outline, find the through-line of your argument, fact-check, suggest transitions, and revise for clarity. If you're doing something in between (a newsletter, a medium post, a wedding toast, a cover letter) AI can help you organize your thoughts, find your voice, and refine until it's right.

Nadia's neighbor, a retired dentist named Harold, had been wanting to write his family's immigration story for years. He had boxes of letters, old photographs, and scattered memories. He didn't know where to start. Nadia showed him how to use Claude. He pasted in a few translated letters and asked: "Help me organize these letters into a timeline and suggest a narrative structure for a family memoir." Within minutes, he had a chronological framework and three possible ways to tell the story. Harold cried. Not because the AI wrote his memoir. Because it showed him the shape of one. He'd been looking at pieces for twenty years and couldn't see the whole. AI helped him see it.

The key is understanding what AI is good at and what it isn't. AI is great at generating options quickly. It's great at analyzing structure. It's great at suggesting improvements. It's terrible at knowing your authentic voice. It can't know what's true in your life the way you do. It can't care about your story the way you do. Your job is to use AI as an amplifier of your own judgment, not a replacement for it.

Here's a practical way to think about it. If you ask AI to "write a blog post about gardening," you'll get something generic and forgettable. If you ask AI to "I've been gardening for fifteen years in North Carolina clay soil. I've learned that most gardening advice doesn't work here. Help me outline a blog post about what I've learned that contradicts conventional wisdom," you'll get something useful. The difference is you. Your experience. Your perspective. Your specificity. AI amplifies what you bring to it.

Nadia started keeping a document of her favorite prompts. For brainstorming plot options, she used: "My protagonist is in this situation. Here are three constraints. What are eight possible decisions she could make, and what would happen as a result? Think about options that are surprising, not obvious." For editing, she used: "I'm going to paste a scene. Tell me: What's the emotional core of this moment? Where is the conflict? What could be stronger?" For dialogue, she used: "My character is trying to do X, and the other character is trying to do Y. What's a conversation where both of them say what they actually feel, not what they think they should say?"

By Chapter 50, Nadia realized something. She'd finished the book. She'd been using AI as a thinking partner through the home stretch. Not every chapter. Not even most chapters. But when she was stuck, it was there. When she needed to test an idea, it was there. And every conversation made her a better writer, because she had to be precise about what she wanted, and precision made her understand her own story better.

A word about the editing process, because this is where AI really shines and most people don't think to use it. Nadia had a complete first draft. One hundred thousand words. She knew it was messy. Every first draft is messy. But she didn't have money for a professional developmental editor (those run $2,000 to $5,000 for a novel-length manuscript).[47] So she did something clever. She pasted her novel into Claude one chapter at a time and asked specific questions. "What's the pacing like in this chapter? Where does it drag?" "Is my protagonist's motivation clear, or does she seem to act without reason?" "Highlight any sentences that are unnecessarily wordy." The AI wasn't as nuanced as a professional editor, but it caught things she'd missed after reading the same pages forty times. Fresh eyes, even artificial ones, make a difference.

She also discovered a trick for finding her own verbal tics. Every writer has them. Words or phrases you overuse without realizing it. Nadia asked Claude: "Read this chapter and tell me which words or phrases I use too often." Turns out she wrote "something about" approximately four hundred times in her manuscript. And "slightly." And "suddenly." Once she could see the pattern, she could fix it. That kind of analysis would take a human reader hours. AI did it in seconds.

One more important thing about using AI for writing: the ethics. Your writing is still your writing. The ideas are yours. The voice is yours. The revision is yours. If you're publishing something, and AI helped you write it, you should be honest about that, especially in professional contexts. But there's no dishonesty in using AI as a creative tool. You're not claiming the machine wrote your novel. You're just saying you had a collaborator. Writers have always had collaborators. Editors. Friends who read drafts. Writing groups. AI is just another form of collaborative feedback. The question isn't whether you used tools. It's whether the final product is authentically yours. And if you've done the thinking, made the choices, and put in the revision work, it is.

TRY THIS NOW: Unstick Your Writing

Take something you're stuck on. A novel chapter. A blog post. An email. A wedding toast. Describe the problem to AI: what you're trying to do, where you're stuck, what you've tried already. Ask for 5-8 different approaches to the problem. Read the suggestions. Most will be generic. One or two might spark something. Use that spark. The point isn't to use the AI's solution exactly. It's to get unstuck. Once you're unstuck, your own creativity takes over.

✦✦✦

Image Generation 101

Nadia's sister texted her a photo. At first she thought it was a real image, a gorgeous birthday card. Watercolor style. Warm tones. A stack of books with flowers coming out of them. Calligraphy that read: "Happy Birthday to a Woman Who's Written a Novel Inside Her Heart (And Now It's on Paper)." It was beautiful. Nadia assumed her sister had hired a designer.

"I made this," her sister said. "Well, I described it to an AI, and the AI made it, and then I tweaked it a little."

Nadia was stunned. She'd been thinking of AI images as obviously fake, obviously robot-made. This didn't look fake. It looked like art.

Her sister talked her through it. You describe what you want. The AI generates it. If you don't like it, you refine your description and try again. That's it. Nadia opened ChatGPT and, feeling slightly silly, tried it herself.

"Create an image for a bookmark. It should show a woman reading in a cozy library nook. Warm afternoon light coming through tall windows. Books everywhere. She's holding a cup of tea. Watercolor style. Soft, peaceful feeling."

ChatGPT generated four images in seconds. The first one was close. The second one was better. The third was exactly what she'd been picturing. She refined: "Make the woman more diverse. Darker skin tone. Curly hair. Keep the peaceful feeling." Second attempt. One of the four was perfect. She printed it, laminated it, and used it as a bookmark while editing her novel.

Here's what you need to know about AI image generation in 2026: it's democratized visual creativity in a way that's genuinely remarkable. Ten years ago, if you wanted a custom illustration, you hired an artist. That cost thousands. Now you describe what you want, and a machine makes it in seconds. For free or cheap.

The major players: ChatGPT has built-in image generation (as of early 2026, it uses its native generation model, not DALL-E 3 anymore).[48] It's the easiest entry point. Free tier gets you 2-3 images per day. Plus tier gets unlimited. Midjourney is the highest quality. The images are stunning. But it costs money ($10 a month to start).[49] Google also has their Nano Banana image generation model. Google allows 20, 50, 100, and 1000 images per day for the free, AI Plus, Pro, and Ultra tiers respectively.[50] Adobe Firefly is designed for commercial use if you're creating images for a business, this is the safest bet legally.[51]

What can you realistically do with image generation? Custom greeting cards. Book covers. Blog illustrations. Social media graphics. Product mockups. Personalized wall art. Storyboards for videos. Visual brainstorming. Holiday cards with your family's names on them. T-shirt designs for your kid's birthday party. Illustrations for a children's story you're writing with your grandkids. The applications are practically endless, and new ones pop up every week.

Nadia's 10-year-old son got in on the fun too. He was doing a school project on the solar system and wanted a poster. Instead of cutting out magazine pictures, he sat with Nadia and described what he wanted: "A dramatic view of Saturn from one of its moons. Realistic style. You can see the rings up close. Stars in the background. Make it look like a NASA photo but more colorful." The image that came back was stunning. His teacher asked where he found it. When he said he'd made it with AI, the whole class wanted to try.

The art of the image prompt is knowing what details matter. Vague: "A nice landscape." Better: "A misty forest at dawn. Tall pine trees. Morning light filtering through fog. A deer in the distance. Moody, peaceful. Digital painting style." The difference is the same as the difference between telling a photographer "take a nice picture" and saying "I want a close-up of the flower with the morning dew, shallow depth of field, golden hour light." Specific details about style (watercolor, digital painting, photography, sketch), lighting, composition, mood, and color palette make a huge difference in what you get back.

The PRIME framework applies directly here. Your initial Prompt should include the subject, style, mood, lighting, and composition. When you Refine, tell the AI specifically what to change: "The lighting is too cool. Make it warmer. Move the figure to the left third of the frame. Make the background less busy." The IDEA loop helps you Imagine what the perfect version looks like, Diagnose what's missing in the current version, Enhance with specific instructions, and Act on the best result. Master means fine-tuning the last 10%. Maybe adjusting colors or cropping. And Execute means downloading, printing, posting, or using the image for its intended purpose.

By the way, there are current limitations you should know about. Hands still look weird sometimes. Count the fingers on any AI-generated image and you'll often find too many or too few. Text in images has improved dramatically but still isn't perfect. Ask for a sign that says "Happy Birthday" and you might get "Hapyy Birthdday." Creating multiple images that are consistent with each other (same character, different poses, different scenes) is genuinely hard. If you need a series of illustrations with the same person, you'll need patience and creative prompting. But these limitations are improving fast. In six months, they'll be better. In a year, unrecognizable. The trajectory is clear: these tools are getting dramatically better, dramatically fast.

Nadia used image generation for a practical project: her novel's cover. She'd been saving for a professional cover designer. That's expensive. Instead, she spent an evening with ChatGPT. She described the feel she wanted: "Minimalist. Modern. A woman walking away from the camera. Cherry blossoms falling. Japanese aesthetic but contemporary. Warm tones. Her back should be strong, not fragile. The title would go at the top in elegant sans-serif." Six attempts. The fourth one was the winner. She spent another two hours with an AI design tool (more on that in a bit) refining the text and layout. Total cost: $0. Total time: three hours.

Professional designer cost: $500+.[52] Time saved: 20 hours of back-and-forth.

TRY THIS NOW: Create Your First AI Image

Open ChatGPT. Start simple. Ask it to generate an image: "A watercolor painting of a cozy reading nook with warm afternoon light coming through the window. Books stacked on wooden shelves. A comfortable armchair. Soft, peaceful feeling." Look at the results. Pick the one closest to what you wanted. Now refine: "That's close! Can you make the light more golden? Add a cup of tea on the side table?" Iterate. In three or four rounds, you'll get something you love. You've just done what used to require commissioning an artist.

✦✦✦

Music, Audio, and Podcasting

Nadia's 13-year-old daughter showed her Suno on a Friday night. "Mom, you have to hear this," she said, pulling up the website on her phone. "I asked it to write a song, and it made it."

She played it. It was a short indie-folk song about their cat, Lord Fluffington. The production was clean. The vocals were recognizable AI but not obviously so. The lyrics were weirdly charming. It was unquestionably a song. A whole song. Created by describing an idea to a machine. Nadia was blown away.

"Can you ask it to make something for my novel?" Nadia said. "Like a theme song?"

Ten minutes later, there was an instrumental theme. Haunting. Japanese-influenced (fitting for her protagonist). Perfect mood. Something Nadia would have spent hours finding on royalty-free music sites. Done in seconds.

Music generation is one of the fastest-moving areas in AI. At the time of this writing, Suno is one of the leading music generation tools. It creates studio-quality audio at 44.1kHz. That's CD quality, for those keeping score. You describe what you want; a vibe, a style, lyrics, an instrument, and it makes a song. Seriously. It makes a whole song. Three to four minutes. With vocals. With production. Actual music. You can even write your own lyrics using tags like [Verse], [Chorus], and [Bridge], and Suno will perform them for you.[53]

Let that sink in for a moment. Twenty years ago, producing a song required a recording studio, instruments, musicians, an engineer, and thousands of dollars. Ten years ago, you could do it on a laptop with GarageBand, but you still needed musical knowledge and hours of work. Today, you describe what you want in plain English, and a full song appears in thirty seconds. We are living in genuinely wild times.

The practical uses: background music for videos. Podcast intros and outros. Personal playlists. Marketing videos. Short films. Ambient background music for studying or working. Custom songs for special occasions, imagine a personalized anniversary song, or a funny birthday tune that references inside jokes. Nadia made one for her husband's birthday: a country ballad about his obsession with smoking brisket. He laughed so hard he nearly fell off the deck. Cost: free. Effort: ten minutes. Joy: priceless.

If you're into podcasting, or even thinking about starting one, AI is revolutionizing the workflow. Automatic transcription (services like Otter or even built-in YouTube transcription) turns your audio into text in minutes. AI can generate show notes from the transcript. It can suggest chapters and timestamps. It can help you edit. AI can even remove background noise and smooth out the audio quality. For someone running a solo podcast, this saves hours every episode.

Nadia's friend from her old teaching days had been wanting to start a podcast about children's literature for years. She never did because the production work felt overwhelming. Recording was the easy part. It was everything else; editing out the "ums," writing show notes, creating episode descriptions, making cover art for each episode. Nadia showed her the AI workflow. Record the episode. Upload the audio to a transcription service. Paste the transcript into Claude and ask for show notes, a one-paragraph episode description, three suggested pull quotes for social media, and a list of books mentioned. What used to take three hours of post-production now took thirty minutes. Her friend launched the podcast the following month.

Then there's text-to-speech and voice cloning. ElevenLabs is the leader here. You can type text, and it'll read it in an AI voice that sounds astonishingly human, natural pacing, emotional variation, the works. Or you can clone your own voice (with a short audio sample), and the AI will read text in your voice. The quality is shockingly good. Nadia recorded herself reading a paragraph, uploaded it, and then had the AI read back a different paragraph in her voice. She played it for her husband without telling him it was AI. He didn't notice. That's how good it is.

The use cases are exciting: creating audiobook versions of your writing without spending twenty hours in a recording booth. Making videos with voiceovers without recording yourself. Accessibility features, imagine someone with a speech disability using voice cloning to have conversations in their own voice. Creating content in multiple languages. For podcasters, it means you can produce polished intros and sponsors reads without re-recording when you fumble.

But there's an ethical note worth mentioning: voice cloning and text-to-speech with recognizable voices is powerful. Use it responsibly. Don't create audio of someone saying something they didn't say. That's a deepfake, and it's harmful. But using it for legitimate purposes (reading your own novel, creating content in your own voice) that's fine. The capabilities are remarkable. And so are the risks. We'll talk more in Chapter 9 about the other side of this technology, what happens when voice cloning is used not for birthday songs, but for scam calls targeting your parents.

▶ **TRY THIS NOW: Generate a Song**

Go to suno.com. Sign up free. Describe a song you want created. Try something like: "An upbeat acoustic folk song about Sunday morning coffee, warm and nostalgic. Fingerpicking guitar. Soft vocal delivery. Main chorus about the comfort of ritual." Hit generate. In 30 seconds, there's a full song. Listen. Refine your prompt. Try again. You've just composed and produced a song. A few iterations in, you'll have something you actually love.

✦✦✦

Video: The Next Frontier

Video is where AI is moving next. This is the most rapidly changing area, so fair warning: the landscape today might be different by the time you're reading this. But here's where things stand in early 2026.

AI video generation is impressive but still maturing. The quality has improved dramatically in the last year. The major players: Runway offers one of the industry-leading video generation models, widely considered to have excellent quality. Google's Veo creates 4K video with synced audio, which is wild. Kling generates longer clips at affordable prices. And OpenAI was running Sora, but the AI video generation landscape is in rapid flux with changing tools and availability. Check the companion site at practicalaibook.ai for the current state of video AI.[54, 55, 56]

What you can realistically do right now: short clips (10-60 seconds), social media content, product demos, animated photos, simple transitions, and mood pieces. Some tools can even generate synchronized audio alongside the video. What's still hard: long-form videos longer than a couple of minutes, consistent characters who look the same across multiple clips, complex narratives with multiple scenes, and perfectly lip-synced dialogue. But "still hard" in AI terms means "probably solved in six months." The pace of improvement is staggering. However, if you are good with Video editing software, you can string multiple videos together and leverage techniques like frame to video where you take the last frame of a video and use it as the start frame with your video along with a prompt. Google has Flow which leverages Veo engine, but is a studio like experience that makes creating longer videos easier.

Nadia tried making a short video trailer for her novel. She described the mood: "Quiet morning in Kyoto. Rain on leaves. A woman staring out a window. Contemplative. Japanese cinematography. The words 'Some Stories Find You' appear on screen in elegant text." It generated a 30-second clip that was haunting. Not perfect, the rain looked slightly off, and the text timing was wrong. But as a rough cut? Amazing. She spent thirty minutes polishing it in a video editor. The result: a professional-looking book trailer created in hours instead of weeks.

For most people reading this book, video AI is the area to watch rather than the area to dive deep into right now. The tools are powerful but still require patience and iteration to get good results. Think of where image generation was two years ago, impressive but inconsistent. Video is at that stage now. By the time this book is in paperback, video generation will likely be as accessible and reliable as image generation is today.

The honest truth: video AI will look completely different soon. Check the companion website (practicalaibook.ai) for updates and tutorials on the current state of video generation. This space is moving too fast to be definitive in print. What I can tell you with confidence is that if you're curious about video, start experimenting now. The people who learn these tools early will have a significant advantage as they mature.

▶ **TRY THIS NOW: Animate a Photo**

If you have a Canva account, open a photo and try the "Animate" feature. It turns still photos into short videos. Or search for "free AI video generator" and experiment with a short clip. Describe a simple scene. Start with something basic: a sunrise, a person walking, falling snow. The quality might surprise you. In six months, it'll be even better.

✦✦✦

Design Without Being a Designer

Nadia needed a book cover for her manuscript. Not to print, just something professional looking to send to agents. A real cover design costs $300 to $800. She didn't have that. So she figured: if I can generate an image, can I design a book cover?

The answer is yes. And the tool is Canva with AI magic design.[57]

Canva has a feature called Magic Design. You describe what you need, and it generates design options. For a book cover, Nadia said: "Minimalist literary novel. Contemporary design. A woman silhouette in the center. Soft watercolor aesthetic. Title: 'Some Stories Find You.' Cherry blossoms in the corners. Warm color palette. Elegant and modern." Canva generated five design options. Three were forgettable. Two were strong. She took one, tweaked the font, adjusted the spacing, and ten minutes later she had a professional-looking book cover.

This is now accessible to anyone. You don't need to be a designer. You don't need to hire a designer. You need to describe what you want, iterate, and know enough about design to recognize what looks good. AI handles the technical part.

Other practical applications: event flyers, birthday invitations, holiday cards, social media graphics, presentation slides for work or school or church, menus for dinner parties, programs for school plays, signs for yard sales. The framework is always the same. Describe what you want. Refine until it's right. Download. Print or share.

Nadia's holiday cards became a family legend. Every December, she'd struggled with the annual family card. Picking a photo everyone looked good in. Finding a template that didn't look like everyone else's. Writing a message that was personal but not braggy. This year, she used AI to generate a custom illustration of her family's house in winter, snow on the roof, warm lights in the windows, their cat sitting on the porch. It looked like a hand-painted Christmas card. She added her family's message in a hand-lettered font through Canva. The result was so beautiful that three neighbors asked who she hired. "I made it," she said. "With AI." Two of them asked her to show them how.

The PRIME framework works beautifully here. Your Prompt needs to be specific: not just "design a flyer" but "design a flyer for a garage sale, Saturday 8am-3pm, families welcome, lots of color, fun but not cartoony, include my phone number, bright primary colors." You Refine by looking at what the AI generated and saying what's working and what isn't. The IDEA loop: In the design, you're asking "what impression does this give?" Does it feel like what I'm selling? The Master stage is the detail work, tweaking fonts, adjusting sizing, moving elements slightly. And Execute is hitting download and using it.

One more note on logo creation: AI can get you started. It can generate logo concepts quickly, and for personal projects or rough concepts, that might be enough. But if you're using a logo for a real business (one that'll go on your website, business cards, truck, and invoices) you'll probably want professional refinement. A logo matters. It's how people recognize your business. The sweet spot is using AI to generate ten or twenty concepts quickly, narrowing to two or three you love, and then hiring a designer to refine the winner into something polished and versatile. You'll save hundreds of dollars in the exploration phase and still get a professional result.

Nadia also used AI design for presentation slides for a book talk she was doing at a local library. Instead of making slides from scratch, she told Canva what she wanted: "Ten slides about my novel writing journey. Modern design. The main character's name is Akiko. Include typography, negative space, one illustration of a woman in a moment of contemplation. Color palette: warm but sophisticated." Canva generated slide templates with the text she wanted and beautiful layouts. She added her own quotes from the book, adjusted the images, and had a presentation she was genuinely proud of. Two hours instead of ten.

TRY THIS NOW: Design Something

Open Canva (free account is fine). Click "Magic Design." Type a description of something you need: a birthday invitation, a flyer for your garage sale, a social media post announcing something you care about. The more specific you are, the better. "A flyer for a community garden tour. Friendly but professional. Natural colors. Include date, time, location, free admission, everyone welcome." Review the designs. Pick one. Tweak it to match your vision exactly. Download. You just designed something without being a designer.

✦✦✦

It was a Tuesday night in December when Nadia realized what had happened. She'd finished her novel. Actually, truly finished. One hundred and ten thousand words. Akiko's story, told start to finish. In Chapter 47, the scene that had paralyzed her for weeks, Akiko made a choice. Nadia's choice. Informed by AI brainstorming, but entirely hers.

She'd used AI throughout the editing process. Not to write, but to think. To brainstorm. To refine. To polish. The novel was entirely her voice, her story, her vision. But the tools had made her better at expressing it.

She'd also made a custom birthday card for her mom. Used AI image generation to create a watercolor painting of the two of them reading together, something that never actually happened but felt true to who they were. Her mom cried when she opened it. The good kind of cry.

And her 13-year-old daughter had discovered a passion for music. They'd spent Saturday afternoons creating silly AI-generated songs together. "Mom, what if we made a song about our cat solving mysteries?" Her daughter was thinking creatively, experimenting, playing. The AI wasn't replacing her creativity. It was awakening it.

Nadia wasn't afraid of AI anymore. She wasn't afraid it would replace human creativity. Instead, she'd discovered something simpler: it was just a tool. A very good tool. A collaborative tool. Like a pencil for a writer, but smarter. Like a camera for a photographer, but capable of things cameras can't do. Like a musical instrument, but one that helps you express ideas faster than your fingers could normally move.

She thought about her sixteen years as an English teacher. She'd always told her students that the hardest part of writing wasn't the writing, it was the thinking. Getting clear about what you wanted to say. Finding the structure that supported the story. Understanding your characters deeply enough that their choices felt inevitable. AI didn't do any of that thinking for her. But it helped her think faster. It helped her get unstuck. It helped her see options she wouldn't have considered on her own. And sometimes, that's all you need.

The novel was hers. The birthday card was hers. The song she and her daughter made was theirs. The tools didn't diminish that. They magnified it. They made creativity faster, more accessible, less lonely. They were the collaborators who showed up at two in the morning with ideas. They were the second set of eyes. They were partners in the work.

And the most important thing Nadia learned was this: the tools work best when you know what you want. When you have a vision. When you're clear about what you're trying to accomplish. The PRIME framework works for creativity exactly like it worked for business. Clear Prompt. Refine based on what you get. Use the IDEA loop to understand what works and what doesn't. Master the details that matter. Execute in the real world. Those principles made her a better writer. They also made her a better collaborator with machines.

But creativity and productivity aren't the whole story. Because as AI gets better and more integrated into our lives, new questions emerge. Questions that should keep you up at night if you're thinking about this clearly. Privacy. Safety. The possibility of deepfakes and misinformation. What happens when AI gets things wrong? What happens when AI is used to hurt people instead of help them? In the next chapter, we're going to have the harder conversation. Not about what AI can do for you. But about what AI can do to you if we're not thoughtful about it. Because using AI well doesn't just mean using it creatively or productively. It means using it wisely.

9

STAYING SAFE AND SMART

THE STUFF THEY DON'T PUT IN THE MARKETING MATERIALS

Frank Medina carried mail in suburban Phoenix for thirty-one years. Not just any mail, he was the guy who knew everyone on his route. He'd chat with Mrs. Chen about her grandkids, help Mr. Patterson bring in his packages, remember that the Rodrigues family always ordered their Christmas gifts in November. When he retired last year, people came to his farewell. He was that kind of neighbor.

On a Tuesday afternoon in February, Frank's mother Carmen called him. She was eighty-two, lived alone in Tucson, and prided herself on being sharp. But she sounded shaken.

"Frank, honey, I need your help," she said. "I'm so scared. You've been in an accident."

Frank's stomach dropped. But the voice on the other end was him. Not close. Him. The same cadence. The same slight Arizona accent. The same way he said "mom" when he talked to her every Sunday.

"Carmen, I've been in a car accident in Phoenix," the voice said. "Medical bills are piling up. I need five thousand dollars wired to an account right away. Don't tell anyone."

Carmen was already reaching for her purse when something stopped her. It wasn't the money. It wasn't even the secrecy. It was this: the voice on the phone said he couldn't remember the name of the family dog they had when Frank was growing up. Biscuit. A golden retriever who lived to be fourteen and Frank had loved like a brother.

Frank wouldn't forget Biscuit. The voice wasn't Frank.

Carmen hung up and called the real Frank. That's when Frank learned what he'd been nervous about, the AI stuff you hear about in the news, had shown up at his own doorstep. Specifically, at his mother's door. Someone had taken a video Frank posted on Facebook from his retirement party (thirty seconds of him telling a terrible joke to a crowd of neighbors) and used it to clone his voice. Then they used that voice to try to scam his mother out of five thousand dollars.

The voice was artificial. But it sounded more like Frank than Frank's own brother would've recognized.

Frank sat down at his kitchen table that night and thought about what he'd been learning about AI. ChatGPT. Claude. The AI stuff he'd been playing with. He'd asked ChatGPT to help him understand his mom's Medicare paperwork. He'd pasted pages of her medical history into the chatbox. He'd thought it was private, like talking to his tax guy. He'd been wrong.

This chapter is the one I wish I didn't have to write. But Frank's story, and millions like it, make it the most important one in the book. Not to scare you. Not to make you throw your laptop out the window. But to open your eyes. Because the same remarkable intelligence that can help you draft an email or explain a medical bill can also be weaponized by people with bad intentions. And the people you love the most, your parents, your kids, your friends, are often the targets.

So let's talk about what you need to know. Eyes wide open. Common sense in hand.

✦✦✦

Section 1: What AI Companies Do With Your Data

The first thing Frank wanted to understand was this: when he pasted his mom's Medicare information into ChatGPT, where did it go? And the answer matters more than you might think.

Here's the plain truth. Most AI companies use your conversations to train their AI systems. Think about it this way. Every time you ask ChatGPT a question, you're giving them a training example. Feed enough training examples from enough people, and the AI gets smarter. That's how they built these systems in the first place.

But here's where it gets tricky. Different companies have different policies. And the default settings are almost never in your favor.

Let's talk about data retention policies first. Each major AI platform has its own approach, and these policies change frequently. Some platforms keep conversations for safety review, others delete them after a period, and the default behaviors vary widely. The key principle: assume your conversations are being stored unless you explicitly opt out.[58]

Each platform handles this differently: some default to keeping conversations (and require you to opt out), while others delete them by default (requiring opt-in for retention). Some platforms allow human reviewers to access conversations for safety purposes, while others don't. The specifics matter, and they change.

Some platforms also integrate conversations with other data you generate on that platform, creating a comprehensive digital profile. And here's the kicker: different platforms have different policies about whether human reviewers can access conversations, and those policies can change. Transparency varies widely across the industry.

There's one bright spot: enterprise and business tiers across all these platforms have stronger privacy protections. They don't use conversations for training by default. But here's the problem, you probably don't have access to those. The consumer tier is what most of us use. And the consumer tier is absolutely not the place to share medical records, bank information, passwords, or anything else that someone could use against you.

When Frank realized he'd been putting his mother's healthcare information into a system that Google, OpenAI, and others could potentially access, he felt sick. It's not that these companies are villains. They're not sitting in a dark room plotting to steal your grandmother's Medicare number. But data is valuable. And valuable things attract thieves.[59]

So what do you do about this? Start with one simple step: find the privacy settings in each AI tool you use. ChatGPT has a settings menu where you can opt out of training. Claude has a clear opt-in button. Google Gemini has privacy controls buried in your Google account settings. The steps are different for each one. But they all have them.

Read the settings. Understand what you're opting into and what you're opting out of. And make decisions based on what you're actually sharing. If you're asking about a recipe? Probably fine. If you're asking about your health insurance? You should probably have a conversation with yourself about whether you really need to be sharing that.[60]

▶ TRY THIS NOW: Check Your AI Privacy Settings Right Now

If you use ChatGPT: Log in and look for Settings. Find "Data Controls." Toggle off "Improve model for everyone" if you don't want OpenAI training on your chats.

If you use Claude: Look for the opt-in button for "Allowed to use this conversation to improve Claude." You control whether you're training the model.

If you use Google Gemini: Check your Google Account privacy settings. Review what data is being collected and how long it's being kept.

Write down your choices. Share them with someone in your family. Make it a habit, not a one-time thing.

✦✦✦

Section 2: Hallucinations: When AI Lies With Confidence

Frank's wife Linda is a fourth-grade teacher. She's been using ChatGPT to help plan her history lessons. Last month, she asked it to tell her about a historical figure who'd changed education policy in the 1950s. ChatGPT wrote back with a beautiful, compelling story. Real name. Real dates. Real accomplishments. It read like it came straight out of a textbook.

She used it in her lesson. Told the kids about this figure. Assigned them a homework project. Two days later, one of her students came up to her with a confused look. "Ms. Medina, I can't find anything about this person in my research."

Linda dug deeper. Nothing. The person didn't exist. ChatGPT had made them up. It didn't say, "I don't know." It didn't hedge. It just invented a person, complete with plausible details, and delivered it with absolute confidence.

This is called a hallucination. And it's one of the most insidious problems with AI systems right now.

Here's what's happening: AI models are pattern-matching machines. They've learned patterns from billions of words. When you ask them a question, they're not actually retrieving knowledge the way a database does. They're predicting the next most likely word, and then the next, and the next. Sometimes those patterns lead them to completely fabricated information. And because they don't actually "know" they're wrong, they deliver false information with the same confidence as true information.[61]

Think of it like a professor who is incredibly smart but has read zero books. He's so confident, so articulate, so convinced of what he's saying that you believe him. But he's making stuff up. That's your AI.

The problem has gotten serious enough that it's reached the courts. In July 2025, two attorneys representing MyPillow CEO Mike Lindell cited fake court cases generated by AI in a federal court brief. The judge fined them three thousand dollars each.[62]

That same year, attorneys from Ellis George and K&L Gates were ordered to jointly pay thirty-one thousand one hundred dollars after submitting a brief containing hallucinated citations. Same problem: made-up cases, delivered with confidence.[63]

These aren't isolated incidents. These are canaries in a coal mine.

If AI can fool lawyers (people whose entire job is to verify facts) then what hope do the rest of us have?

The hallucinations come in three flavors. Sometimes AI invents facts entirely: a person who never existed, a date that never happened, a statistic that came from nowhere. Sometimes it takes real sources and makes up quotes that were never in them. "Einstein said [something Einstein never said]" with a real source that doesn't actually contain that quote. And sometimes it takes a real case or real person and adds unsupported arguments or claims.

So how do you protect yourself? The same way you'd fact-check anything. Verify independently. If ChatGPT tells you about a historical figure, Google them. If it cites a study, find the actual study. If it gives you a statistic, see if you can find it from an original source. Be especially skeptical of overly confident language. The more certain the AI sounds, the more you should verify.

Don't stop using these tools. Just use them the way you'd use a smart colleague who hasn't done the research yet. They're great for brainstorming, drafting, and thinking through problems. But for anything that matters, anything where accuracy is important, you need to do the verification work yourself.

TRY THIS NOW: Spot the Hallucination

Ask your AI tool a factual question: "Who won the Academy Award for Best Picture in 2024?" or "What was the population of Denver in 2020?"

Get the answer from the AI.

Now verify it independently using Google or another reliable source.

Did the AI get it right? Great. But if it didn't, you've just learned a valuable lesson about when to trust and when to verify.

✦✦✦

Section 3: Deepfakes and Misinformation

Let's go back to Frank's mom and that call. The voice cloning she experienced isn't science fiction anymore. It's here. It's real. And it's already costing people billions of dollars.

In 2024, deepfake losses hit one point one billion dollars. That's a threefold increase from three hundred and sixty million in 2023.[64] The problem is getting worse, not better. And voice cloning is the most efficient weapon in the scammer's toolkit.

Here's the scary part: you only need about three to five seconds of someone's voice to clone it with eighty-five percent accuracy.[65] That video you posted on Facebook of your retirement party? That Facebook Live of you singing happy birthday? That podcast appearance from five years ago? Any of those are enough. Feed them into a voice-cloning tool (and these tools are widely available online) and someone can make you say anything.

The scams follow a predictable pattern. Someone calls a senior with a voice that sounds like their grandchild. They're in trouble. They need money. Fast. Now. Don't tell anyone. Wire it to this account. Grandparents have lost their entire life savings to this scam. Some of them have lost their homes trying to repay the money they wired to criminals.

Voice cloning is just one flavor of deepfake. Video deepfakes are getting better too. In 2026, we're heading into midterm elections. And for the first time in American history, there's widespread concern about AI-generated political content. Twenty-eight states have already passed legislation trying to regulate deepfakes.[66] Celebrity deepfakes are everywhere, fake videos of famous people promoting crypto scams, fake announcements, things that never happened.[67, 68]

None of this is meant to terrify you. But it is meant to wake you up to what's possible. Because knowledge is your best defense.

So what do you do? Start with this: establish code words with your family for emergency situations. Frank taught his mother to use the dog's name, Biscuit, as a test. If someone claims to be Frank and can't answer the Biscuit question, it's not Frank. Pick something that only you and the people you love would know. A childhood nickname. A secret joke. Something personal.

Second, if someone calls claiming to be a family member in crisis, hang up. I'm serious. Hang up and call them back at a number you know is real. Call their cell phone. Call their office. Call their spouse. This simple step stops ninety-nine percent of these scams in their tracks. Real people will understand. Real family members will be relieved you're confirming it's actually them.

Third, be skeptical of emotional content. If something makes you feel an intense emotion very quickly, panic, fear, excitement, love, slow down. Scammers are targeting your emotions, not your logic. Take a breath. Verify independently. There's almost never a reason to act on an emergency in the next five minutes.

Finally, reverse image search is your friend. If someone sends you a photo or video of someone famous, drop it into Google Images or TinEye and see where it came from. If it's a deepfake, you might find traces. If it's real, you might find the original source. Check URLs carefully. Is it actually CNN.com or is it CNN.co or cnn.net? Scammers use lookalike domains all the time.

TRY THIS NOW: Establish Your Family Safe Word or Phrase

Pick something personal that only your close family would know. A childhood pet's name. A family joke. A place you all went together.

Tell your family this is your emergency verification code.

If someone calls claiming to be a family member in crisis, use the code word. Real family will know it. Scammers won't.

Practice this with your spouse, your kids, your elderly parents. Make it normal, not weird.

✦✦✦

Section 4: Bias in AI: Real But Manageable

AI bias is one of those topics that makes people's eyes glaze over. But it's important. Not because it's an abstract social issue. But because it could directly affect you or someone you love.

Here's how bias works in AI: AI systems learn from data. Data comes from the real world. And the real world is full of historical biases. So when you feed an AI system training data from the real world, it absorbs those biases. It's not malice. It's mathematics. Patterns in, patterns out.

Let's talk about hiring. Stanford researchers in October 2025 tested AI resume-screening tools. They fed the same resumes through the system multiple times, but changed the names on them. When the name was a traditional male name, the AI flagged the resume as a strong candidate. When the same resume had a female name or a name that suggested the candidate was Black, the selection rate plummeted.[69]

One study found near-zero selection rates for Black male names. Not because the resumes were different. But because the training data that AI system learned from reflected decades of discriminatory hiring practices. The AI wasn't inventing discrimination. It was amplifying discrimination that was already buried in the data.

Healthcare is even scarier. There's an AI system for detecting skin cancer. Sounds great, right? Early detection saves lives. But here's the problem: the system was trained on over one hundred and six thousand images. Only ten of those images were of people with brown skin. One was of someone with dark brown or Black skin.[70]

So the AI learned to detect skin cancer on pale skin. When you run it on someone with darker skin, it fails. It misses cancers. People die of skin cancer that could have been caught early if the AI had been trained on diverse data. This isn't a theoretical concern. When a diagnostic tool trained overwhelmingly on light skin encounters a patient with dark skin, it doesn't flag its own uncertainty, it just gets it wrong, confidently. The consequences fall hardest on the people who were invisible in the training data.

Or consider the UnitedHealth nH Predict algorithm. It was being used to determine post-acute care coverage for Medicare Advantage patients. A ninety-one-year-old man in Wisconsin fractured his leg and ankle in a fall, and the algorithm cut off his nursing home rehabilitation coverage after just nineteen days of physical therapy, against his doctors' recommendations. His family paid roughly twelve to fourteen thousand dollars a month out-of-pocket for nearly a year until he passed away. His estate joined a class action lawsuit. But how many others couldn't afford to fight back? How many people got their coverage cut because an algorithm was biased in ways no one could see?[71]

So what do you do? First, recognize that AI bias is real. If you're using an AI tool to make an important decision about your life (hiring someone, deciding on medical treatment, choosing a college) don't rely on the AI alone. Cross-reference. Get a second opinion. Think critically.

Second, be especially careful when AI is making decisions about people. An AI writing a greeting card? Not a huge deal. An AI deciding whether someone gets a job, a loan, or medical treatment? That's serious. Push for transparency. Ask what data the system was trained on. Ask how it was tested. Ask to see the results broken down by demographic groups.

And here's the important framing: bias in AI is manageable when you know it's there. You're not helpless. You're not at the mercy of the algorithm. You're just aware that you need to think a little harder, ask a few more questions, and not blindly trust a system just because it sounds smart.

✦✦✦

Section 5: Scams and Social Engineering

We've talked about voice cloning. But that's just one way bad actors use AI. Let's talk about the other attack vectors because they're getting more sophisticated by the week.

AI-generated phishing emails are a huge problem. An AI can write an email that sounds like it came from your bank, from Amazon, from your boss. It can personalize it with details pulled from your social media profile. It can include the exact language your bank uses. The links look right. The urgency feels real. And you're clicking on a malicious link before you even think about it.

Fake customer service chatbots are another one. You have a problem with your cable company, so you go to their website and chat with what you think is customer service. But it's actually a chatbot controlled by scammers. It asks you for your account number. Then your password. Then your credit card information. You've just handed your entire digital life to criminals.

Romance scams with deepfake video have become disturbingly effective. Someone creates a deepfake of an attractive person. They build a relationship with you online. They become your friend, your confidant, your romantic interest. Then they ask you to send money. Just this once. For a plane ticket to come see you. For a medical emergency. For a business opportunity. By the time you realize it's a scam, you've sent thousands of dollars and your heart is broken.

In January 2026, security researchers at Check Point discovered ninety AI-generated "experts" operating in controlled messaging groups. These fake experts were directing victims to install fraudulent trading apps. Victims lost millions thinking they were following investment advice from real people.[72]

Here's a real case: in Hong Kong, someone impersonated the CFO of a major firm using AI-generated deepfake video. The scammer conducted a full video call with employees of the company. The call felt real. The person looked right. The orders made sense. The company wired twenty-five point six million dollars to fraudulent accounts based on a deepfake video call.[73]

These aren't hypotheticals. These are things happening right now.

So what are the red flags? Urgency is the biggest one. Scammers create artificial time pressure. You have to act now. The offer expires today. Your account will be closed. Your package will be returned. Real organizations usually give you time to think. Real emergencies with people you know happen in person or through trusted channels you can verify independently.

Secrecy is another red flag. Don't tell anyone. Don't talk to your spouse. Don't ask your accountant. Anyone telling you to keep something secret from people you trust is probably running a scam.

Unusual payment methods are a warning sign too. Real bills can be paid through normal channels. Scammers ask for wire transfers, gift cards, cryptocurrency. Payments that can't be reversed. Payments that disappear into the internet and can't be traced.

And emotional manipulation is the glue that holds it all together. Scammers study psychology. They know how to make you feel afraid, excited, in love, grateful. They trigger the emotions that override your logical brain.

Frank taught his mom these lessons. They went through her email together. They looked at requests that had come in over the years. Things that seemed normal at the time but had all the hallmarks of scams. Urgency. Requests for money. Secrecy. She started seeing patterns she'd missed.

Different age groups are vulnerable to different scams. Older adults are often targeted with grandparent scams and Medicare scams.[74] Middle-aged people are targeted with tech support scams and investment scams. Younger people are targeted with romance scams and fake job offers. There's no age that's immune. There's just different ways that scammers learn to prey on different people.

▶ **TRY THIS NOW: Practice the Pause and Verify Technique**

The next time you get an email, a text, or a call that creates a feeling of urgency, stop. Don't click. Don't respond.

Pause for at least five minutes. Breathe. Let the emotion pass.

Verify independently. If it's from a bank, call the bank's official number. If it's from a family member, reach out through a channel you know is real. If it's a work thing, talk to your manager.

Nine times out of ten, if you pause and verify, the scam falls apart. Real emergencies can wait five minutes.

✦✦✦

Section 6: Your Digital Footprint in the Age of AI

This distinction matters: while Deepfakes focuses on how AI-generated media can deceive, Your Digital Footprint examines the raw material that makes deception possible in the first place, the personal data we voluntarily share.

Everything you post online is training data for potential bad actors. Every photo. Every video. Every voice message. Every comment. Someone, somewhere, could use it against you.

That video of Frank at his retirement party seemed harmless. Just him telling a joke to neighbors. Thirty seconds. But it was enough to clone his voice. It was enough to potentially traumatize his eighty-two-year-old mother.

This doesn't mean you should become a hermit and never post anything again. But it does mean you should be thoughtful about what you share.

Start with an audit. Go through your social media profiles. Look at what you've shared. Look at what's public. Look at what's private. Ask yourself: if someone wanted to create a scam that targeted me or someone I love, would this content help them?

Photos with your kids' names visible? That's information a scammer could use. Videos of your voice? That's voice-cloning material. Posts about your mother's maiden name or your childhood pets? That's the answers to security questions.

Be especially careful with video and audio content. Text can be attributed to anyone. But video and audio feel authentic in a way text doesn't. If someone has video of you saying something, people believe it. Even if you didn't say it. Even if it's a deepfake. The visceral reaction to video is stronger.

Here's a practical guide: think about limiting public video and audio content. You don't have to be completely silent. But that TikTok or YouTube video or podcast appearance? Maybe make those private or friends-only. Review the privacy settings on your photos. Do you really need everyone to see pictures of your family? Or could that be limited to people you actually know?

And when you're tempted to share something personal online, ask yourself a simple question: would I be okay with a criminal using this? Because that's a realistic possibility now. Not because the world is evil. But because AI has made it easier for bad actors to weaponize personal information.

This brings us to the framework I mentioned at the beginning of this chapter. It's called GUARD, and it was originally developed to help people avoid financial scams. But it works for digital safety in general.

The GUARD framework is: Get the facts. Understand the source. Assess the risk. Research independently. Defend and educate others.

Get the facts means stop before you react. When you get a message that feels urgent or emotional, take a breath. Most scams rely on you acting before you think. If you pause, you're already more protected.

Understand the source means verify things independently. Check multiple sources. Call the actual company using a number you looked up yourself. Ask a trusted friend. The more you verify, the safer you'll be.

Assess the risk means look for red flags. Weird phrasing. Poor grammar. Requests for unusual payment methods. Pressure to act fast. Requests for secrecy. The more red flags you spot, the less likely you should trust something.

Even Dave Kowalski (who once thought the biggest risk of AI was it writing bad poetry about plumbing) now knows to pause before clicking links that promise free estimates from "verified contractors." His rule of thumb: "If it sounds too good to be true, it probably learned that trick from the internet." The red flags aren't just theoretical anymore. They're practical survival skills.

Research independently means take control of your privacy and security. Check your privacy settings. Limit what you share. Use strong passwords. Enable two-factor authentication. You can't control everything that happens online. But you can control what you put out there and what you protect.

And Defend and educate others means share what you learn. Tell your family. Tell your friends. Tell your neighbors. Talk to your grandkids about how they share things online. The more people who understand these dangers, the harder it is for scammers to succeed.

Coming Full Circle

Frank spent a Saturday afternoon installing privacy settings on his mother's phone. They went through her email accounts. They talked about what she could safely share and what she should keep private. And they established their code word: Biscuit.

The following Tuesday, Frank started something new. He called it "Tech Safety Tuesday" at the community center where he volunteers. He taught his neighbors about deepfakes. About social engineering. About how to verify that a call is really from a family member. He didn't try to scare them. He just gave them the same information he'd learned.

Forty people came to the first session. His mail route friends. Neighbors he'd known for decades. People from his church. They had questions. They had their own scam close calls to share. And they wanted to know how to protect the people they love.

That's the thing about knowledge. It spreads. It compounds. It creates a culture of awareness. Once you know how these scams work, once you understand the dangers, you start seeing the patterns. And once you see the patterns, you can protect yourself.

Frank's mom still uses AI. But now she's aware of what it can and can't do. She knows that urgency is a red flag. She knows that a real emergency can wait five minutes to verify. She knows that the person on the phone might sound like her son but might not actually be her son.

And Frank has learned that the same tools that can be weaponized to hurt people can be used thoughtfully by people who care. He's still curious about AI. He still experiments with it. But he's thoughtful. He's aware. He's protected the people he loves.

This is what staying safe and smart truly means. Not paranoia. Not avoidance. But eyes-wide-open awareness. Knowledge of the dangers. And a commitment to sharing that knowledge with the people you care about.

You picked up this book because you wanted to understand AI. Not to be scared of it. Not to be a victim of it. But to use it thoughtfully. To benefit from it without being harmed by it. Staying safe is part of that. It's not the end of the conversation. It's the foundation of it.

Which brings us to the final chapter. We've talked about what AI is, how it works, where it's going, and now how to protect yourself from its dangers. But the bigger question remains: how do you actually weave AI into your daily life in a way that makes things better? Not just safer. But actually better. More productive. More creative. More connected. In the next chapter, we're going to put everything together. We're going to take the knowledge you've gathered and show you how to build a life where AI is working for you.

10

BUILDING YOUR AI WORKFLOW

PUTTING IT ALL TOGETHER INTO DAILY HABITS

Rosa Gutierrez sits at her kitchen table with a cup of café con leche, the morning light just starting to break over the garden she tends. She opens her iPad (the same one her granddaughter helped her set up three years ago) and taps into the routine that has become as natural as brushing her teeth.

First, she asks ChatGPT to give her a three-sentence summary of the news she cares about: political developments in her district, local weather that matters for her garden, and one story from her hometown in Colombia that the algorithm has learned she follows. Thirty seconds of reading. No more.

Then she opens her "Today's Plan" prompt (one she's written and refined over months) and types in what's on her agenda. Teaching a three-hour class at the community center. Lunch with a friend. A video call with her son in Tampa. The AI takes those rough inputs and transforms them into a timeline: when to prep, when to eat lunch to have energy for the evening call, what to pack. Rosa doesn't follow it exactly; she just uses it to think more clearly about the shape of her day.

By the time she's finished her café, she's checked in with ChatGPT one more time, asking it to suggest one way she could make her teaching class more interactive today. She writes down the suggestion: "Ask students to talk to their own AI helper about their biggest challenge, then share what the AI said. Compare notes."

This entire routine takes twelve minutes.

"I used to spend an hour with the newspaper," Rosa told me when I first learned about her morning ritual. "Now I'm more informed and less anxious. I know what actually matters to my life, not just what the news thinks should scare me." She smiled. "And I have time to talk to my plants before class."

This is what building an AI workflow really means. Not fancy automation or complex integrations. Just the thoughtful practice of weaving AI into the moments when you actually live your life, when you need to think clearly, move faster, or see something in a new way.

We spent the first nine chapters learning the pieces. How to ask good questions. How to find AI tools that fit your life. How to think through whether AI is even the right answer. Now comes the harder part: putting it together. Making it stick. Building it into the fabric of your days so thoroughly that you stop thinking of it as "using AI" and start thinking of it as "thinking better."

This chapter is about that. The workflows. The habits. The practical choreography of your life with AI.

✦✦✦

The Morning AI Routine

Rosa didn't set out to create a formal morning routine. It emerged.

For years, she woke up and did exactly what she watched her mother do: coffee, newspaper, and a slow scroll through the anxiety of the world. She's always been a curious person, a teacher by temperament, someone who wanted to stay informed. But there was a cost. By the time she left her kitchen, her mind was jumbled, six different stories competing for attention, a vague dread about things she couldn't control, and no clear sense of what she needed to do with her day.

The first shift came by accident. Her granddaughter, exasperated after watching Rosa worry about something, said: "Nuela, just ask ChatGPT. It's like having a smart friend you can talk to in the morning."

So she did. She asked: "What are the three most important things happening in politics today that would affect my voting?" She got a clear answer. It took ninety seconds. She felt smarter, not more anxious.

That worked. So she tried it again the next day. And asked another question. Then another. And slowly, over the course of months, she discovered that each question worked best at a specific time, in a specific way, paired with a specific intention.

This is what an effective morning routine with AI looks like: intentional, not magical.

Here's what Rosa does:

The Briefing (5 minutes). Coffee in hand, she opens ChatGPT and uses a simple prompt she's saved in her notes app:

> "You know I care about: politics in California, gardening, news from Medellín, and climate news. Give me three sentences on each that matter to me today. Keep it under 200 words total. Nothing scary, just what I need to know."

She reads, absorbs, and closes the app. She doesn't go down rabbit holes. The AI helps her stay current without the psychological toll of opening seventeen different news apps.

The Planning (5 minutes). She opens her "Daily Plan" document, a template she's refined over time, and types in her schedule for the day in rough form. Her prompt is saved:

> "I'm going to [list activities]. Given that I have [energy level, high/normal/tired], what order should I do these in? When should I eat? When should I take breaks? Give me a suggested timeline."

The AI doesn't know her body as well as she does, but it thinks systematically about energy and flow in a way that her tired morning brain might not. She uses it as a thinking partner, not a rule book.

The Inspiration (2 minutes). Before she closes her laptop, she asks one question specific to what she's working on that day. If she's teaching, she asks for an idea. If she's working on a project, she asks for a different angle. If it's a normal day, she might ask: "What's one thing I could do today that would make my granddaughter proud of me?"

This last one might seem sentimental, but Rosa is serious about it. That question focuses her toward what she actually cares about, not what she thinks she should care about.

This entire routine takes twelve minutes, and it has reshaped Rosa's relationship with information and her own clarity.

The pattern here is the key. Notice what she's

not doing. She's not asking the AI to make decisions for her. She's not outsourcing her thinking. She's using it as a structured conversation partner, a way to externalize her thoughts, think them through systematically, and come back to her own judgment with more clarity.

This is the real morning routine pattern that works:

1. Intake. Get information on your terms, not the algorithm's. Use AI to filter, summarize, and prioritize. Five minutes max.
2. Planning. Use AI as a thinking partner to map out your day logically. This is not about control, it's about clarity. Five minutes max.
3. Inspiration. Ask for one idea, one perspective, one reframe that connects to what you care about. Two minutes.

The total? About twelve minutes of your morning, before anything else starts happening. In that time, you've become more informed, clearer about your day, and more connected to your intentions.

Now, the details matter. Rosa uses ChatGPT because it's what she knows. You might use Claude, Gemini, Perplexity, or something else entirely. The tool isn't the point. The structure is.

And the routine only works because Rosa is disciplined about stopping. She has her prompts saved. She reads the output once. She closes the app. She doesn't scroll. She doesn't ask seven follow-up questions. She doesn't let the AI routine become a rabbit hole that eats her morning.

Many people fail at morning routines because they treat them like magical solutions. Rosa succeeds because she treats them like a tool, useful, time-bound, and part of a larger life that AI is not the center of.

▶ TRY THIS NOW: Start Your Own AI Morning Routine

Pick one moment this week—tomorrow morning is ideal. You'll need five minutes and access to a chat AI (ChatGPT, Claude, Gemini, whatever you're comfortable with).

1. Write down three things you want to know or think about in the morning. Examples: current news in an area you care about, your schedule and optimal timing, one idea for a project you're working on, one question about your own life.

2. For each one, write a simple prompt—two or three sentences max. Save it to a note app or document. Examples:

"Summarize today's news about [topic] in one paragraph."

"I'm going to [list activities]. What's the best order and when should I take breaks?"

"I'm working on [project]. What's one approach I haven't considered?"

3. Tomorrow morning, use one prompt. Just one. Read the answer. Close the app. Don't scroll. Don't follow up.

4. Do this for a week. If it helps, add another prompt the next week. The routine only works if you keep it short and intentional.

✦✦✦

Automation for the Non-Technical

Marcus Chen owns a landscaping business. After a strong year of growth, he now employs fifteen people, manages over fifty residential clients, and has the kind of life that pulls at him constantly from a dozen directions.

Two years ago, his daughter Emma (in one of those moments of technological charity that adult children perform for their parents) handed him his phone and said, "Dad, I set you up on ChatGPT. Use it. You'll like it."

He was skeptical. Marcus is a hands-on guy. He finds comfort in dirt under his fingernails and things you can fix with a wrench. "Artificial intelligence" sounded like technology for people who sit in offices.

But Emma was right. He found uses. In Chapter 7, we looked at how Marcus uses ChatGPT to write better estimates for clients, how the AI helps him find the right tone and hit the right details. That worked so well that he kept looking for places to use it.

By last year, Marcus had a different problem. He was using AI in bits and pieces, but none of it was connected. He'd write an estimate in ChatGPT, then copy and paste it into an email. He'd get a text from a client confirming an appointment, and he'd manually add it to his calendar. He'd finish a job and manually type up an invoice. These weren't hard tasks. But there were dozens of them every week, and together they ate hours.

"I was doing the same thing over and over," he told me. "I'd think, 'There's got to be a better way.' But I also thought, 'That would take a programmer, and I can't afford that.'"

Then he discovered no-code automation tools. And everything changed.

Marcus doesn't need to know how to code. What he needed was permission to connect the tools he was already using (his email, his calendar, his invoicing software) in ways that let them talk to each other. That's what no-code automation does. It's the bridge that connects different apps so they can pass information back and forth without anyone in the middle doing the typing.

The simplest one is Zapier. Marcus uses it. Here's how it works:

You connect the apps you already use: Gmail, Google Calendar, your invoicing software, whatever. Then you create a "Zap", which is basically an instruction that says, "When X happens in App A, automatically do Y in App B."

For Marcus, his first Zap was simple: "When I send an email from my Gmail account with the subject line 'APPROVED ESTIMATE,' copy that email and add it to a 'Job Status' spreadsheet I keep in Google Sheets."

Used to be, he'd finish an estimate in ChatGPT, polish it in Gmail, send it to the client, and then manually type the date, client name, and estimated price into a spreadsheet so he could track what he'd quoted. Now? The Zap does it. He sends the email. Done. The data appears in his spreadsheet automatically.

That saved him maybe twenty minutes a day.

His second Zap: "When a client texts me a photo of a damaged area in my front yard, send that photo and the text to my 'Client Issues' folder in Google Drive, and email me so I see it immediately."

His third: "When I create a new job in my invoicing software, automatically add it to my business calendar and send a reminder to my team chat."

None of these required him to learn any code. They're just thinking about his workflow (about the places where he does repetitive data entry) and letting the computer do that instead.

Zapier's free plan lets you create two-step Zaps (one app triggering one other app) and handles 100 tasks per month.[75] That's enough to start. If you need more, the Starter plan is $19.99 a month and gives you unlimited two-step Zaps and 750 tasks per month. For a small business like Marcus's, that's plenty.

There are other tools like this too. IFTTT (If This Then That) has a free tier that lets you set up two applets. Make.com (formerly Integromat) is more powerful and gives you 1,000 operations per month for free. If you're building something more complex, Make is better. If you're just starting, Zapier or IFTTT are less intimidating.[76, 77]

If you're in the Apple ecosystem, iOS 26 Shortcuts now integrate with Apple Intelligence, letting you build on-device AI automations for summarizing PDFs, generating images, and editing text directly on your iPhone or Mac.[78]

The magic of these tools is that you don't need to understand APIs or webhooks or any of the technical plumbing. You just think about your workflow:

What repetitive data-entry task do I do at least twice a week?

That's your target. Fill out a form? Copy information from one app to another? Manually type something into a spreadsheet? That's what automation is for.

Here's what Marcus's automation has freed him to do: things that require his judgment. Client calls. Job site planning. Thinking about how to grow. Staff management. These are the things that make the business better. The data entry doesn't make the business better. It's just a cost. Why pay that cost if a computer can handle it instead?

Priya Sharma, the marketing manager from Chapter 5, took this idea further. She and her team built an entire content-to-social-media pipeline using Make.com.

Here's how it works:

1. Priya drafts a blog post in Google Docs
2. When she changes the status to "PUBLISHED," a Make automation triggers
3. The automation extracts the title, key points, and a link from the doc
4. It automatically creates a LinkedIn post, a Twitter post (shorter version), and a snippet for Slack (#announcements)
5. It sends these drafts to Priya's manager for approval
6. Once approved, the manager clicks a button and the posts go live

Before this automation, someone on the team spent three hours a week rewriting content for different platforms. Now that person spends thirty minutes reviewing drafts that the computer generated.

The other two and a half hours? Priya has those people doing original thinking instead.

"It's not about replacing people," Priya emphasized. "It's about moving people toward the work that's actually valuable. My team member is smarter than a robot. I want her thinking about

why this message matters, not rewriting the same message for the fifth platform."

This is the second key insight about automation: it's not about replacement. It's about moving your attention, and your people's time, toward the thinking work that requires human judgment.

▶ **TRY THIS NOW: Find Your First Automation Target**

Look at your week. Look for one task that fits this criteria:

1. You do it at least twice a week
2. It involves copying information from one place to another
3. It takes more than five minutes total per week
4. The steps are always the same

Examples might be:

- Copying a client response email into your project tracker
- - Typing event details into a calendar when you get a confirmation
- - Manually updating a spreadsheet from data in another app
- - Filing documents into folders based on their name or date
- - Sending the same reminder message to multiple people

Once you've found it, sign up for a free Zapier account. Look through their templates (they have hundreds). You might find one that already does what you need. If not, spend fifteen minutes building your first Zap. It will probably save you two to five hours per week.

That's your minimum viable automation. Start there.

✦✦✦

Creating Your Personal AI Playbook

By now, if you've been paying attention throughout this book, you've probably asked ChatGPT or Claude a few hundred times. Some of those conversations have been brilliant. Some have been mediocre. Some have been completely useless.

The difference usually isn't the AI. It's the prompt.

A good prompt is specific about what you need, clear about the context, and honest about constraints. A bad prompt is vague, assumes the AI understands what you mean, and hopes for the best.

After nine chapters, you've probably figured out what works for you. You might ask better questions in certain areas, maybe you've gotten really good at using AI for brainstorming, but less good at using it for editing. Maybe you've found certain phrasings that always work, and others that always disappoint.

A personal AI playbook is just a living document where you write down your best prompts and workflows. It's not complicated. It's powerful.

Marcus keeps his in a Google Doc. He has sections:

- Estimate Writing: The exact prompt he uses to draft estimates, including the tone he wants, the information he needs to include, and the specific formatting his clients expect
- Client Communication: Prompts for different situations, how to say "we can't do that," how to explain a delay, how to suggest an upsell in a way that feels helpful not pushy
- Hiring: The prompt he uses when he needs to write a job posting or review an applicant's qualifications
- Troubleshooting: When something goes wrong, his prompts for thinking through the problem systematically

Each prompt has a title, the actual text of the prompt, and sometimes a note about when to use it. "This one is for first-time clients who seem nervous. This one is for repeat clients who trust us." Context matters.

Priya's playbook is much larger. She has prompts for:

- Topic ideation for her blog
- Writing different types of social posts (announcement, question, teaching moment, story)
- Analyzing campaign performance
- Drafting newsletters
- Brainstorming positioning statements
- Competitor analysis
- Writing product descriptions

Each one has been refined over time. She's tried different structures, different lengths, different levels of detail. The final version in her playbook is the one that consistently works.

Rosa has the smallest playbook, just four prompts, but she's very disciplined about it. Her prompts are:

1. The morning briefing prompt (news)
2. The daily planning prompt
3. A teaching prompt (for creating interactive lessons)
4. A health research prompt (she wants accurate medical information but explained clearly, so she has a specific structure she uses)

She doesn't improvise much. She knows what she wants from each AI interaction, and she's written a prompt that gets her there.

The point of a playbook is this: once you've found something that works, you don't have to rediscover it. You don't have to spend three minutes setting up context that you've already figured out. You just open your playbook, find the prompt, maybe customize one detail, and go.

This is how AI becomes a tool instead of a hobby. It becomes something you use, not something you tinker with.

Here's how to build your own:

Pick three areas of your life where you use AI regularly. Could be work, could be personal projects, could be health, relationships, learning, anything where you ask AI questions more than once a month.

For each area, go back through your conversation history. Which questions got you the best results? What did you ask for? What context did you provide? What structure made the answer most useful?

Write down the best version of that prompt. Be specific. Include the context. Include any constraints or special instructions. If tone matters ("professional but friendly"), say so. If length matters, say so. If there's a specific format you want the answer in, say so.

Test it twice. Use the prompt again and see if it still works. If something doesn't land right, refine it.

Put it somewhere you'll use it. A Google Doc. A note in Notion. A simple text file. Somewhere you'll think to go before you ask the AI a question. Marcus keeps his in Google Drive. Rosa keeps hers in Apple Notes. Priya has a Notion database. The tool doesn't matter. Accessibility matters.

The guitar analogy that we've been using throughout this book applies perfectly here. A guitarist doesn't reinvent how to play a chord progression every time they play a song. They have their techniques. They have their fingering patterns. They have their standard tunings. All of that frees them up to focus on the musicality, on what's actually interesting about this particular song.

A playbook does the same thing. It handles the mechanics so you can focus on what matters.

✦✦✦

When NOT to Use AI

This might seem like a strange section to include in a book about AI. But it's the most important one.

Rosa discovered this almost by accident. She was asking ChatGPT to help her think through a conflict with a friend. The friend had said something hurtful, and Rosa was trying to decide whether to bring it up or let it go.

ChatGPT gave her a reasonable answer. Balanced. Options. Thoughtful.

But it missed something that her daughter understood immediately when Rosa called her: that Rosa had been hurt, and what she needed more than a logical framework was to feel understood by someone who knew her.

> "The AI can't know me," Rosa said to me later. "It can't know that I've been friends with Martita for forty years, and that we've weathered hard things before. It can't know that I might be overreacting because my son said something critical yesterday and I'm still raw. The AI sees this one conflict in isolation."

This is the deepest limit of AI: it doesn't have continuity with your life.

There are categories of tasks where human judgment (especially human judgment from someone who knows you or knows the situation deeply) is stronger:

Decisions that carry emotional weight. Whether to end a relationship. Whether to take a risky job. Whether to move to a new city. How to grieve. AI can help you think through the logical factors. But the part of you that lives with the consequences? That part is yours alone. You'll need human counsel, a friend, a therapist, a mentor, someone who knows you.

Situations that require real accountability. If something goes wrong, who's responsible? You are. If you outsource a decision to AI, or claim the AI made you do something, you've abandoned your own judgment. This matters especially in professional contexts. Don't use AI to avoid responsibility for your own decisions.

Things that require genuine creativity. AI is good at variations on a theme. It's not good at genuine novelty. If you're an artist, a writer, a designer (someone whose actual value is your unique voice) don't outsource to AI. Use it as a thinking partner. But the work has to come from you. When people can tell your art was generated by machine, they can feel it. They lose trust.

Situations where the context is dense and personal. Parenting advice. Medical decisions. How to communicate with someone you love. Yes, use AI to help you think. But you know your kid better than any AI ever will. You know your body. You know the person you're talking to. The AI brings frameworks. You bring understanding.

When speed would be a mistake. Some things are worth sitting with. Some decisions are worth sleeping on. Some conversations are worth struggling through. If you use AI to shortcut the struggle, you might get an answer faster, but you might also miss something important about the process itself.

Priya learned this one recently.

Her company was planning a rebranding. The color palette. The messaging. The overall feel. Priya asked Claude to suggest some directions based on their current brand and their new market positioning. Claude gave her four solid options. They were all defensible. They were all fine.

But they were all derivatives. They were all variations on existing brand aesthetics. They all felt, when Priya looked at them objectively, like they could be any B2B software company in her space.

She realized that what she needed was not an AI suggesting variations. She needed her team in a room (her designer, her writing person, the executive who understood the market shift) talking through what felt true about the rebrand. What they were

trying to say that was different.

So she ran a workshop instead. Didn't use AI. Just gave the team the prompt: "What's the one thing about this pivot that's genuinely new?" They fought about it. They talked in circles. They eventually landed on something that changed everything about how they thought about the rebrand.

Then, once they knew that core insight, Priya asked Claude to help design a visual and verbal language around it.

The AI came afterward, not before. It was a tool in service of human thinking, not a replacement for it.

"Sometimes," Priya told me, "the thing I need from AI is to validate and polish what I already know. Not to tell me what I should think."

This is the maturity mark of someone who's truly integrated AI into their workflow. It's knowing where AI makes you faster and smarter, and knowing where it would make you worse.

✦✦✦

Staying Current Without Drowning

The AI space moves fast. New models come out. New tools launch. New capabilities appear weekly. If you wanted to, you could spend forty hours a week just staying on top of what's new.

Some people do. They've made AI their hobby. That's fine if that's what you want.

But most of us have lives. We have jobs and families and gardens and businesses. We don't want to become full-time AI researchers. We just want to be aware enough that we're not blindsided. That we know when something meaningfully changes our tools. That we're not missing an opportunity because we didn't know it existed.

So how do you stay current without it eating your life?

Rosa has a system. Once a week, specifically, Sunday evening, she subscribes to four AI newsletters:

1. **Practical AI Book** (free, weekly): practical updates and tool changes that affect the exercises she learned in the book
2. **WOCxO** (free): articles about technology, leadership, and health
3. **The Neuron** (free, daily, beginner-friendly): plain-language coverage of the week's biggest developments
4. **The Batch** (free, weekly, from Andrew Ng): more academic, but clear and thoughtful

She reads whichever one is delivered that week, usually just one, because they cover similar ground. She takes notes if something seems like it might matter to her. And she moves on.

That's about thirty minutes per week. In that time, she's aware of the landscape. She knows what's shifting. She knows what new capabilities are available.[79]

Marcus doesn't read newsletters. He doesn't have time. Instead, he's told Priya (who loves this stuff) to "tell me if something happens that would change how I run my business." She does. Once every month or two, she'll send him a link and say, "This could be useful for you," or "This is coming, just so you know."

That's his way of staying current. He doesn't read every newsletter. But he has a trusted person who does, and who filters it for him.

Priya, predictably, spends more time on this. She reads several newsletters with different focuses. She follows three people on social media who share AI developments. She's part of a Slack group with ten other marketing leaders where they share what they're learning. She probably spends three to four hours per week on this.

But she gets value from it. She found Claude's marketing helper before most marketers knew it existed. She discovered a new approach to content testing through an essay someone shared in her Slack group. For her, this investment in staying current returns dividends.

The framework is simple:

1. Choose a cadence. Weekly, monthly, or less frequently. Be honest about what you'll do.
2. Choose one or two sources that match your interests. Don't subscribe to ten newsletters. That guarantees you'll read zero.
3. Set a specific time. Sunday evening. Monday morning. Friday afternoon. Somewhere on your calendar. If it's not scheduled, it won't happen.

4. Skim, not dive. You're looking for signal, not getting a PhD. Read the headlines. Read the first paragraph. If something seems relevant to you, dive deeper. Otherwise, move on.
5. Have a filter for your life. If you're not going to act on it, you probably don't need to know about it. Rosa filters for things that touch education or accessibility. Marcus filters for business tools. Priya filters for marketing. Each of them is staying current in their lane, not trying to know everything.

The paradox of staying current in AI is that the more you try to know everything, the further behind you fall. Too much information causes paralysis. So instead, choose your lane, choose your sources, commit to a small regular practice, and let that be enough.

It will be.

✦✦✦

AI as an Accessibility Tool

This might be the most powerful section in this entire chapter, and I want you to sit with it.

Rosa is 68. For the first time in her life, she's not limited by her near vision. She can ask ChatGPT to enlarge the text, or to simplify something that's too dense, or to read it aloud. For someone whose eyesight has been declining, this is actually more enabling than any glasses prescription.

But it goes deeper than that.

Rosa has dyslexia. She's lived with it for sixty-eight years. She's incredibly smart, but certain kinds of reading and writing have always been slower for her. Now, she can ask ChatGPT to help her organize her thoughts before she writes. She can read text aloud while looking at the transcript, double encoding that actually helps her brain process better.

"I was ashamed of this for so long," she told me. "I thought I was just stupid. Now I know I'm not. I think differently. And for the first time, I have a tool that works with my brain instead of against it."

This is one of the most important uses of AI, and it doesn't get nearly enough attention.

Live Transcribe, a free tool from Google available for Android phones, transcribes speech in real-time in over 70 languages. For someone who is deaf or hard of hearing, this changes conversations. Not perfectly, it misses things, it misinterprets, but it gives access where there was none before.[80]

Ava is specifically built for captioning phone calls and in-person conversations for Deaf and hard of hearing people. It's not perfect, but it enables connection.[81]

Be My Eyes uses AI to describe images to people who are blind or low vision. Point your phone camera at something, and a combination of AI and human volunteers will tell you what it is.[82]

JAWS (Job Access With Speech) is a screen reader that has been around for decades. It reads web content and applications aloud. Newer versions integrate with AI to provide more intelligent navigation.[83]

Voiceitt uses AI to recognize non-standard speech patterns, voices affected by cerebral palsy, stroke, Parkinson's, other conditions that affect how someone sounds. It translates non-standard speech into standard speech that other voice systems can understand.[84]

Each of these tools removes a barrier. Each one says: "Your disability doesn't have to stop you from doing this thing."

And here's the thing that the tech industry is only beginning to understand: accessibility helps everyone. The captions that were originally built for deaf users? Hearing people use them in loud environments. The voice-to-text technology that helps someone with Parkinson's speak? It helps someone who has their hands full or is driving. The text-to-speech that assists blind users? It helps someone who needs to listen while cooking.

Rosa's discovery that ChatGPT helps with her dyslexia? It also helps her when she's tired. It helps her when she's trying to do something while teaching. It helps her think more clearly across the board.

The best workflows are inclusive workflows. They're designed for how actual humans work, not for a mythical average person who doesn't exist.

If you have a disability, visible or invisible, don't think of AI as something you're permitted to use. Think of it as something built for you. The accessibility capabilities are not secondary features. They're core.

And if you're designing workflows for others (whether you're building systems at work, or helping a parent use a new technology, or writing instructions for a team) think about accessibility from the start. How would this work for someone who can't see the screen? Someone who can't hear the audio? Someone with dyslexia? Someone with ADHD who needs things simplified?

The workflows that work for everyone start by thinking about the people who need the most support.

▶ **TRY THIS NOW: Audit Your AI for Accessibility**

Think about one way you use AI regularly. It could be reading news, writing emails, brainstorming, learning something new—anything.

Now ask yourself:

- 1. What if I couldn't see the screen? (Could I listen to the output with audio?)
- 2. What if I couldn't read quickly? (Could I ask the AI to simplify?)
- 3. What if I couldn't type? (Could I use voice input?)
- 4. What if I got tired easily? (Is this tool speeding me up or slowing me down?)
- 5. What if English wasn't my first language? (Can I ask the AI to explain more simply?)

You don't need to rebuild your entire workflow. But pick one of those questions that resonates with you, and see if your AI tools have features that make it more accessible. They probably do, and you probably haven't noticed.

✦✦✦

Putting It Together

It's a Tuesday morning in March. Rosa wakes up earlier than she needs to, which at 68 is almost never. She has the kind of sleep that comes from peace, she's teaching a class on aging and technology at the community center, and something shifted in her this semester. She's not nervous about it anymore. She knows the material. She knows her students. She knows what she's trying to do.

She makes her café con leche and sits at the kitchen table.

She opens her iPad and runs through her morning routine: three-sentence news briefing (politics, gardening, Colombia), daily timeline, and one teaching idea. Twelve minutes. She knows what her day looks like. She's ready.

By 8:15, she's texted with Marcus, his business has been growing, and Rosa advises him on hiring. He followed his own workflow from Tuesday night: he built an automation that screens job applications into categories, so he's not manually reading fifty bad fits. He's sitting on his porch with a coffee, looking at the ten applications that actually matter.

He sends Rosa a picture of his garden. Hers is blooming a week earlier this year. They trade jokes about the weather.

By 10:00, she's teaching. She's weaving in an idea the AI gave her, she asked her students to describe their biggest barrier to using technology, and she had each one ask ChatGPT the same question. Now they're comparing notes. Why did the AI ask certain clarifying questions? Why did it misunderstand? What did it get right? It's become a lesson about how to work with AI, and also about their own barriers. The class feels alive. It's the kind of teaching she dreamed about, and she's 68 years old, and it's happening now.

At lunch, she gets a message from Priya. Priya has been writing about AI in marketing, and she'd like to use one of Rosa's teaching experiences as an example. Could they talk? Rosa agrees. They're building a friendship across their different worlds. Rosa's classroom, Priya's corporation, bound together by curiosity about how AI actually serves human work.

In the afternoon, Rosa revises her personal AI playbook. She adds a note to her teaching prompt: "Don't ask the AI to give you activities. That's your job as a teacher. Ask the AI to help you think through what your students need, but you design the activity." The distinction is subtle, but it matters. After a few months of using AI, she's gotten much clearer about what she wants from it.

By evening, she has dinner with her son on a video call. They talk about everything: his work, her class, his kids, her garden. As they're winding up, he says, "Nuela, I've been watching how you've learned this stuff. I'm kind of proud of you."

She smiles. Not because an AI told her to smile. But because she's spending her last decades awake and engaged in the world. Because she's learning. Because she's teaching. Because she's connected to people who matter, in her kitchen, in her classroom, in video calls, in text messages and coffee meetings.

The AI is there, woven through. But it's not the point. The point is her life.

This is what a real workflow looks like. Not fancy. Not optimized to its maximum potential. Not following some guru's ten-step system. Just thoughtfully integrated. Questioned regularly. Refined over time. Serving what actually matters.

Your workflow will look different. Marcus's business needs are not Rosa's teaching needs. Priya's marketing challenges are not your life. But the principle is the same:

Use AI to move toward the thinking work. Away from data entry, away from organizing information, away from endless scrolling. Toward decisions that matter. Toward creativity. Toward connection.

Build systems you'll stick with. A morning routine that works is better than a perfect morning routine you never use. An automation that saves one hour per week is better than an automation framework that saves five hours per week but requires a PhD to set up.

Treat it as one tool in a larger life. Not the solution. Not the magic. One tool, alongside people and books and gardens and walking and work that matters.

Stay honest about what you can't outsource. Your judgment. Your values. Your relationships. The decisions that only you can make. Bring the AI in as a thinking partner, but keep yourself at the center.

Build in regular check-ins. Does this still work? Is this still serving my actual life? What would I change?

Rosa does this. Every three months, she reviews her prompts. Every month, she assesses her morning routine, is it still twelve minutes, or have I let it drift? Every week, she decides which newsletter she's going to read.

The workflow is not set it and forget it. It's a living practice. It evolves as your life evolves. When Rosa retires from her teaching role next year, her workflows will change. When Marcus brings on a manager, automation options will shift. When Priya's marketing team scales, her playbook will expand.

This is the final chapter before the conclusion, and I wanted it to be this: practical, grounded, focused on the life you're living.

You've learned to ask good questions. You've learned what tools exist. You've learned to think critically about whether AI is the right answer. You've learned from real people who are doing this.

Now go forward to the part that only you can do: the actual living. The actual building. The actual integration of these tools into the days and weeks and months of your life.

In Chapter 11, we'll look at what's coming next in AI. But I want you to finish this chapter knowing this: you don't have to wait for the next breakthrough. You don't have to understand everything. You don't have to be an expert. You just have to start with one thing (your morning routine, or one automation, or one prompt you write down) and build from there.

Start small. Stay real. Build toward what matters.

That's the workflow that works.

11

WHAT'S COMING NEXT

A grounded look at the near future

Dave Kowalski is standing in a customer's kitchen in Mechanicsburg, Pennsylvania, staring at a dishwasher that won't drain. This is his world, copper pipes and PVC fittings, water pressure and gravity, problems you can see and fix with your hands. He's been a plumber for twenty-three years, and there's a deep satisfaction in the work: something is broken, you figure out why, you make it right.

But Dave has changed since we first met him in Chapter 1.

Back then, he was skeptical. His college-age daughter Megan had shown him ChatGPT over Thanksgiving dinner, and he'd been politely unimpressed. "Great," he'd said. "It can write a poem about plumbing. Can it snake a drain?"

That was two years ago.

Now Dave uses AI every day. Not in dramatic ways (he's not building robots or automating his business with no-code platforms. But he asks ChatGPT to help him write estimates for bigger jobs, because Megan was right: his estimates used to sound like he was filling out a police report. He uses it to troubleshoot unusual problems) last month, a customer had a recirculating system he'd never seen before, and he asked Claude to explain the manufacturer's wiring diagram. He even uses it to draft texts to customers when he's running late, because "Sorry, the job before yours turned into a nightmare" doesn't sound as professional as what the AI suggests.

"I still can't believe I'm saying this," Dave told me recently, "but it's like having a really smart apprentice who knows a little about everything. Doesn't know plumbing worth a damn. But knows how to write, how to explain things, how to think through a problem out loud."

He paused. "What I want to know is: what's next? My daughter keeps telling me things are changing fast. My customers are asking me about smart water heaters and leak detection systems that call your phone. What's actually coming, and what do I need to pay attention to?"

That's the question this chapter answers. Not with science fiction. Not with apocalyptic warnings about robot overlords. Just an honest, grounded look at what's actually arriving in the next one to three years, the stuff that's going to show up in your life whether you're ready or not.

But here's the good news: the single best thing you can do right now to prepare for what's coming is exactly what you've already been doing. If you've been working through this book, you've already built the most important skill for navigating the future of AI: the ability to work with these tools thoughtfully, critically, and on your own terms. The PRIME framework doesn't expire when the next model launches. The habit of verifying AI output, understanding its limitations, and keeping your judgment at the center of the process—that's what separates people who ride the wave from people who get knocked over by it. Everything in this chapter builds on that foundation.

✦✦✦

AI Agents: Your Digital Assistants

Everything we've talked about in this book so far has one thing in common: you ask the AI a question, and it gives you an answer. You're in charge. You type, it responds. You decide what to do with the response.

That's about to change.

The next big shift in AI is something the industry calls "agents." An AI agent doesn't just answer your question, it takes action. You give it a goal, and it figures out the steps, executes them, checks its own work, and comes back to you with results.

Here's what that looks like in practice. Right now, if you want to book a trip, you might ask ChatGPT: "What are the best flights from Philadelphia to Denver next Friday?" It gives you information. You take that information, go to an airline website, compare options, enter your payment details, and book the flight yourself. The AI helped you think. You did the doing.

An AI agent would handle the whole thing. You'd say: "Book me a flight to Denver next Friday, arriving before noon, under $400. Use my United frequent flyer number. I prefer aisle seats." The agent would search flights, compare prices, select the best option based on your preferences, book it, add it to your calendar, and send you a confirmation. You'd approve the final step, the actual purchase, but everything else happened without you.

This isn't hypothetical. It's already starting.

In early 2026, the major AI companies all launched their versions of agents. OpenAI released Operator, which can navigate websites and complete tasks on your behalf, like filling out forms, making purchases, scheduling appointments. Google introduced Project Mariner and Astra, which work inside your browser and across Google's apps. Anthropic built computer-use capabilities into Claude with Claude Desktop, letting it control your screen, opening files, clicking buttons, moving between applications like a very fast, very patient assistant sitting at your desk.[85, 86, 87]

Microsoft embedded agents throughout its entire product suite. Copilot can now draft your emails, schedule your meetings, pull data from your spreadsheets, and create presentations. Not just suggesting content, but building the files and sending them where they need to go.[88]

Dave's daughter Megan is already using some of this. She's a marketing coordinator at a mid-size company in Philadelphia, and she uses an AI agent to monitor her company's social media mentions, draft initial responses, and flag anything that needs a human touch. "It's like having an intern who never sleeps," she told her dad. "Except I have to check its work, because sometimes it's confidently wrong."

That last part is critical. AI agents are powerful, but they inherit every limitation we talked about in Chapter 9. They can hallucinate. They can misunderstand your intent. They can take an action you didn't want. The difference is that when an agent makes a mistake, the consequences can be bigger, because it's not just giving you bad information, it's potentially doing something with that bad information.

Think of it like this: if your GPS gives you wrong directions, you notice and course-correct. But if your GPS were driving the car, that wrong turn could take you somewhere you really don't want to be.

So here's the practical advice for agents, as they become more available over the next year or two:

Start with low-stakes tasks. Let an agent organize your email, draft routine responses, or schedule appointments. Don't hand it your tax return or your medical decisions on day one.

Always keep a human in the loop for anything that matters. The best agents are designed with approval steps, moments where they pause and ask you to confirm before taking an irreversible action. Use those guardrails. Don't turn them off.

Watch for the "automation trust gap." The more an agent does correctly, the more you'll trust it. That's natural. But it means you might stop checking its work on the one task where it makes a serious mistake. Stay engaged, especially for financial transactions, communications sent in your name, or anything involving personal information.

Dave listened to Megan explain all of this and had the most Dave reaction possible: "So it's like hiring a new guy. You don't hand him the complicated jobs on his first day. You start him on simple stuff, watch how he works, and gradually give him more once you trust his judgment."

That's exactly right. And just like a new hire, the agent gets better as it learns your preferences, and you get better at knowing what it can and can't handle.

▶ **TRY THIS NOW: Meet an AI Agent**

If you're curious about what AI agents feel like in practice, here's a safe way to try one:

1. **Open ChatGPT (free tier works).** Ask it to help you plan a dinner party for six people. Give it your dietary restrictions, your budget, and when you're hosting.

2. Instead of accepting its first suggestion, say: *"Now create a shopping list organized by grocery store section, and estimate the total cost."*

3. Then say: *"Create a cooking timeline so everything is ready by 7pm."*

Notice what's happening: you gave it a goal, and it's breaking it into steps and executing them. This is the basic pattern of an agent, goal in, steps out. The difference with true agents is that soon, you'll be able to say all of that in one sentence, and the AI will handle the rest.

✦✦✦

AI in Your Doctor's Office, Car, and Kitchen

AI isn't just living inside your phone and laptop anymore. It's moving into the physical world, the places where you eat, drive, and get medical care. Some of this is already here. Some of it is arriving this year. Almost none of it looks like the robots from the movies.

Your doctor's office. The FDA has now approved over 1,400 AI-enabled medical devices, with nearly 300 new ones cleared in 2025 alone. The vast majority, approximately 76% for radiology, help with diagnosis, not treatment. That means when you get an X-ray, an MRI, or a CT scan, there's a growing chance that an AI system is helping your radiologist spot things that human eyes might miss: tiny tumors, hairline fractures, early signs of disease.[89]

Dave's wife, Maria, experienced this firsthand. During a routine mammogram last fall, the imaging center used an AI screening tool that flagged a cluster of calcifications the radiologist wanted to look at more closely. It turned out to be benign, but the AI caught something that might have been easy to overlook in a busy practice reviewing hundreds of scans a day.

"The technician told me the computer flagged it," Maria said. "I didn't even know they used AI for that. But I'm glad they do."

This is where healthcare AI is making its biggest impact right now: not replacing doctors, but giving them a second pair of eyes. Think of it like spell-check for medical imaging. The doctor still makes the diagnosis. The AI just makes sure nothing gets missed.

That said, remember what we discussed in Chapter 4 about ChatGPT Health: AI still under-triages in emergency situations, and it doesn't know your full medical history the way your doctor does. The AI in your doctor's office is a tool for your doctor, not a replacement for one.

Your car. Self-driving cars have been "five years away" for about fifteen years now. So let me be honest about where things stand in 2026.

Most cars you can buy today operate at what the industry calls Level 2 autonomy. That means the car can steer, accelerate, and brake on its own, but you have to keep your hands on the wheel and your eyes on the road. Tesla's Full Self-Driving, Ford's BlueCruise, and GM's Super Cruise all fall into this category. They're impressive driver-assistance systems. They are not self-driving cars.[90, 91]

True driverless vehicles, no human behind the wheel, exist in limited geographic areas as taxi services. Major companies operate fully driverless robotaxis in a handful of U.S. Cities with growing ride volumes. If you live in one of those cities, you can experience a driverless ride. It works in those specific areas. It's also geographically limited and not something you can buy for your driveway.[92]

As of this writing, fully autonomous robotaxis operate in a

handful of U.S. Cities, but affordable, personally owned autonomous vehicles remain years away for most people.

For Dave, the practical takeaway is this: you're probably not buying a self-driving car anytime soon. But the car you buy next will almost certainly have more AI in it than the one you drive now, better lane-keeping, smarter cruise control, automatic emergency braking that works in more situations, and maybe parking assistance that lets you stand outside the car while it squeezes into a tight spot. These are real, useful improvements. They're just not the science fiction version.

Your kitchen. Smart home technology has been promising to change your life for a decade, and mostly it's given us the ability to yell at a speaker to set a timer. But AI is starting to make smart home devices smart enough.

The newest smart refrigerators can track what's inside, suggest recipes based on ingredients you have, and add items to your shopping list when you're running low. Smart ovens can recognize what you've put inside them and adjust temperature and cooking time automatically. Leak detection systems, this is Dave's territory, can now use AI to learn your home's normal water usage patterns and alert you (or shut off the water) when something looks wrong, potentially preventing thousands of dollars in water damage.

"Those leak detectors are the real deal," Dave said. "I've installed maybe thirty of them in the last year. Customer had one go off at 2 AM, a supply line under the kitchen sink had cracked. The system shut off the water automatically. Saved her floor, her cabinets, probably ten grand in damage. That's AI doing something useful."

The pattern across all of these, healthcare, cars, homes, is the same: AI is most useful when it's embedded in something you already use, doing a specific job better than the non-AI version did. It's least useful (and most overhyped) when it's trying to replace an entire human system that we're not ready to give up control over.

✦✦✦

Jobs and Careers in an AI World

This is the section a lot of you turned to first. I get it. The question of whether AI is going to take your job, or your kid's future job, is the one that keeps people up at night. So let me be as honest as I can.

Here's what the data actually says, as of early 2026:

About 15 percent of U.S. Jobs, roughly 23 million positions, have already crossed a threshold where at least half of their tasks could be automated by AI. That doesn't mean 23 million people are about to be fired. It means the nature of those jobs is changing. The tasks that can be automated are being automated. The humans doing those jobs are being asked to do different things, or in some cases, they're being let go.[93]

Throughout 2025, significant job cuts were explicitly linked to AI. The trend continues into 2026. These numbers are real, and they represent real people.[94]

At the same time, AI is creating jobs. The World Economic Forum estimates that AI will create 170 million new roles globally by 2030. Demand for analytical, technical, and creative positions grew 20 percent after ChatGPT's debut, even as openings for routine, automation-prone roles fell 13 percent.[95]

So which is it? Is AI creating jobs or destroying them?

Both. And the honest answer is that economists don't yet have definitive proof that AI is causing net job loss across the economy as a whole. What they do see is a massive reshuffling, certain kinds of work are declining, while other kinds are growing.[96]

Let me make this concrete with people Dave knows.

His buddy Steve worked as a data entry specialist at an insurance company for eleven years. Last summer, the company implemented an AI system that processes claims forms automatically, reading handwritten notes, extracting key data, entering it into the system. Steve's entire department of twelve people was reduced to three. Steve was one of the nine who were let go.

"It hit him hard," Dave said. "He's fifty-two. He'd been doing the same thing for over a decade. And the company basically said, 'The computer does this now.'"

Steve is back in school now, studying to become a claims adjuster, a job that requires judgment, negotiation, and human relationships. Jobs that AI can't do. But it took him four months of unemployment and a lot of anxiety to get there. The last time Dave talked to him, Steve was halfway through his cybersecurity certification and had already landed two interviews.

On the other side, Dave's daughter Megan was recently promoted. Her ability to use AI tools effectively (to write better copy faster, to analyze data she couldn't have tackled before, to automate routine parts of her job so she could focus on strategy) made her more valuable to her company, not less. She didn't just survive the AI transition. She's thriving in it.

The difference between Steve and Megan isn't intelligence. Steve is smart. The difference is that Steve's job was primarily composed of tasks that AI can now do better and faster, while Megan's job is primarily composed of tasks that AI makes her better at.

This is the key distinction that matters for your career:

If your job is mostly routine tasks with clear rules and predictable inputs, AI is coming for those tasks. Not necessarily your job tomorrow, but the tasks that make up your current role. Data entry, basic bookkeeping, simple customer service scripts, routine document processing, basic content writing to a template. These are the tasks that AI does well and cheaply.

If your job requires judgment, relationships, physical presence, creativity, or navigating ambiguity, AI is more likely to help you than replace you. Plumbers, nurses, teachers, therapists, salespeople, managers, skilled tradespeople, artists, strategic thinkers, these roles involve things that AI is genuinely bad at: reading a room, understanding context that isn't written down, making decisions when the data is incomplete, and building trust with humans.

Dave's plumbing business is a good example. No AI can crawl under a house to find a leaking pipe. No AI can look at the way water stains on a ceiling and instantly diagnose whether it's a roof leak or a plumbing leak based on twenty years of experience. No AI can calm down a panicking homeowner whose basement is flooding.

But AI can help Dave write better estimates, manage his schedule more efficiently, troubleshoot unusual systems, and communicate more professionally with customers. The tasks around his core work get better. The core work itself (the judgment, the craft, the customer relationship) remains human.

Here's what concerns me, and I want to be straight with you about it. The people most vulnerable to AI displacement are often those who can least afford it. Research from UNC Kenan-Flagler Business School found that 79 percent of employed women in the U.S. work in jobs with high automation risk, compared to 58 percent of men. Entry-level positions, disproportionately filled by younger workers, are especially exposed. If you're just starting your career, the job you're training for may look very different by the time you're established in it.[97]

I don't say this to scare you. I say it because the people selling you on AI are usually the ones who benefit from its adoption. They have every incentive to tell you it's all going to be fine. I want to tell you the truth: it will be fine for many people, but it will be hard for some people, and the difference often comes down to preparation and adaptability. Not talent or intelligence.[98]

Which brings us to the most important question: what can you do about it?

▶ **TRY THIS NOW: Assess Your Own AI Exposure**

Take ten minutes with this exercise. It's not meant to scare you, it's meant to help you think clearly.

1. List the five tasks you spend the most time on at work. Be specific. Not "my job" but the actual activities: writing reports, entering data, responding to emails, managing schedules, visiting clients, etc.

2. For each task, ask: Could AI do this today? Rate it: Easily / Partially / Not really.

3. For each task rated "Easily" or "Partially," ask: What part of this task requires my human judgment? That's where your value is. That's what you should be developing.

4. For each task rated "Not really," ask: Could AI make me

better at this? Maybe AI can't do the task, but it can help you prepare, research, or communicate about it.

This exercise doesn't predict the future. But it helps you see where the future is likely to push, and it points you toward the skills and tasks that make you harder to replace.

✦✦✦

The Skills That Will Matter Most

If AI can write a decent email, create a passable report, and generate a serviceable marketing plan, what's left for humans to be good at?

More than you think.

The skills that are becoming more valuable in an AI world are, ironically, the most human ones. They're the things that AI is famously terrible at, and they're the things that have always separated good professionals from great ones.

Judgment. The ability to look at a situation with incomplete information and make a good call. AI can give you data, analysis, and options. But deciding which option is right (given your specific context, your values, your understanding of the people involved) that's judgment. Dave exercises judgment every day when he decides whether a pipe needs to be repaired or replaced. A doctor exercises it when she decides which test to order. A parent exercises it when she decides how to handle a child's lie. AI can inform your judgment. It cannot replace it.

Communication. Not just writing. AI can write. Real communication: the ability to listen to what someone isn't saying, to adjust your message based on who's receiving it, to have a difficult conversation with empathy, to persuade someone by understanding what they care about. Megan's promotion came partly because she's exceptional at explaining AI-generated insights to executives who don't understand AI. She translates between machines and humans. That skill is gold.

Adaptability. The pace of change means that what you know today may be less relevant in three years. The willingness to learn new tools, develop new skills, and pivot when circumstances change is becoming the most valuable career trait. Business leaders increasingly describe adaptability as the new job security. Dave learned ChatGPT in his fifties. Steve is going back to school at fifty-two. Rosa picked up AI at sixty-six. None of them found it easy. All of them did it anyway.

Deep subject expertise. Here's a paradox: the more AI spreads, the more valuable deep knowledge becomes. AI tools need informed humans to guide them, evaluate their outputs, and apply results in real-world contexts. A lawyer who understands contract law deeply can use AI to draft contracts ten times faster, but only because she knows what a good contract looks like. An AI without that expertise produces plausible-looking garbage. Dave's twenty-three years of plumbing experience aren't threatened by AI. They're amplified by it.

Empathy and emotional intelligence. The ability to understand what someone else is feeling, to connect with them, to make them feel heard. AI chatbots can simulate empathy. They cannot feel it. And humans can tell the difference. Every customer who calls Dave in a panic because their bathroom is flooding needs a human on the other end of the line who says, "I understand. I'm on my way." That's not a skill AI will replace.

Critical thinking. The ability to evaluate whether something is true, useful, and relevant. This has always mattered, but it matters more now because AI generates plausible-sounding nonsense at an extraordinary rate. Knowing how to question an AI's output (to ask "Is this actually right?" rather than accepting it because it sounds confident) is a meta-skill that applies to every job and every part of your life.

If you're a parent wondering what to tell your kids about the future, here's what I'd say: Learn to use AI tools, yes. But invest more in learning to think critically, communicate clearly, work with people, and develop deep expertise in something you care about. Those skills were valuable before AI. They'll be valuable after it. And they're the ones that will determine whether AI is your tool or your replacement.

Dave said it better than I could: "Megan's good with the AI stuff, and that's great. But what makes her good at her job is that she's smart, she works hard, she's good with people, and she pays attention. The AI just makes all of that more powerful."

✦✦✦

Staying Human in a Machine Age

I want to tell you about a Saturday morning at Dave's house.

It's early spring. Dave is in his backyard with his neighbor, Jim, trying to figure out why the rain garden they built last year isn't draining properly. They're standing ankle-deep in mud, arguing about slope angles and soil composition. Dave thinks the issue is compacted clay underneath. Jim thinks the downspout is overwhelming the bed during heavy rain.

Dave could pull out his phone and ask ChatGPT. He's done it before for trickier problems. But he doesn't. Because this (standing in the mud with a friend, turning a problem over together, the satisfaction of figuring something out with your own hands and eyes) this is the good stuff. This is the part of life that doesn't need to be optimized.

We've spent this entire book learning how to use AI effectively. How to ask good questions. How to build workflows. How to think critically about what AI can and can't do. And all of that matters.

But I want to close with something that matters more.

AI is a tool. It's a powerful tool, maybe the most powerful tool most of us will encounter in our lifetimes. But it is a tool. It exists to serve your life, not to become your life.

The things that make life meaningful (connection with people you love, work that engages your mind and your hands, creative expression that comes from your own experience, the slow process of learning something difficult, the satisfaction of helping someone who needs it) none of these are improved by automating them. They're improved by being more present for them.

AI can help you be more present. That's the best case for it. If AI handles the tedious parts of your work, you have more energy for the meaningful parts. If AI helps you organize your thoughts, you can have clearer conversations. If AI gives you back two hours a week that you used to spend on data entry, those two hours can go toward something you actually care about.

But AI can also make you less present. If you're constantly checking what the AI thinks, you might stop trusting your own judgment. If you outsource every piece of writing to a chatbot, you might lose the ability to express yourself in your own voice. If you use AI to avoid the struggle of learning something new, you might miss the growth that comes from that struggle.

The balance is yours to find.

Rosa found hers. Twelve minutes in the morning with her AI routine, then a full day of teaching, gardening, calling her son, living her life. The AI is a thin thread woven through her days, useful, time-bound, in service of what actually matters.

Marcus found his. AI and automation handle the busywork of running his landscaping company. But the dirt under his fingernails, the conversations with clients, the pride of a job done right, those are still his.

Priya found hers. AI makes her marketing team more productive. But the creative breakthroughs, the strategic insights, the mentoring of her junior staff, those come from Priya being fully human, fully present.

Dave is still finding his. And that's fine. You don't have to have it figured out. You just have to stay thoughtful about it.

"You know what I keep coming back to?" Dave said, sitting on his back porch after a long day of service calls. Megan was home for the weekend, and they were grilling burgers, something Dave is very particular about, because he considers grilling to be an art form that no AI could replicate. (He's probably right.)

"I keep coming back to the fact that none of this stuff matters if you lose the plot. The AI can make me a better plumber, sure. It can help me write better, think more clearly, maybe even grow my business. But if I'm spending my whole life staring at a screen asking a computer what to do next, what's the point? The point is the work.

The point is Megan. The point is this." He gestured at the grill, the backyard, the evening light.

"The point is this," Megan agreed. She put her phone down.

✦✦✦

Your Invitation

We started this book with a question: What is AI, really?

Now you know. It's a tool that can write, analyze, create, organize, and soon take actions on your behalf. It's powerful and imperfect. It's changing how we work, learn, create, and communicate. And it's here to stay.

But you also know something more important: you're not a passive bystander in this. You're not at the mercy of technology companies and their timelines. You have agency. You have the PRIME framework. You have the practical skills you've built chapter by chapter. You have a clearer understanding of what AI can do, what it can't, and where the line is between useful tool and lazy crutch.

So here's my challenge to you.

In the next seven days, do one thing with AI that you haven't done before. Not something you read about in this book and thought, "That's interesting." Something you try. Ask it to help you with a real problem. Use it to learn something you've been curious about. Let it help you write something you've been putting off. Build one small automation. Have one conversation with it that surprises you.

In the next thirty days, teach someone else. Show a friend, a parent, a colleague, a neighbor. Sit with them the way Megan sat with Dave. The way Rosa's granddaughter sat with Rosa. AI literacy spreads person to person, not through marketing campaigns. You now know enough to be someone's guide.

In the next year, stay curious. The tools will change. New capabilities will emerge. Some of what I've written in this book will be outdated by the time you read it, that's the nature of this field. But the principles won't change: ask good questions, think critically about the answers, keep a human in the loop, and use AI to move toward the work that matters, not away from it.

And please, visit the companion website at practicalaibook.ai. It exists because books are static and AI is not. The screenshots will be current. The tool comparisons will be updated. The prompt library will grow. It's this book's way of staying honest in a world that keeps moving.

Dave walked me to the door after that Saturday evening. The burgers were done, the dishes were someone else's problem (Megan's, as it happened), and the spring air had that quality it gets when the sun is low and the world seems briefly, perfectly still.

"Thanks for including me in the book," he said. "I still don't totally get all of it. But I get enough. And I'm not scared of it anymore. That's the big thing. I'm not scared of it."

He shook my hand.

"Now if you'll excuse me, I've got a dishwasher to fix in the morning. And no, the AI is not going to help me with that one."

He grinned.

I hope this book has done for you what it did for Dave: not made you an expert, but made you unafraid. Not given you all the answers, but given you the confidence to ask better questions. Not turned you into a technologist, but shown you that you don't have to be one to use these tools well.

The future is coming. It's not as scary as the headlines suggest, and it's not as magical as the advertisements promise. It's just a set of tools, waiting for you to pick them up and use them in service of the life you're actually living.

Sofia Ramirez, for what it's worth, still parks both cars in that garage.

Start small. Stay real. Stay human.

AI TOOL COMPARISON CHART

A REGULARLY-UPDATED REFERENCE FOR CHOOSING THE RIGHT TOOL

This appendix provides a snapshot of popular AI tools as of early 2026. Features, pricing, and capabilities change frequently. For the most up-to-date information, pricing, and new tools that have emerged since publication, visit practicalaibook.ai/appendix/a where we maintain current comparisons and recommendations.

GENERAL-PURPOSE AI ASSISTANTS

ChatGPT (OpenAI)

Best For: Versatile all-rounder
Free Tier: Yes (GPT-4o limited)
Paid Price: $20/mo (Plus)
Key Strength: Largest ecosystem, plugins, image generation

Claude (Anthropic)

Best For: Long documents, nuanced writing
Free Tier: Yes (limited)

Paid Price: $20/mo (Pro)
Key Strength: Thoughtful analysis, 200K context window

Gemini (Google)
Best For: Google integration, multimodal
Free Tier: Yes (with Google account)
Paid Price: $20/mo (Advanced)
Key Strength: Deep Google Workspace integration

Grok (xAI)
Best For: Real-time news and social media insights
Free Tier: Yes (limited prompts)
Paid Price: $10/mo (SuperGrok Lite) / $30/mo (SuperGrok)
Key Strength: Built into X (Twitter), live access to trending posts and breaking news

Microsoft Copilot
Best For: Office productivity
Free Tier: Yes (basic)
Paid Price: $20/mo (Pro)
Key Strength: Built into Word, Excel, PowerPoint

Perplexity
Best For: Research with sources
Free Tier: Yes (limited)
Paid Price: $20/mo (Pro)
Key Strength: Always cites sources, real-time web search

IMAGE GENERATION TOOLS

GPT-4o Image Gen (via ChatGPT)
Best For: Easy text-to-image
Free Tier: Included with ChatGPT
Paid Price: Included

Key Strength: Natural language prompts, integrated chat

Midjourney
Best For: Artistic, stylized images
Free Tier: No
Paid Price: $10/mo (Basic)
Key Strength: Stunning aesthetic quality

Adobe Firefly
Best For: Commercial-safe images
Free Tier: Limited free credits
Paid Price: $4.99/mo (Premium)
Key Strength: Trained on licensed content, Photoshop integration

Canva Magic Design
Best For: Quick social/marketing graphics
Free Tier: Yes (limited)
Paid Price: $13/mo (Pro)
Key Strength: Templates + AI, no design skills needed

Ideogram
Best For: Text in images, logos
Free Tier: Yes (limited)
Paid Price: $8/mo (Basic)
Key Strength: Best at rendering text in images accurately

SPECIALIZED AI TOOLS

Otter.ai
Category: Meeting notes
What It Does: Transcribes and summarizes meetings
Price Range: Free–$16.99/mo

Grammarly

Category: Writing
What It Does: Grammar, tone, clarity suggestions
Price Range: Free–$12/mo

Descript
Category: Audio/Video
What It Does: Edit audio/video by editing text transcript
Price Range: Free–$24/mo

Suno
Category: Music
What It Does: Generate original songs from text descriptions
Price Range: Free–$10/mo

Notion AI
Category: Productivity
What It Does: AI writing and organization inside Notion
Price Range: $10/mo add-on

Zapier
Category: Automation
What It Does: Connects apps with no-code automations
Price Range: Free–$19.99/mo

✦✦✦

HOW TO CHOOSE

Start with free. Every major AI tool offers a free tier worth exploring. There's no risk in trying ChatGPT, Claude, Gemini, or Perplexity for a week to see which one matches how you think and work.

Match the tool to your existing ecosystem. If you live in Google Workspace, start with Gemini. If you're deep in Microsoft Office, Copilot is built right in. If you're platform-agnostic, any of the general-purpose tools work well.

You don't need them all. Pick one general-purpose AI assistant and learn it inside out. Master one tool at 80% before chasing five tools at 20%. Depth beats breadth.

Paid tiers pay for themselves once you use AI daily. If you're experimenting, free is enough. If you're using AI several times per day for work or projects, the $20/month for Pro access to a flagship tool (ChatGPT Plus, Claude Pro, etc.) is a bargain.

Stay current. Visit practicalaibook.ai/tools for the latest pricing, new tools that have emerged, and honest comparisons based on real usage.

✦✦✦

Prices and features change frequently. Visit practicalaibook.ai/appendix/a for the most current version of this chart.

PROMPT LIBRARY

50+ READY-TO-USE PROMPTS ORGANIZED BY CATEGORY

The prompts in this library are designed to be copied and used immediately. For each prompt, replace any text in [brackets] with your specific details. These prompts are built on the PRIME framework from Chapter 3, feel free to adjust them using those principles if you want different results.

Many of these prompts build on examples from earlier chapters. Where applicable, we've noted which chapter introduced that type of prompt so you can find the full context.

You'll find all prompts right here in this appendix—ready to copy, just fill in the bracketed details. We also maintain an updated, searchable version at practicalaibook.ai/prompts, where we'll add new prompts as AI capabilities evolve.

✦✦✦

HOME & DAILY LIFE

The Family Meal Planner

Use case: Plan a week of dinners that fit your budget and family preferences

> You're a nutritionist who specializes in budget-conscious family meal planning. I'm planning dinners for a family of [number]. Here's who we are: [describe each person]. Budget: $[amount] per week. Give me a week of dinners with a combined grocery list organized by store section.

The Pantry Clean Out

Use case: Create meals using what you already have at home

> Here's what I currently have in my fridge and pantry: [list items]. I need to make [number] meals from what I already have, only buying up to $[amount] of additional groceries. Give me recipes that use what's on hand first.

The Travel Planner

Use case: Build a day-by-day itinerary within your budget

> You're a travel agent specializing in family vacations. Plan a 5-day trip to [destination] for two adults and [X] kids ages [ages]. Budget is [amount] not including flights. Present as day-by-day itinerary with estimated costs.

The Decluttering Project Manager

Use case: Organize a room or space with a phased plan

> I have a [space] that's about [size]. It's full of [describe contents]. Give me a phased decluttering plan with timelines, a decision tree for keep/sell/donate/trash, and storage solution recommendations.

The Lab Results Translator

Use case: Understand your medical test results in plain language

> Here are my lab results: [paste values — remove name and identifying info]. Explain what each number means in plain English. Are any outside the normal range? Give me 5 questions to ask my doctor.

The Gift Finder

Use case: Generate creative gift ideas for someone specific

> I need a gift for [person]. They're [age], they love [interests], they hate [things to avoid], and my budget is [amount]. Give me 10 ideas ranging from practical to creative.

The Explainer

Use case: Understand complex topics in plain language

> Explain [complex topic] to me like I'm a smart adult who knows nothing about this subject. Use everyday analogies. Don't use jargon. Keep it under 300 words.

The Fitness Routine Builder

Use case: Create a personalized, progressive fitness plan

> I want to build a fitness routine. I'm [age], [fitness level], with [injuries/limitations]. I can work out [frequency] for [duration]. Goals: [describe]. Create a routine that's safe and progressively challenging.

✦✦✦

WORK & PROFESSIONAL

The Email Drafter

Use case: Write clear, professional emails with the right tone

> Write a [tone] email to [recipient] about [topic]. Include [specific points]. Keep it under [word count]. End with [call to action].

The Tricky Reply

Use case: Handle difficult email situations gracefully

> I need to write an email to [person/role] about [situation]. Here's what happened: [backstory]. I want the email to [list goals]. Tone: [style]. Keep under [word count].

The Thread Summarizer

Use case: Extract the key points from long email conversations

> I was CCed on this email thread with [number] messages. Summarize: what happened, what was decided, and what I need to do. Keep to 5 bullet points.

The Agenda Builder

Use case: Create a structured agenda for productive meetings

> I'm meeting with [who] for [duration] about [topic]. We need to [list objectives]. Generate a detailed agenda with timeboxes. Include a parking lot for off-topic items.

The Transcript Processor

Use case: Turn meeting notes into action items and follow-ups

> Here's a transcript of our meeting about [topic]. Give me: key decisions made, action items with owners and deadlines, unresolved items, and a follow-up email I can send.

The Competitive Analysis

Use case: Research competitors and identify market opportunities

> You're a market research analyst in [industry]. Analyze [companies]. For each: key products, target market, pricing, recent moves, and vulnerabilities. Present as comparison table.

The Report Generator

Use case: Create professional reports from raw data

> Here are our [time period] metrics: [data]. Write a report for [audience]. Include: executive summary, performance, comparison to previous period, key wins, and recommendations.

The Meeting Prep

Use case: Prepare talking points and anticipate objections

> I have a meeting about [topic] with [who]. Give me 5 talking points, 3 questions to ask, and 2 potential objections to prepare for. Format as a one-page cheat sheet.

✦✦✦

PARENTING & EDUCATION

The Socratic Tutor

Use case: Guide students to answers through guided questions

> I'm a [grade level] student working on [subject]. Don't give me the answer. Ask questions that help me figure it out myself. Start by asking what I already know.

The Math Tutor

Use case: Build problem-solving skills without giving answers away

> I'm a [grade level] student working on [math topic]. Walk me through problem-solving steps without giving the answer. When I'm stuck, give a hint, not the solution.

The Lesson Plan Generator

Use case: Create structured, engaging lesson plans

> I'm teaching a [grade level] [subject] unit on [topic]. Create a [number]-day lesson plan with hands-on activity, group discussion, individual reflection, and formative assessment.

The Age-Appropriate Explainer

Use case: Explain topics at a child's level

> Explain [topic] in a way that a [age]-year-old would understand. Use examples from their world—school, friends, games, animals. Keep it to 3–4 sentences.

The Homework Tutor

Use case: Help kids learn rather than just getting answers

> You're a patient tutor for a [grade level] student. My child is struggling with [topic]. Don't give the answer—guide them step by step with questions.

The Test/Quiz Study Partner

Use case: Practice for exams with progressive difficulty

> I have a [subject] test on [topic] on [date]. Quiz me on key concepts. Start easier and get harder. When I get something wrong, explain why.

The AI-Resistant Assignment Designer

Use case: Create assignments that require genuine thinking

> I'm designing a [subject] assignment for [grade level] on [topic]. Help me create one that requires personal experience or multi-step reasoning AI can't fake.

✦✦✦

SMALL BUSINESS

Social Media Calendar

Use case: Plan a month of engaging social media posts

> You're my marketing assistant for [Business Name], a [type] in [location]. I need a social media calendar for [month] with

daily posts. Alternate between: before-and-after, seasonal tips, testimonials, and behind-the-scenes.

Email Response Templates

Use case: Create consistent, professional email responses

> I need email templates for my [type of business]. Create templates for: follow-up after estimate, service delay notification, seasonal reminder, payment reminder, thank-you with review request, and complaint response.

Job Description

Use case: Write an honest job listing that attracts the right people

> I'm hiring a [role] for my [business] in [location]. The role involves [describe]. I don't require [degree]—I train people. I do require: [qualities]. Write an honest job description, about 300 words.

Interview Questions

Use case: Prepare questions that reveal if someone's a good fit

> I'm hiring for [role]. My main concerns: reliability, teamwork, willingness to learn, handling [demands], quality focus. Write 10 conversational interview questions that reveal these qualities.

FAQ Page

Use case: Turn common questions into a polished FAQ

I own a [business] in [location]. Here are questions my team gets constantly with rough answers: [paste]. Turn into a professional FAQ. Clean up language, organize by category.

Standard Operating Procedure

Use case: Document a process so anyone can follow it

Create a standard operating procedure for [task] at my [business]. Here's what we do: [describe]. Write step-by-step that a new employee could follow. Include safety notes and time estimates.

Negative Review Response

Use case: Reply professionally to critical feedback

Help me respond to this negative review: "[paste]". Write a professional response that thanks them, acknowledges frustration without admitting fault, offers to resolve, and invites direct contact.

Estimate/Proposal Writing

Use case: Create a professional estimate for a client

I run a [business]. I need to write an estimate for a client who wants [job]. Include: description, timeline, price breakdown, what's included/not, and a personal touch.

✦✦✦

CREATIVE PROJECTS

Plot Brainstorming

Use case: Develop story ideas that surprise readers

> My protagonist is [describe situation]. Here are three constraints: [list]. What are eight possible decisions she could make, and what would happen? Think surprising, not obvious.

Scene Editing

Use case: Strengthen scenes for emotional impact

> I'm going to paste a scene. Tell me: What's the emotional core? Where is the conflict? What could be stronger? What's missing that would make the reader feel something?

Dialogue Coaching

Use case: Write natural dialogue that reveals character

> My character is trying to [goal], and the other character is trying to [goal]. Write a conversation where both say what they actually feel. Make it natural, not theatrical.

Nonfiction Outlining

Use case: Structure essays and articles for clarity

> I want to write a [blog post/essay/article] about [topic]. My main argument is [thesis]. My audience is [describe]. Help me outline with a compelling opening, 3–4 sections, and strong conclusion.

Custom Image Generation

Use case: Create images for projects or presentations

> Create an image for [purpose]. It should show [subject]. [Style] style. [Lighting]. [Mood/feeling]. [Color palette].

Background Music

Use case: Generate instrumental tracks for videos or focus

> A [mood] instrumental [genre] track. [Instruments]. [Tempo]. Good for [use]. No vocals.

Wedding Toast/Speech

Use case: Craft a meaningful speech for special occasions

> I'm writing a [type of speech] for [person]. They are [describe]. I want it [funny/emotional/both]. About [length]. Help me brainstorm key stories and suggest structure.

✦✦✦

SAFETY & VERIFICATION

Privacy Policy Analyzer

Use case: Understand what a company does with your data

> I'm pasting a privacy policy from [company]. Explain in plain English: what data they collect, how long they keep it, who they share with, can I opt out, what happens if I delete my account.

Verify a Claim

Use case: Think critically about something you read

> I read the following claim: "[paste]". Help me think critically: What would verify this? What are reliable sources to check? Red flags? Most likely alternative explanation if false?

Check AI's Own Work

Use case: Understand where AI is confident or uncertain

> After you answer, rate your confidence (high/medium/low), tell me which parts you're most and least sure about, and suggest 2–3 sources to verify independently.

Analyze a Suspicious Message

Use case: Detect scams and phishing attempts

> I received this message and I'm not sure if it's legitimate or a scam. [Paste]. Check for: urgency tactics, unusual payment requests, suspicious links, impersonation.

Evaluate a News Article

Use case: Assess the trustworthiness of a news story

> Help me evaluate this article: Does it cite sources? Emotional manipulation? What's missing? How could I verify key claims? Trustworthiness 1–10?

✦✦✦

GETTING STARTED & LEARNING

First Contact

Use case: Understand what AI can help you with

> Hi, I'm new to AI and just setting things up. Can you tell me what you're best at?

Simple Factual Question

Use case: Get reliable information on straightforward topics

> What's the difference between baking soda and baking powder?

Refinement Follow-Up

Use case: Adjust results to match what you need

> That's good, but make it a little less formal. I actually like my landlord—I just want the dishwasher fixed.

Interview Practice Partner

Use case: Prepare for job interviews with realistic practice

> I have a job interview for [position] tomorrow. Act as the interviewer and ask me tough questions one at a time. After five questions, give me feedback.

AI Job Exposure Self-Assessment

Use case: Understand how AI might affect your work

> I work as [title] in [industry]. My main daily tasks are: [list]. For each, assess: How likely AI could automate it in 1–3 years? What part requires human judgment? How could AI make me better?

Career Skills Gap Analysis

Use case: Plan your professional development with AI in mind

> I'm a [title] with [X] years of experience. Help me identify: 3 skills to develop, 1 way to use AI in my current role, 1 adjacent specialization that would make me harder to replace.

✦✦✦

BUILDING YOUR OWN PROMPT LIBRARY

The best prompts are the ones you customize for your own needs. As you work through this book, you'll develop favorite patterns and approaches. Save these, build your own library. The prompts here are a starting point, not the destination.

For an updated library, additional prompts shared by readers, and tools to organize your own collection, visit practicalai-book.ai/prompts.

GLOSSARY

Every technical term in this book, explained in plain English

This glossary covers every technical term used in this book. We've kept the definitions simple and practical: this is a glossary for real people, not a computer science textbook. Terms are listed alphabetically.

A

AI (Artificial Intelligence): Software that can learn from examples and make decisions or predictions. Think of it as a very fast pattern-recognition engine, not a thinking brain.
AI Agent: An AI system that can take actions on your behalf, not just answer questions. Like having a digital assistant that can actually book your restaurant reservation, not just tell you where to eat.
Algorithm: A set of step-by-step instructions a computer follows to solve a problem. A recipe is an algorithm for making dinner.
API (Application Programming Interface): A way for different software programs to talk to each other. When your weather app gets data from a weather service, it's using an API.
Automation: Setting up tasks to happen automatically without you

doing them manually each time. Like setting your coffee maker on a timer, but for digital tasks.

B

Bias (in AI): When an AI system consistently favors certain outcomes over others, usually because the data it learned from was skewed. Like a restaurant reviewer who only eats Italian food: their "best restaurant" list will be biased.
Bot: A software program that performs automated tasks. Chatbots are bots designed to have conversations.

C

Chatbot: An AI program you interact with through conversation, like ChatGPT or Claude. You type (or speak), it responds.
ChatGPT: An AI assistant made by OpenAI. One of the most popular and versatile AI tools, capable of text, image generation, and more.
Claude: An AI assistant made by Anthropic. Known for thoughtful, nuanced responses and the ability to work with very long documents.
Context Window: The amount of text an AI can "remember" in a single conversation. Like a desk: the bigger the desk, the more papers you can spread out and reference at once.
Copilot: Microsoft's AI assistant, built into Windows, Office, and Edge. Designed to help with productivity tasks inside Microsoft products.

D

DALL-E: An AI image generator made by OpenAI (available through ChatGPT). You describe what you want in words, and it creates an image.
Data: Information like numbers, text, images, anything a computer can process. AI learns by processing enormous amounts of data.
Deep Learning: A type of machine learning that uses layers of artifi-

cial "neurons" to find complex patterns. It's what powers most modern AI, from voice assistants to image generators.
Deepfake: AI-generated fake video, audio, or images of real people. The technology that can make it look like someone said or did something they never actually did.

F

Fine-Tuning: Taking a general AI model and training it further on specific data to make it better at a particular task. Like a general contractor who takes extra courses in kitchen remodeling.
Foundation Model: A large AI model trained on massive amounts of data that can be adapted for many different tasks. ChatGPT, Claude, and Gemini are all built on foundation models.

G

Gemini: Google's AI assistant. Tightly integrated with Google services like Gmail, Docs, and Search.
Generative AI: AI that creates new content like text, images, music, code: rather than just analyzing existing content. When ChatGPT writes you an email or DALL-E creates an image, that's generative AI.
GPT (Generative Pre-trained Transformer): The technology behind ChatGPT. A type of AI architecture that's particularly good at understanding and generating human language.
Grok: An AI assistant made by xAI, Elon Musk's AI company. It's available through the Grok app and on X (formerly Twitter). It can answer questions, generate images and video, and hold voice conversations, with a notable ability to search the web in real time for current information.
GUARD Framework: The safety framework taught in Chapter 9: Get the facts, Understand the source, Assess the risk, Research independently, Defend and educate others. A practical method for protecting yourself from AI-related scams, misinformation, and privacy risks. Developed by Colossal LLC.

H

Hallucination: When an AI confidently states something that's completely wrong. It's not lying on purpose, it's generating text that sounds right based on patterns, even when the facts don't check out. Always verify important information.

I

IDEA Loop: Part of the PRIME framework (Chapter 3): Imagine what perfect looks like, Diagnose the gap, Enhance with specific instructions, Act on the result. A systematic way to improve AI output.

IFTTT (If This Then That): A no-code automation platform. "If this happens, then do that": like "if I get an email from my boss, send me a text notification."

Image Generation: Using AI to create images from text descriptions. You describe what you want in words, and the AI produces a picture.

L

Large Language Model (LLM): The technology behind modern AI chatbots. A massive AI system trained on billions of words of text to understand and generate human language. Think of it as an incredibly well-read assistant that's read most of the internet.

M

Machine Learning: A type of AI that learns from examples rather than following pre-written rules. Instead of programming "if temperature > 90, say it's hot," you show the system thousands of weather reports and let it figure out the pattern.

Midjourney: An AI image generation tool known for producing especially artistic and stylized images. Accessed through Discord.

Model: In AI, the trained system that does the actual work. When people say "GPT-4" or "Claude 3," they're referring to specific models.

Multimodal: An AI that can work with multiple types of input: text, images, audio, video. Like being able to show your AI a photo and ask questions about it.

N

Nano Banana: Google's AI-powered image generator and photo editor, built into the Gemini app and Google Search. Type a description of what you want, or upload a photo and describe how you'd like it changed, and Nano Banana creates or edits the image for you. As of 2026, the latest version is Nano Banana 2, powered by Google's Gemini models.

Natural Language Processing (NLP): The branch of AI focused on understanding human language. It's why you can talk to AI in normal sentences instead of computer code.

Neural Network: An AI system loosely inspired by how brain cells connect. Layers of mathematical "neurons" that process information and learn patterns. The foundation of most modern AI.

No-Code: Tools that let you build automations or simple apps without writing any programming code. Drag-and-drop interfaces for non-programmers.

O

Open Source: Software whose code is publicly available for anyone to use, modify, and share. Some AI models are open source, meaning anyone can run them.

P

Parameter: A setting or value the AI learns during training. When people say a model has "175 billion parameters," they're describing its complexity. More parameters generally means more capable, but also more expensive to run.

Perplexity: An AI-powered search engine that answers questions with cited sources. Like Google Search meets ChatGPT.
Plugin: An add-on that gives an AI tool extra capabilities, like accessing the web, reading files, or connecting to other services.
PRIME Framework: The prompting method taught in this book: Prompt (build with the 5-Part Formula), Refine (treat first response as a draft), IDEA (Imagine-Diagnose-Enhance-Act loop), Master (fine-tune details), Execute (put the result to work). Developed by Colossal LLC.
Prompt: The text you type into an AI tool to tell it what you want. The better your prompt, the better your results. Think of it as giving instructions to a very capable but very literal assistant.
Prompt Engineering: The skill of crafting effective prompts to get the best results from AI. What Chapter 3 of this book teaches you.

R

RAG (Retrieval-Augmented Generation): A technique where AI searches through specific documents before answering, so its response is based on real information rather than just its training data. Like an assistant who checks the filing cabinet before answering your question.

S

Smart Speaker: A device like Amazon Echo or Google Nest that uses AI to respond to voice commands.
Suno: An AI tool that generates original music from text descriptions. Describe the mood, genre, and style, and it creates a song.

T

Temperature: A setting that controls how creative or random an AI's responses are. Low temperature = predictable and focused. High temperature = creative and surprising. Like a dial between "play it safe" and "get weird."

Token: The basic unit AI uses to process text. Roughly, one token equals about three-quarters of a word. When AI tools have limits, they're usually measured in tokens.

Training Data: The information an AI learned from. ChatGPT was trained on billions of words from books, websites, and other text. The quality and breadth of training data shapes what the AI knows and how it responds.

Transformer: The AI architecture that powers most modern language models (the "T" in GPT). A breakthrough in how computers process sequences of text.

V

Voice Cloning: AI technology that can replicate a person's voice using just a few seconds of recorded audio. Used legitimately in entertainment and accessibility, but also exploited in scams where criminals impersonate family members or colleagues. See Chapter 9 for how to protect yourself.

Voice Assistant: An AI you interact with by speaking, like Siri, Alexa, or Google Assistant.

Z

Zapier: A popular no-code automation platform that connects different apps and services. "When X happens in App A, automatically do Y in App B."

Zero-Shot Learning: When an AI performs a task it wasn't specifically trained for, just from your description. Like asking someone who's never played chess to figure out the rules by watching one game, except AI is surprisingly good at it.

RESOURCES & FURTHER READING

CURATED RECOMMENDATIONS FOR READERS WHO WANT TO GO DEEPER

This is a hand-picked list of resources for continuing your AI journey. We've focused on sources that share our philosophy: practical, accessible, and honest about both the potential and the limitations. Everything here is free unless noted.

The AI landscape changes fast. For our most current recommendations, visit practicalaibook.ai/resources. We update this list monthly.

Newsletters

The Batch (deeplearning.ai/the-batch)

Andrew Ng's weekly newsletter. The most readable summary of AI news, written by one of the field's most respected educators. Free.

TLDR AI (tldr.tech/ai)

A daily 5-minute newsletter covering AI news, tools, and research. Skimmable and well-curated. Free.

Superhuman (superhumanai.com)

Practical AI tips, tools, and use cases delivered weekly. Focused on productivity. Free.

Ben's Bites (bensbites.com)

Daily roundup of AI developments with a friendly, accessible tone. Great for keeping up without feeling overwhelmed. Free.

One Useful Thing (oneusefulthing.org)

Ethan Mollick's blog and newsletter. Thoughtful, research-backed takes on how AI affects work, education, and daily life. Free.

✦✦✦

YouTube Channels

Matt Wolfe (youtube.com/@mreflow)

Weekly roundups of new AI tools with hands-on demos. Great for seeing tools in action before you try them.

AI Explained (youtube.com/@aiexplained-official)

In-depth but accessible explanations of AI developments. The channel for understanding the "why" behind the headlines.

Fireship (youtube.com/@Fireship)

Fast-paced tech explainers, including excellent AI coverage. Each video is under 10 minutes and packed with information.

The AI Advantage (youtube.com/@TheAIAdvantage)

Practical tutorials on using AI tools for everyday tasks. Step-by-step walkthroughs you can follow along with.

✦✦✦

Podcasts

Hard Fork (nytimes.com/hard-fork)

Kevin Roose and Casey Newton discuss the week in tech, with substantial AI coverage. Entertaining and informative.

Practical AI (changelog.com/practicalai)

Making AI practical, productive, and accessible. Interviews with researchers and practitioners.

Latent Space (latent.space)

More technical but excellent for readers who want to go deeper. Interviews with the people building AI.

✦✦✦

Online Communities

r/ChatGPT (reddit.com/r/ChatGPT)

Active community sharing tips, prompts, and use cases. Good for seeing how real people use AI. Note: these communities range from beginner-friendly to extremely technical. Look for threads tagged [Beginner] or [Help] for the most accessible discussions.

r/ClaudeAI (reddit.com/r/ClaudeAI)

Community focused on Anthropic's Claude. Helpful for Claude-specific tips and workflows. Same caveat as r/ChatGPT: quality varies, so stick to beginner-tagged threads when starting out.

Hugging Face (huggingface.co)

The largest open-source AI community. More technical, but great for exploring free AI models and tools.

AI Tool Report Community ((Facebook group and newsletter))

Community focused on practical AI tool discovery.

✦✦✦

Books for Going Deeper

Co-Intelligence (by Ethan Mollick)

The best book on living and working with AI. More academic than ours, but deeply thoughtful. Essential reading for anyone who wants the bigger picture.

The Alignment Problem (by Brian Christian)

For readers curious about AI safety and the challenges of making AI systems behave as intended. Readable and important.

Artificial Intelligence: A Guide for Thinking Humans (by Melanie Mitchell)

The best plain-English explanation of how AI works under the hood. Written by a computer scientist who respects her audience.

Atlas of AI (by Kate Crawford)

A critical look at the social and environmental costs of AI. Important perspective for balanced understanding. For readers who want a more challenging, academic read.

The Coming Wave (by Mustafa Suleyman)

By a co-founder of DeepMind, about where AI is heading and what it means for society. Thought-provoking without being alarmist. More advanced than our book, but rewarding for readers who want to go deeper.

✦✦✦

Official Documentation & Learning

OpenAI Help Center (help.openai.com)

Official guides for ChatGPT and DALL-E. The authoritative source for features and updates.

Anthropic's Claude Docs (docs.anthropic.com)

Official Claude documentation. Clear and well-written.

Google AI Essentials (grow.google/ai-essentials)

Free course from Google covering AI fundamentals. Well-produced and beginner-friendly.

Elements of AI (elementsofai.com)

Free online course from the University of Helsinki. Designed for non-technical learners. Over a million students enrolled.

Khan Academy + AI (khanacademy.org)

Khan Academy's AI tutor (Khanmigo) and educational content about AI. Excellent for parents and students.

NOTES

The AI landscape changes fast. For the most current versions of these sources, visit practicalaibook.ai/sources.

A Note on Sources

What Is AI, Really?

1. Alan Turing posed the question "Can machines think?" in his 1950 paper "Computing Machinery and Intelligence," published in the journal *Mind*.

2. The Dartmouth Workshop of 1956 is conventionally considered the founding of artificial intelligence as a field of study.

3. A modern smartphone has millions of times the computing power of the Apollo Guidance Computer. "Your Mobile Phone vs. Apollo 11's Guidance Computer," RealClearScience, July 2019; "Smartphone Power Compared to Apollo," ZME Science.

4. ChatGPT was released on November 30, 2022. "This Day in History: ChatGPT Released by OpenAI," HISTORY.com; "ChatGPT," Wikipedia.

5. ChatGPT reached one million users within five days. Statement

by Sam Altman, CEO of OpenAI; "ChatGPT: The AI Chatbot Taking TikTok and the Internet by Storm," CBS News.

6. ChatGPT reached one hundred million users within two months, making it the fastest-growing consumer application in internet history. UBS analyst note, February 2023; "ChatGPT Is the Fastest-Growing Consumer Application in History," TIME, February 2023.

7. TikTok took nine months and Instagram took approximately two and a half years to reach one hundred million users. "Fastest Growing App: ChatGPT vs. TikTok and Instagram," Interesting Engineering.

Your AI Starter Kit

8. ChatGPT Plus, Claude Pro, cost $20/month as of March 2026. Google Gemini Advanced (a.k.a. Google AI Pro) is $19.99/month. Prices mentioned are the entry level prices for paid subscriptions. Most Foundation model providers also offer higher subscription tiers with more tokens and features. ChatGPT pricing at chatgpt.com/pricing; Claude pricing at claude.com/pricing; Gemini pricing via Google One AI Premium.

9. ChatGPT free tier includes approximately 10 messages per 5 hours on the latest model, then unlimited on a lighter model. ChatGPT Pricing page; IntuitionLabs plan comparison.

10. ChatGPT's free tier began showing ads in some U.S. regions as of February 9, 2026. Reported by tldv.io and felloai.com.

11. Claude's free tier offers approximately 30–100 messages per day on the flagship model. Claude pricing page; glbgpt.com pricing guide.

12. Gemini's free tier includes image generation, code execution, and Google ecosystem integration. FreeAcademy.ai Gemini comparison, March 2026.

13. Gemini Advanced includes 2TB of Google storage, a 1-million-token context window, Deep Research, and Gems. FreeAcademy.ai Gemini comparison, March 2026.

14. Perplexity's free tier includes unlimited basic searches and 5 Pro searches per day; Pro costs $20/month. Perplexity Help Center; PanelsAI pricing guide.

15. ChatGPT's advanced voice mode uses natural-sounding speech, picks up on tone, and allows interruptions. "ChatGPT Can Now See, Hear, and Speak," OpenAI announcement.

Talking to AI: The Art of the Prompt

16. The PRIME framework (Prompt, Refine, IDEA, Master, Execute) was developed by the author and his team at Colossal, LLC for this book. IDEA stands for Imagine, Diagnose, Enhance, Act.

17. "Few-shot prompting" is a standard term in machine learning for the technique of providing examples within a prompt to guide AI output. Widely documented across Anthropic, OpenAI, and Google prompting guides.

AI at Home

18. OpenAI launched ChatGPT Health in January 2026, allowing users to connect medical records and wellness apps. "Introducing ChatGPT Health," OpenAI announcement, January 2026; CNBC, January 7, 2026.

19. Research shows ChatGPT under-triaged in 52% of emergency cases. "ChatGPT Might Give You Bad Medical Advice, Studies Warn," NPR, March 2026; Euronews Health, March 2026.

20. Prior to the launch of ChatGPT Health, OpenAI reported that approximately 40 million people were already using ChatGPT daily for health-related questions. OpenAI, January 5, 2026; MedicalXpress, February 2026.

21. The 2026 Medicare Plan Finder includes provider directories for the first time. CMS.gov HPMS memo; AARP; Rise Health.

22. AI translation tools have achieved near-professional accuracy for medical and legal documents in common language pairs. ChatGPT, Claude, and Google Gemini support real-time translation in

over 50 languages. A 2024 systematic review found that large language models achieved translation accuracy comparable to professional human translators for clinical and public health materials, though quality varies by language pair and document complexity. Munoz-Miquel et al., 'Machine Translation and AI in Medical Translation,' Journal of Medical Internet Research, 2024; Google AI, 'Supported Languages,' ai.google.

23. More than one in three adults over 65 experience loneliness, and social isolation significantly increases the risk of dementia, heart disease, and depression. The National Academies of Sciences, Engineering, and Medicine reported that social isolation is associated with a 50% increased risk of dementia and a 29% increased risk of coronary heart disease. National Academies of Sciences, Engineering, and Medicine, 'Social Isolation and Loneliness in Older Adults,' 2020; AARP Foundation, 'Loneliness and Social Connections,' aarp.org.

AI at Work

24. The average office worker spends 28% of the workday on email. McKinsey Global Institute.

25. Otter.ai achieves up to 95% transcription accuracy under ideal conditions; its free tier offers 300 minutes per month. Otter.ai blog and pricing page, March 2026.

26. Fireflies.ai achieves 90–93% transcription accuracy; its free tier offers unlimited transcriptions, but only 800 minutes of stored recordings per month and supports 100+ languages. TheBusin essDive comparison; Alfred.ai comparison, March 2026.

27. ChatGPT accepts .xlsx and .csv file uploads up to 50MB. OpenAI Help Center, March 2026.

28. ChatGPT for Excel add-in was in beta as of March 2026. "ChatGPT for Excel," OpenAI announcement.

29. Microsoft 365 Copilot Business pricing ranged from $18–21 per user per month (promotional pricing through June 2026); Copilot Enterprise at $30/user/month; Copilot Pro at $20/user/month is an

individual/consumer product for non-business users and may lack features compared to other licenses. Microsoft pricing page; EASI blog.

30. Illinois requires employers to disclose the use of AI for hiring and promotion decisions as of January 2026. Illinois Human Rights Act amendment; McDonald Hopkins analysis.

31. The Colorado AI Act was originally scheduled to take effect February 1, 2026, but Governor Polis signed SB 25B-004 on August 28, 2025, delaying the effective date to June 30, 2026. Additional legislation may further delay substantive obligations to 2027. The act regulates AI used in 'consequential decisions.' Foley & Lardner analysis; TrueFuture Media.

AI for Parents & Educators

32. Multiple school districts reported incidents involving AI-generated intimate images of students during 2024–2025. At Lancaster Country Day School in Pennsylvania, AI-generated nude images of female students circulated in November 2024, prompting student protests, a criminal investigation, and the departure of school leaders (U.S. News & World Report, November 19, 2024). In a related Pennsylvania case, two students generated 347 fake pornographic images featuring 60 classmates, most under 18, leading to criminal charges (WHYY; NewsNation, 2024). At Cascade High School in Iowa, students created AI-generated nude images of female classmates in April 2025, resulting in a law enforcement investigation (KCRG News, April 24, 2025).

33. AI detection tools have been shown to produce both false positives (flagging human-written text as AI) and false negatives (missing AI-written text). Multiple studies; acknowledged by GPTZero, Turnitin, and others.

34. Carol Ann Tomlinson's differentiated instruction framework is a standard reference in education research and is widely accepted as best practice.

35. AI-powered text-to-speech tools have evolved significantly

beyond earlier robotic-sounding readers, now offering natural pacing, appropriate emphasis, and emotional tone that makes listening a genuine alternative to reading for students with dyslexia. Tools such as NaturalReader, Read&Write, and the built-in accessibility features in ChatGPT and Google can adjust speed and voice to individual preference. Research shows that listening to text while following along visually improves word recognition and comprehension for students with reading difficulties. EdTech Magazine, 'AI Assistive Technology Improves Inclusion in K–12 Environments,' February 2026; University of Michigan DyslexiaHelp, 'Text-to-Speech Readers,' dyslexiahelp.umich.edu.

36. The International Dyslexia Association estimates that 15–20% of the population has some symptoms of dyslexia, making it the most common learning disability. A hallmark of dyslexia is a significant gap between a student's verbal ability and their written output — students often demonstrate strong comprehension and reasoning in conversation while producing written work that does not reflect their actual understanding. International Dyslexia Association, 'Dyslexia Basics,' dyslexiaida.org; National Center for Learning Disabilities, 'What Is Dyslexia?' ncld.org.

37. Research shows that combining speech-to-text with AI-powered organization tools can significantly improve written output for students with dyslexia without doing the thinking for them. A systematic review by Svensson et al. (2023) found that students using assistive technology reported improved academic performance, reduced anxiety related to schoolwork, and increased engagement. A meta-analysis by Wood et al. (2018) found significant improvements in reading comprehension when students used text-to-speech tools, allowing them to process and retain information more effectively. The Windward School, 'Leveraging Technology to Empower Students with Dyslexia,' July 2025; Wood et al., 'Does Use of Text-to-Speech and Related Read-Aloud Tools Improve Reading Comprehension for Students with Reading Disabilities? A Meta-Analysis,' Journal of Learning Disabilities, 2018.

38. AI assistants can help students with ADHD manage executive

function challenges including organization, time management, task initiation, and sustained focus. AI-powered tools can break assignments into smaller steps, create visual schedules, send reminders, and help students get started on tasks by asking structured questions. CHADD (Children and Adults with Attention-Deficit/Hyperactivity Disorder), 'Can AI Revolutionize Education for Students with ADHD?' August 2025; Psychology Today, 'ADHD, Executive Functions, and AI: A New Era in Treatment,' March 2025.

39. AI chatbots are emerging as low-stakes practice environments for students on the autism spectrum to rehearse social interactions, including how to ask questions in class, join group conversations, or express disagreement respectfully. The AI provides consistent, patient, nonjudgmental responses and can repeat scenarios as many times as needed. These tools are not a replacement for professional therapy or human interaction but serve as a complement, similar to how a pianist practices scales before performing. SchoolAI, 'How to Use AI Tools for Neurodivergent Students,' 2025; Understood.org, '6 Ways AI Can Help You Manage ADHD Symptoms,' July 2025.

40. AI-powered image description tools can describe photographs, diagrams, charts, and other visual content in detail, making it accessible through text or speech for students with visual impairments. Be My Eyes, powered by GPT-4, serves over 900,000 blind and low-vision users worldwide by providing AI-generated visual descriptions. Built-in accessibility features in iOS (VoiceOver) and Android (TalkBack) also incorporate AI to describe on-screen content. Be My Eyes, bemyeyes.com; Apple Accessibility, apple.-com/accessibility/vision.

41. Real-time AI captioning has become remarkably accurate, with tools built into Google Meet, Zoom, and Microsoft Teams providing live transcription of classroom discussions, lectures, and group work. Google Live Transcribe, a free Android app, supports over 120 languages and dialects for everyday conversations. Dedicated captioning apps like Ava provide human-assisted AI captioning for deaf and hard-of-hearing users in both phone calls and in-person settings. Google Play Store, 'Live Transcribe'; Ava, ava.me.

42. Schools are increasingly incorporating AI-based assistive technology into Individualized Education Programs (IEPs) and Section 504 accommodation plans. AI tools can qualify as assistive technology under the Individuals with Disabilities Education Act (IDEA), which requires schools to consider assistive technology for every student with an IEP. Parents who advocate for specific AI tools and bring examples of what is available often accelerate the process of getting accommodations approved. EdTech Magazine, 'AI Assistive Technology Improves Inclusion in K-12 Environments,' February 2026; Understood.org, 'Assistive Technology for Kids with Learning Disabilities.'

43. Excessive passive screen time in children is associated with attention problems, sleep disruption, and reduced physical activity. American Academy of Pediatrics, "Digital Ecosystems, Children, and Adolescents," *Pediatrics*, February 2026; American College of Pediatricians, "Media Use and Screen Time — Its Impact on Children, Adolescents, and Families," September 2025.

AI for Small Business Owners

44. A basic digital marketing package for a small business typically costs $500 to $2,000 per month, while full-service agency retainers generally range from $2,500 to $15,000 per month. MTHD Marketing, 'Marketing Agency Pricing Guide,' February 2026; InfluenceFlow, 'Digital Marketing Agency Pricing Guide 2026,' January 2026.

45. Google Business profiles with recent activity and review responses tend to rank higher in local search results. Moz Local Search Ranking Factors; BrightLocal research.

46. A lawyer's review of a simple business contract typically costs $300 to $1,000, with issue-specific reviews (explaining a few clauses) as low as $150 to $350. The average flat fee for a contract review is approximately $470 to $608, based on marketplace data from thousands of transactions. ContractsCounsel, 'Business Contract Review Cost,' September 2025; ContractsCounsel, 'Contract Review Cost,'

August 2024; LegalCounselPA, 'Lawyer Contract Review Cost Guide,' January 2026.

AI for Creative Projects

47. A professional developmental editor typically charges $2,000, $5,000 for a novel-length manuscript. General industry range.

48. In March 2025, OpenAI replaced DALL-E 3 with GPT-4o's native image generation as the default in ChatGPT, unifying text and image capabilities in a single model. In December 2025, the model was upgraded to GPT Image 1.5, with DALL-E 3 fully deprecated. 'Introducing 4o Image Generation,' OpenAI, March 25, 2025; 'The New ChatGPT Images Is Here,' OpenAI, December 16, 2025.

49. Midjourney, widely regarded as the highest-quality image generation tool for artistic and photorealistic output, starts at $10/month as of March 2026. GurhkaTech; SurePrompts comparison.

50. Google's Gemini image generation uses the Nano Banana model. Daily image limits by subscription tier: free (20 images), AI Plus (50 images), AI Pro (100 images), and AI Ultra (1,000 images). Limits reset daily and may change without notice. Google Support, "Gemini Apps limits & upgrades for Google AI subscribers," support.google.com/gemini/answer/16275805.

51. Adobe Firefly is designed with an explicit commercial licensing model, making it the safest option for business use of AI-generated images. Adobe documentation.

52. Professional book cover design typically costs $300 to $1,250, with the average falling around $880 based on an analysis of over 9,600 projects. Genre matters: fantasy, romance, and science fiction covers tend toward the higher end, while nonfiction covers cost less. Reedsy, 'Book Cover Design Costs: Professional Rates for 2026,' December 2025; Miblart, 'How Much Does It Cost to Design a Book Cover?' March 2026.

53. Suno version 5 creates studio-quality audio at 44.1kHz (CD quality) and supports lyric formatting tags like [Verse], [Chorus], and

[Bridge]. Suno, 'Introducing v5,' September 2025; AI Song Creator, 'Suno AI Review 2026,' January 2026.

54. Runway Gen-4.5 was widely considered the top-rated AI video model as of March 2026. DigitalApplied comparison.

55. Google Veo creates 4K video with synchronized audio. DigitalApplied comparison, March 2026.

56. In March 2026, OpenAI announced the shutdown of the standalone Sora app effective April 26, 2026. eWeek; Vo3AI, March 24, 2026.

57. Canva's Magic Design feature generates designs from text descriptions. canva.com/magic-design; Labla.org review, March 2026.

Staying Safe and Smart

58. By default, ChatGPT uses your conversations to train its AI models. Users can opt out through Settings → Data Controls, but OpenAI retains data for 30 days even after opting out. OpenAI Help Center; "AI Chatbot Privacy Concerns," Stanford Report, October 2025.

Note on GUARD Framework: Chapter 9 presents the GUARD safety framework (Get the facts, Understand the source, Assess the risk, Research independently, Defend and educate others) as a practical approach to managing AI-related risks. This framework was developed by Colossal LLC, drawing on established cybersecurity and media literacy principles including the NIST Cybersecurity Framework, the SIFT method (Mike Caulfield, University of Washington), and the National Cyber Security Alliance's Stay Safe Online guidelines.

59. In August 2025, Anthropic shifted Claude's consumer data policy to an opt-out model. Opting out means conversations are deleted after 30 days; opting in allows retention for up to 5 years. "Updates to Consumer Terms and Privacy Policy," Anthropic announcement; AMST Legal analysis.

60. Google Gemini conversations are saved for 18 months by default. Human reviewers may examine conversations for safety and improvement. Gemini data is integrated with your broader Google account, including Gmail and search history. Google Gemini FAQ;

"The Truth About AI Chatbot Data Privacy," Medium, February 2026.

61. There are at least 700 court cases that now involve AI-generated hallucinations or fabricated content and the number continues to grow rapidly. Damien Charlotin AI Hallucination Cases Database; Bloomberg Law.

62. In July 2025, a federal judge ordered two attorneys representing MyPillow CEO Mike Lindell to pay $3,000 each after they filed a brief containing AI-generated fake case citations. "AI Courts Lawyers MyPillow Fines," NPR, July 10, 2025.

63. Attorneys from Ellis George LLP and K&L Gates LLP were ordered to jointly pay $31,100 after submitting a brief containing hallucinated citations generated by AI tools including CoCounsel, Westlaw Precision, and Google Gemini. "AI Hallucinations Strike Again," LawSites, May 2025.

64. In 2025, deepfake-related losses in the United States reached $1.1 billion, tripling from $360 million in 2024. "Deepfake Statistics 2025," DeepStrike.io; "Deepfake Statistics and Trends," Keepnet Labs.

65. Modern AI can clone a person's voice with approximately 85% accuracy using just 3–5 seconds of audio, such as from a social media video, voicemail greeting, or online recording. "What Are AI Scams? A Guide for Older Adults," National Council on Aging; "Protecting Seniors from AI Voice Cloning Scams," Kathie Brown Roberts P.C.

66. As of March 2026, 28 states have passed legislation addressing the use of AI in political ads. "AI Deepfakes Blur Reality in 2026 U.S. Midterm Campaigns," Detroit News, March 28, 2026.

67. Voters are expected to face unprecedented levels of AI-generated misinformation during the 2026 U.S. midterm elections. "Voters to Face Unprecedented Levels of AI-Generated Misinformation in 2026," WITF, December 2025; "How Political Misinformation Deepfakes Threaten 2026 Elections," AI CERTs.

68. Beginning in 2024 and continuing through 2025, multiple deepfake videos of Elon Musk circulated across YouTube and X (formerly Twitter), promoting fraudulent cryptocurrency giveaways. "Top 5 Ways Scammers Have Used AI and Deepfakes in 2025," Norton.

69. In October 2025, researchers from UC Berkeley and Northwestern University found that ChatGPT, when generating and evaluating resumes, assumed women were younger with less experience and rated older male candidates as more qualified than female candidates with identical qualifications. Separately, University of Washington researchers found AI resume-screening tools favored white-associated names 85% of the time and never favored Black male-associated names. 'Age and Gender Distortion in Online Media and Large Language Models,' *Nature*, October 8, 2025; Wilson et al., University of Washington, presented at AAAI/ACM Conference on AI, Ethics, and Society, October 2024.

70. Researchers at the University of Oxford examined 21 open-access datasets used to train AI skin cancer detection algorithms and found severe underrepresentation: among 106,950 total images, only 10 were from people with brown skin and just 1 was from an individual with dark brown or Black skin. "Real-World Examples of Healthcare AI Bias," Paubox.

71. UnitedHealth's subsidiary NaviHealth used an algorithm called nH Predict to determine post-acute care duration for Medicare Advantage patients. In May 2022, 91-year-old Gene Lokken of Wisconsin fractured his leg and ankle in a fall. After nineteen days of physical therapy in a skilled nursing facility, the algorithm cut off his coverage against his doctors' recommendations. His family paid $12,000 to $14,000 per month out-of-pocket for nearly a year until his death in July 2023. His estate joined a class action lawsuit alleging the algorithm had a 90% error rate. Casey Ross and Bob Herman, "UnitedHealth Faces Class Action Lawsuit Over Algorithmic Care Denials," STAT News, November 14, 2023; Estate of Gene B. Lokken et al. v. UnitedHealth Group, Case No. 0:23-cv-03514 (D. Minn. filed November 14, 2023).

72. In January 2026, Check Point researchers exposed an operation using 90 AI-generated "experts" to populate controlled messaging groups, directing victims to install mobile apps displaying fabricated trading returns. "Internet Scams 2026: $16.6B Crisis & AI Deepfake Threats," Axis Intelligence; "AI Scams in 2026," Vectra AI.

73. In 2024, a finance employee at engineering firm Arup in Hong Kong was deceived by an all-deepfake video call that included the apparent CFO, resulting in 15 separate transactions totaling $25.6 million to fraudulent accounts. "Top 5 AI and Deepfake Scams," Norton; "Are Successful Deepfake Scams More Common Than We Realize?" IBM.

74. In 2024, Americans over age 60 lost nearly $4.9 billion to cybercrime, a 43% increase from the previous year. Yahoo News / AARP; FBI IC3 Annual Report.

Building Your AI Workflow

75. Zapier's free plan includes 100 tasks per month and two-step Zaps (one trigger, one action). The Starter plan costs $19.99/month (annual billing) and includes 750 tasks per month. Zapier consolidated its product ecosystem in 2026, bundling Tables, Forms, and MCP into every plan tier. Zapier pricing page, March 2026.

76. IFTTT (If This Then That) offers a free tier with 2 applets, a Pro plan at approximately $3/month with 20 applets and multi-action capabilities, and a Pro+ plan with unlimited applets (pricing varies from approximately $8.49 to $14.99/month depending on billing period). IFTTT pricing page, ifttt.com/plans; The Digital Project Manager, 'IFTTT Pricing Tiers & Costs,' October 2025.

77. Make.com (formerly Integromat) offers a free plan with 1,000 credits per month and a Core plan at $10.59/month (or $9/month billed annually) with 10,000 credits. Native AI integrations with OpenAI and Claude are available on all paid plans. Make.com pricing page; Make.com Help Center, 'Adjustments to Plans and Pricing,' November 2025.

78. iOS 26 Shortcuts integrate with Apple Intelligence, supporting on-device AI models for summarizing PDFs, generating images, editing text, and ChatGPT via Private Cloud Compute. The "Use Model" action brings AI into Shortcuts workflows. Requires iPhone 15 Pro or later, iPad with M1+, or any Mac with Apple silicon. Apple Support; Cult of Mac, March 2026; Tom's Guide, March 2026.

79. Recommended AI newsletters: Practical AI Book (weekly, companion to this book); WOCxO (weekly, by the author, wocxo.-com); The Neuron (daily, beginner-friendly); The Batch (weekly, by Andrew Ng / deeplearning.ai); Ben's Bites (daily, curated by Ben Tossell). Zapier "Best AI Newsletters"; Publuu "Best 24 AI Newsletters for 2026"; Readless "12 Best AI Newsletters."

80. Google Live Transcribe is a free accessibility app providing real-time captions for everyday conversations, supporting over 120 languages and dialects. Available on Android. Google Play Store listing; InnoCaption "Top 10 Accessibility Apps," 2026.

81. Ava provides real-time captioning for phone calls and in-person conversations for deaf and hard-of-hearing users, with human-assisted AI captioning (Ava Scribe). iAccessibility listing; Ava website.

82. Be My Eyes uses AI to describe images and surroundings to people who are blind or have low vision. The app combines AI visual descriptions with human volunteer assistance. Be My Eyes website.

83. JAWS (Job Access With Speech) is a screen reader for blind and low-vision users. Newer versions integrate AI for more intelligent navigation of web content and applications. Freedom Scientific / Visme "Best AI Accessibility Tools," 2026.

84. Voiceitt uses AI to recognize non-standard speech patterns affected by conditions such as cerebral palsy, stroke, and Parkinson's, translating them into standard speech that other voice systems can understand. Voiceitt website; Visme "Best AI Accessibility Tools," 2026.

What's Coming Next

85. OpenAI released Operator on January 23, 2025, an AI agent that can navigate websites and complete tasks on behalf of the user. By July 2025, Operator's capabilities were integrated into ChatGPT as 'agent mode,' and the standalone Operator site was sunset on August 31, 2025. 'Introducing Operator,' OpenAI, January 2025; Axios, 'AI 2025 trends: bubbles, agents, demand for ROI,' January 2025.

86. Google introduced Project Mariner and Astra, agentic AI systems that work inside the browser and across Google's apps. Google Cloud Blog, "What Google Cloud announced in AI this month," 2026.

87. Anthropic built computer-use capabilities into Claude, allowing it to control a user's screen (opening files, clicking buttons, and moving between applications). "AI agents arrived in 2025 - here's what happened and the challenges ahead in 2026," The Conversation, December 2025.

88. Microsoft embedded Copilot agents throughout its entire product suite, enabling multi-step task execution across Office applications. Microsoft 365 announcements, 2025–2026.

89. The FDA has authorized over 1,450 AI-enabled medical devices, with 295 new authorizations in 2025 alone. The majority are used for diagnostic purposes, with radiology accounting for approximately 76% of all authorizations. FDA, 'Artificial Intelligence-Enabled Medical Devices'; Innolitics, '2025 Year in Review: AI/ML Medical Device 510(k) Clearances,' December 2025; Sivakumar et al., *JAMA Network Open*, November 2025.

90. Waymo operates fully driverless robotaxis across 10 U.S. metropolitan areas, including Phoenix, San Francisco, Los Angeles, Austin, Atlanta, Miami, Dallas, Houston, San Antonio, and Orlando. The company completed over 500,000 paid rides per week as of March 2026, doubling from 250,000 rides per week in April 2025, with a target of 1 million rides per week by end of 2026. Waymo operates a fleet of approximately 3,000 vehicles and has logged over 200 million fully autonomous miles. TechCrunch, 'Waymo's Skyrocketing Ridership in One Chart,' March 27, 2026; Waymo, '2025 Year in Review,' December 2025.

91. Tesla launched a paid robotaxi service in Austin in June 2025 using modified Model Y vehicles with in-car safety monitors. By early 2026, the Austin fleet comprised approximately 30 to 42 vehicles, the majority still carrying safety monitors. Tesla began testing a small number of unsupervised vehicles (without in-car monitors but with remote oversight) in December 2025, though as of March 2026 only 4

to 10 vehicles operated without a safety monitor at any given time. Tesla's Full Self-Driving system remains classified as SAE Level 2, requiring human supervision. Electrek, 'Tesla Expands Unsupervised Robotaxi Area,' March 31, 2026; Austin Today, 'Tesla's Unsupervised Robotaxi Fleet Shrinks,' March 14, 2026.

92. Most consumer vehicles in 2026 operate at Level 2 autonomy, including Tesla Full Self-Driving (Supervised), Ford BlueCruise, and GM Super Cruise. Ford has targeted Level 3 eyes-off driving for 2028. ACV Auctions, "The Best Self-Driving Cars of 2026"; GreenCars, "State of Self-Driving in 2026."

93. Approximately 15% of U.S. jobs (roughly 23.2 million positions) have crossed the threshold where at least 50% of their tasks are automated. However, 63% of all jobs include nontechnical barriers that would prevent complete automation displacement, such as client preferences for human interaction, regulatory requirements, and cost-effectiveness considerations. SHRM, 'Automation, Generative AI, and Job Displacement Risk in U.S. Employment,' October 2025.

94. In January 2026, approximately 7,600 layoffs were directly attributed to AI adoption. Through 2025, over 55,000 U.S. job cuts were explicitly linked to AI. HIGH5 Strengths Test, "AI and Automation Job Loss Statistics in the U.S. (2024–2026)"; SQ Magazine, "AI Job Loss Statistics 2026."

95. The World Economic Forum estimates AI will create 170 million new roles globally by 2030. Demand for analytical, technical, and creative positions grew 20 percent after ChatGPT's debut, while openings for routine, automation-prone roles fell 13 percent. Index.dev, "AI Job Growth Statistics 2026"; HBR, "Research: How AI Is Changing the Labor Market," March 2026.

96. Economists have not yet found measurable evidence that AI is causing net job loss across the U.S. economy as a whole, though significant reshuffling is occurring. Yale Budget Lab, "Evaluating the Impact of AI on the Labor Market"; Dallas Fed, "AI is simultaneously aiding and replacing workers," February 2026.

97. Seventy-nine percent of employed U.S. women work in occupations susceptible to disruption and automation by generative AI,

compared to 58 percent of men. This disparity exists because a higher percentage of working women hold white-collar positions (approximately 70%), while men are more evenly split between white- and blue-collar occupations. Mark McNeilly et al., 'Will Generative AI Disproportionately Affect the Jobs of Women?' UNC Kenan-Flagler Business School / Kenan Institute of Private Enterprise, April 2023; CNN, 'Nearly 80% of Women's Jobs Could Be Disrupted by AI,' June 2023.

98. Business leaders increasingly describe adaptability as "the new job security" in an AI-driven economy. Red Hat, "Future-proof your tech career: 6 essential human skills for the AI era"; Phys.org, "Time to retrain? How to future-proof your career in the AI age," March 2026.

ACKNOWLEDGMENTS

Writing a book about technology is easy. Writing a book that makes technology feel approachable to real people is much harder, and I couldn't have done it without the people who kept me honest along the way.

To my early readers: Alex, who struggled through every chapter with the eyes of someone who writes for the heart, not just the head. And my Mom, who reminded me what it actually feels like to encounter AI for the first time. Also thank you to Andrew Wright for help put into words the vision that became PRIME.

To Alex. Thank you for inspiring me to finally write my own story, and for your patience through every late night it took to finish it.

To our kids. You are the reason the future matters.

And finally, a note of genuine gratitude to the AI tools that helped design, draft, and refine this book. It felt only right that a book about practical AI should be shaped by it. They were, in many ways, my most tireless collaborators.

And to every reader who picked up this book feeling uncertain about AI: you were my audience from the very first word.

ABOUT THE AUTHOR

Jeff Kuehn is the Chief Technology Officer at Colossal LLC, where he leads AI practice development and builds artificial intelligence solutions for government and enterprise clients. With more than a decade in federal technology, he has spent his career at the intersection of complex technology and the people who actually need to use it.

Jeff and his team developed the PRIME framework; a practical, five-step approach to working with AI tools, that forms the backbone of this book and has been adopted by organizations looking to make AI accessible and useful across their workforces.

He writes about technology, fitness, and the human side of innovation at wocxo.com, where he has built a community of readers who appreciate straight talk about complicated subjects. He is also a proud supporter of Mission 22, an organization dedicated to veteran mental health and suicide prevention.

When he is not building AI solutions or writing about them, Jeff can be found in Maryland, where he lives with his wife Alexandra (a children's book author) and their two daughters, Harper and Vivienne.

Practical AI for the Rest of Us is his first book.